What People are saying about
Transforming Your Business

This book is an amazing tool for an area that most business owners know nothing about. Few have even thought about examining the spiritual foundations of their business. With this tool, you can take an accurate inventory of your business; discover both strengths and weaknesses, and trouble shoot what needs to be fixed. *Transforming Your Business* opens the door for the power of God to propel you to an unbelievable future!

Dr. C. Peter Wagner
Presiding Apostle, International Coalition of Apostles
President, Global Harvest Ministries
Chancellor, Wagner Leadership Institute

This book is a revolutionary approach to establishing Kingdom of God businesses. Based on my 52 years as a minister, working with people of all walks of life, I would say that this is the first book of its kind on how to eliminate the things that keep businesses from becoming successful and then maintaining that success indefinitely.

Dr. Bill Hamon
Founder, Christian International Ministries Network

The precepts taught in *Transforming Your Business* will serve as invaluable tools to bring transformation to your business, organization and even church. Carol and I have for a long time seen amazing fruit as a result of ministry to the heart of individuals. Chester Kylstra is now directing these same healing concepts to the "heart" of businesses, organizations and churches. Attitudes of sin, ungodly beliefs, arrogance and unforgiveness are destructive even at a corporate level, whereas, prayer, repentance and humility, in tandem with a strategic plan, can dramatically turn everything around. Your business and employees need this book.

John Arnott
Toronto Airport Christian Fellowship
Partners In Harvest Network

Chester Kylstra has done it again! He has written a marvelous book for not only *Transforming your Business*, but for transforming your life. I highly recommend this revolutionary book.

Che Ahn
President, Harvest International Ministry

I am very excited about the impact *Transforming Your Business* is going to have to bring righteousness to the marketplace. The work is timely and the principles are well tested. The central message is Biblically-based, practical ways of changing your organization "at the roots," all done under the transforming power of the Holy Spirit.

Dr. Carle M. Hunt
Regent University Professor
Business/Organization Consultant

Have you tried process improvement, change management, hired the best marketing consultants, etc… and yet you still are plagued with unexplained challenges and poor results? Then take a look at the spiritual dynamics of your business using *Transforming Your Business.* I have no doubt that it will help you discover spiritual roots that are affecting your bottom line.

Tim Taylor
Founder, Watchman Ministries International

Transforming Your Business is a must read for anyone involved in the business arena. The possibilities for success increase exponentially after applying the principles clearly revealed. I don't know how a person can truly succeed in business or in their personal life without the wisdom contained in this book. *Transforming Your Business* needs to be part of every business person's arsenal of books.

Dr. Nick Pappis
President, World Impact Ministries
World Impact Business Network

This revolutionary book has the potential of being a major power tool to help transform businesses. Chester has done an excellent job of showing that it will not be done instantaneously, but it will be done step by step, precept by precept.

Heeth Varnedoe, III
Retired CEO, Fortune 500 Company

Daniel and Joseph acted under God's power and authority in their otherwise "secular" callings. For a leader, the appropriation of God's power and authority for our businesses requires us to act in humility, faith, and conviction, with listening ears. In *Transforming Your Business*, Chester has captured the scriptural foundations to simultaneously clean the wax from our spiritual ears and remove the spiritual debris that inhibits our progress. He has shown us an orderly process that can elevate the business into an even greater place of blessing.

Leaders of units within larger multinational corporations face unique challenges, but God's favor is poured out on those who strive to give Him His rightful place. The larger organization is blessed by the faithfulness of the few, or as stated in *Transforming Your Business*, the whole organization is blessed by the tithe.

Kenneth W. Porter
Coordinating Elder, Immanuel Church
Global Finance Director, large multinational corporation

Chester Kylstra has written a ground-breaking book, applying the life changing principles of *Restoring the Foundations* to the world of business. In this season in which the Holy Spirit is highlighting the importance of marketplace ministry, Chester gives clear, practical, and insightful solutions to break free from the demonic and hindering influences that the evil one uses to keep organizations from entering into their destiny in the Kingdom. The section on the role of intercessors and their relationship to the leaders was particularly meaningful to me because of our experiences with intercessors in businesses in Korea. While reading *Transforming Your Business*, I was deeply convicted of my responsibility as a leader to face head-on the issues raised in this book, both in my personal life and in our ministry.

Steve Stewart
Founding Director, Impact Nations International Ministries

Chester Kylstra has hit another home run!!! *Transforming Your Business* is a cutting edge pioneering effort of colossal proportion. It is a must read for anyone looking to take the quantum leap into the next generation of Kingdom expansion. He has taken the time tested process of *Restoring the Foundations* and applied it magnificently to the world of business and organizational development.

Truly, healthy people will create healthy leaders, which will in turn create healthy organizations. And healthy organizations will create the resource base to impact the world for the sake of the Kingdom of God!!! For such a time as this, *Transforming Your Business* has come to elevate leaders and organizations to "go to the next level!"

Dr. J. Patrick Fiore
Aprecis Group Leadership Services

Transforming Your Business is well written, uses biblical examples and principles, and applies tested and proven principles of *Restoring the Foundations*. With this book, you have the solutions as well as being able to identify the roots of the problems.

Ralph A. Beisner
Retired New York Supreme Court Judge
President, Wall Street Paradigm Corp.

This book is an excellent resource for every marketplace leader. Chester has masterfully woven the proven principles of *Restoring the Foundations* for effective ministry to individuals into a plan for incorporating them into the marketplace organization.

Bruce E. Mow, M.P.A.
President, Maximum Significance International, Inc.

Transforming Your Business

How To Change Your Organization For Good

By
Chester Kylstra

Proclaiming His Word Publishing

Transforming Your Business
How To Change Your Organization For Good

Author: Chester Kylstra

Published by:

Proclaiming His Word Publishing
2849 Laurel Park Highway
Hendersonville, NC 28739
828-696-9075
877-214-8076
office@phw.org
www.phw.org

Former Address:

PO Box 2339
Santa Rosa Beach, FL 32459

Layout by Chester Kylstra, Editing by Marsha Capo, Cover by Paul Greenwood.

Unless otherwise noticed, Scripture quotations are from the King James Version of the Bible.

First Edition, July 2006   ISBN-13:   978-0-964939-88-2
                               ISBN-10:   0-964939-88-6

Table of Contents

Acknowledgments

Where to begin? The last acknowledgment we wrote was in September, 2000, as we finished the second edition of *Restoring the Foundations*. So much has happened in the intervening years. We have been blessed with many incredible people in our lives. We have outstanding mentors who have blazed the trail and prepared the way for us. It is hard to know where to start.

So without any attempt to order by importance, let us just begin.

We want to acknowledge and thank the Restoring the Foundations ministry teams of the Healing House Network and the Restoring the Foundations church teams for catching the vision of a Bride without spot or wrinkle. Together we can do our part to prepare the Bride.

The members of our Advisory Board have stood with us and encouraged us as the vision continued to expand, first internationally, then to an International Training Center, and now to ministering to businesses/organizations. Thank you for verifying the Word of the Lord with us and investing your very lives into the reality of a place where accelerated Restoring the Foundations training is happening.

A very big "Thank You" goes to the Echo Mountain Inn staff and the ministry staff for "carrying on" as our focus was on "the book" during these finishing months.

Thank you, Bishop Bill Hamon and Evelyn, for believing in us and being an encouragement to us for the past 13 years. Thank you for your life and examples.

We want to thank Carle Hunt for "spirit-storming" with us as we sat around the kitchen table many years ago. We were discussing the vision of bringing the Restoring the Foundations ministry to businesses and other organizations and what it would look like. You were extremely instrumental in launching the concept of this book. Thank you!

We want to acknowledge and bless Pastors Gary and Danice Duda, and Oliver and Kellie Halterman, for believing in the Transforming Your Business (TYB) ministry approach and inviting us to "practice" on their church. Likewise, thank you Rector John Roddam for opening up Saint Lukes Episcopal Church to host a TYB seminar as we "sharpen" the presentation.

Editor Marsha Capo corrected our "Eastern Oregon" English and brought both insightful suggestions and great encouragement. We thank you, Marsha, and the Readers thank you, for the help in bringing greater clarity to the content.

Thank you, Reviewers, for so generously giving of your time to help this book be the best possible, the most useful to the reader.

Thank you, Endorsers, for your strong validation of what God has put on our hearts. We will continue on to help the Bride make herself ready.

Friend Simon Harrison generously provided his company of graphic artists to create the cover for the book and to "take it to the next level." Thank you, Simon and Catherine.

And Betsy. Thank You Lord for Betsy. You have encouraged me and stood with me as we together have labored many hours to bring forth this revelation of how to apply the Restoring the Foundations ministry approach to groups of people, i.e., businesses/ organizations, so they too could become all that God has called them to be. It is a wonderful privilege to partner with you in this ministry.

Foreword

In this book Chester Kylstra presents truths for transforming one's business into greater success and prosperity. His approach is a step beyond what others have written. These are truly workable principles that have been proven to be a transforming experience for thousands of individuals. Some may wonder if the truths that transformed individuals to a better life could work as effectively with a business or organization. The simple answer is, "Yes," because businesses and organizations are established and managed by people. If you can help the leadership, you can help the business.

In the early 1990s, I heard that Chester and Betsy were bringing great help and transformation to individuals and married couples. I sent one of the 25 couples that serve on my Board of Governors to receive ministry from them. The Kylstras' ministry helped this couple so much that I required all my Board of Governors to go through their Restoring the Foundations ministry, as did my wife and myself. It was worth all the money and time spent to receive their ministry. Several couples felt that it brought such truth and transformation into their lives that things were "adjusted" that could have led to failure in their lives and marriages had they not received this ministry.

Anyone willing to participate in the truths and practices found within this book cannot help but be blessed, adjusted and transformed for a more victorious life and greater success in business. Based on my 52 years as a minister, working with people of all walks of life, I would say that this is the first book of its kind on how to eliminate the things that keep businesses from becoming successful and then maintaining it indefinitely. This book is a revolutionary approach to establishing Kingdom of God businesses. Jesus said that He would lay the axe to the root of any tree that was not bringing forth good fruit (Matthew 3:10). Chester reveals how to find the root causes of a business not being profitable. He then enables the business leaders to put the axe to those hidden problems. When this is done properly, it will bring transformation to any business. God bless you, Chester, for having the revelation, passion and courage to make these truths available to those who really want to see their business transformed into a continuing success.

This book could become one of the greatest tools ever to bring positive transformation to organizations and businesses. May each reader receive such a clear understanding that it will motivate them to act upon these principles which will produce tremendous benefit.

Dr. Bill Hamon
Founder of Christian International Ministries Network
Founder of Christian International Business Network
July 2006

Author of:
The Eternal Church
Prophets and Personal Prophecy
Apostles and Prophets and the Coming Moves of God
The Day of the Saints
Who Am I and Why Am I Here...

Preface

Dear Reader,

Initial Edition
What you hold is the initial edition of *Transforming Your Business*. We feel an urgency to put into your hands these important revelations, concepts, and "how to" sections. We believe that in publishing this edition we are providing you an opportunity to begin to implement these spiritual principles and understandings in your business or organization. As you do so, we expect you to begin to see your business/organization transformed. Let us know what you experience. We may ask permission to include your story in the next edition that others may benefit and grow.

We plan to work closely with two businesses over the next couple of years applying the Transforming Your Business approach. We will carefully monitor the changes and prepare detailed case studies for inclusion in the next edition. It will be exciting to see what God can do when we apply His truths to organizations.

Spiritual Understanding
This book is written to those who have obtained a basic level of spiritual understanding. If the topics in this book are new to you, we recommend you obtain and study our book *Restoring the Foundations*, and the other books we have listed at the end of this book in the Bibliography and References. You will gain insight into the fall of man, resulting curses, sowing and reaping, Satan and demonology, spiritual warfare, authority of the believer, and other such topics that you should know and "be living" before you engage negative spiritual forces desiring to destroy you and your business.

Whatever you do, please read the Warning page before you start page 1. This is a real caution for you and it should not be taken lightly.

Our Hope and Prayer
We hope and pray that the revelation(s) in *Transforming Your Business* will enable you to make a big step forward in removing the negative influences and increasing the positive flow in your business. As you apply these principles we believe that your company will prosper even more, overcoming deficits or failure, and fulfilling its destiny. Further, you personally will be able to fully accomplish God's purpose for you during your stay here on the earth.

Chester Kylstra
July 2006

office@TransformingYourBusiness.org

www.TransformingYourBusiness.org
www.RestoringTheFoundations.org

WARNING
THIS BOOK MAY BE HAZARDOUS
(This is the "fine" print!)

The material you are about to read may be hazardous to you, your business, and the people associated with you in your business. Depending on your current awareness of and operation within the spiritual realm, it may provide new understandings and revelations that you may not be willing or able to handle. It may mark you as a "no-longer-ignorant" enemy of the negative spiritual realm, causing it to single you out for spiritual attacks.

If you choose to continue reading, there is only one safe way to handle the spiritual warfare that will come. First, we implore you and the other leaders in your business to insure your "right standing" with God before making the decision to put these principles and procedures into practice. This means to be in relationship with God through Jesus Christ His Son who He sent for you. In Christ a New Covenant was established to free you from the oppression and entrapping of the negative spiritual realm.

If your relationship with Jesus Christ is in question and you want a vital relationship with God, please find a person who knows

> *We do not want to cause you more trouble, we want to help you get free of the trouble you already have.*

and loves Jesus Christ to help you obtain this Life. Then follow through by finding a Bible believing church to be in fellowship with and become involved. This is the only safe place from which to implement these spiritual principles and engage the enemy of our souls and businesses. *Without the "new birth," the inheritance of the saints, and the knowledge of how to conduct spiritual warfare, you will be defeated before you even start.*

Our goal for writing this book is to help you recognize the strategies of the "evil one." Our desire and motivation is to give you God's solution and empowerment to remove the evil

one out of your life, your family, and your business. This means "spiritual warfare" in the negative spiritual realm. However, the evil one does not give up easily. He hates God, he hates you and he hates to lose. So things may get worst before they get better. How bad things get will depend very much on "whose you are" and what you do.

If you decide to proceed with reading this book, thereby gaining spiritual understanding and revelation, the enemy will immediately begin to escalate the spiritual warfare to discourage you, dissuade you that he is even real, and defeat you–anything to stop you from moving forward gaining freedom. It is important that you decide quickly, and begin to wage the necessary spiritual warfare to stop the enemy even before he has opportunity to attack. It is important that you seal all Open Doors through which he has access to you, so that he cannot use them before the time when you can eliminate them.

Again, if this is all new to you, please re-read the preface to see what fundamentals you need to learn and put into practice. It is important to have your spiritual defense in place before proceeding.

This hands-on book has been written so you may know the reality of the spiritual realm. It has been published to provide understandings and strategies, with the hope that you may obtain healing and freedom for yourself and your business and all your surroundings. However, we can take no responsibility for your choosing to read or not read this book. We take no responsibility for whether you have experienced "being born from above" or not, whether you do the spiritual warfare or not, or whether you implement or do not implement the understandings, revelation(s), or procedures contained herein. We can not be responsible for the outcome, whether good or bad, for you and your business. In short, we desire to help, but what you do with this book and its material is beyond our ability to control thus we release all responsibility and liability to you.

Beginning

Have you ever wondered why certain things happen that just do not make sense? Even with great efforts to avert them, the same negative result repeatedly happens. Here are but a few examples: the same type of financial crisis continually repeats, a personal conflict erupts time after time (even with new employees who know nothing about the previous conflict), a specific department keeps making the same costly mistake, or even one business failure after another. If you have ever wondered about such things, you have come to the right place.

Let us share with you a personal experience that did not make sense to us.

The Puzzle
To give you a little background, in the mid-1980's we were called out of our careers in business/engineering into the ministry. We first went to a wonderful Bible College maturing under its influence. While there, God gave us a ministry of healing and freedom. Along the way, an interesting thing happened. A crisis among the leadership developed and within two years the Bible College closed its doors. It never reopened!

The crisis developed around the founder of the Bible College and Senior Pastor of the church associated with the school. These two had acquired different visions. Cooperation and then unity between the two organizations suffered. From the forces at work, the college suffered a fatal blow, and the church came very close to closing its doors. How could two organizations that had so positively impacted thousands of lives suddenly fail?

Eleven Years Later
Eleven years later the mystery intensified. Another Bible College, also closely connected to a church, bought the land and buildings of the previous school. Again, the leadership of both organizations are known for vision and integrity. Again, dis-

1

agreement came between the church leader and the Bible College leader. Again both church and college took a severe blow with students, congregation, and leaders being split, scattered, and left confused and hurt. Again, thousand of lives were impacted.

The similarities between the two devastations were too strong to disregard. What was happening? Is there a common thread?

What you are about to read will give you deeper insight into these and like situations that seemingly do not make sense. You see, there are reasons behind these types of problems. However, once the roots of the problems are exposed, there are solutions that can be implemented.

A. Goal: Real Solutions to Real Problems

This book is about problems. Actually, to be more accurate, it is about solutions to problems. It is about achieving real solutions to real problems, solutions that actually eliminate the problems. It is about keeping organizations from coming apart, about helping them maintain stability and productivity. It is about gaining new freedom, allowing achievement of purpose and function. It is not about learning how to cope or cover or some other false hope to "make it go away" approach, rather it is about digging to find the real roots, the source and causes of problems. Since these roots are spiritual in nature, this book is about applying spiritual principles that bring spiritual solutions to real, everyday spiritual problems.

> *Implementing Real Solutions to Real Problems.*

What organizations are you a part of, and what is dear to your heart? Are there problems that have resisted solution by more traditional means? If so, then please join us as we journey through a non-traditional yet effective problem solving process.

In order to base this journey on a sure foundation, let's first make sure we are "on the same page" as part of getting started.

Goal of this Book

Our goal is to help your business achieve its potential and full destiny. Our goal and desire is that you come into the fullness of all that God has called you to be. In this book, we will emphasize and present an approach and application for solving problems characteristic of many businesses. These principles equally apply to other types of organization such as a family, churches, social clubs, or even governmental units.

Current World View

We encourage you to read and study the principles and key concepts presented in this book even if you have a different world view. We know from first-hand experience that these principles and key concepts work regardless of one's world view. They work because God has built them into the fabric of the universe. They represent His nature and character. As we journey through the problem-solving process, you may experience a paradigm shift as your world view adapts to the truths expressed in these principles.

B. What is a Business?

Let us begin at the beginning and find common ground as we define some key words.

Groups, Organizations, and Businesses: What is the Difference?

Let's look at the definitions of these words (concepts): "Group," "Organization," and "Business." While these are similar concepts, they have important distinctions. In this book we will use these words somewhat interchangeably, as if they are "close" synonyms, but we still want to be aware of the differences.

A **Group** is two or more people. It is a collection of people. The Group is not necessarily organized nor has a purpose. A group may be a bunch of people walking through the park, those shopping at the local store, or perhaps a gathering at a baseball game. Each person is doing "his own thing." Yet they can be part of a "Group."

An **Organization** takes the definition of a group one step further. It is a group of people that have order. They are "organized," having structure and relationship. We would expect an organization to have a plan, a purpose, a reason for existing. It is an "organ" doing something functional, fulfilling its purpose, as does a heart or a kidney. The organization might be a business, a church, a civic club, an outing club, etc.

Business

This book focuses on a particular type of organization called a "business." The business is "organized" for a particular purpose. It is "busy," "in business," to "make money," hopefully to produce a "profit." Producing a profit is not the only reason for the creation of a business, but this must be at least one of the reasons or it is not a "business." Often a business is started because someone gets a "good idea," a vision, a call, that stirs him because it is a part of his destiny. It causes him, and the others that he draws into the vision, to commit their time, energy, money, and passion to the achieving of the vision. It includes the potential for "making money," "becoming wealthy," which adds to the excitement and passion of pursuing one's vision.

Profit

Now, making a profit is not a bad thing. So many people decry the "capitalistic" urge to make a profit. They do not know that this is a God-instilled desire. God Himself makes it clear in His Word, the Bible, that He desires profit; only He calls it "fruit." God likes fruit, lots of fruit![1]

This desire to "make money" can get out-of-hand, be perverted and corrupted (like any other human characteristic or drive). We have the admonishment that the "love of money is the root of all evil,"[2] not money itself. God wants us to accomplish His purpose for our lives, but He wants our love fixed on Him and not on temporal things such as money.

---

[1] One example is the parable of the talents, etc., Matthew 25:14-30.

[2] This is found in 1 Timothy 6:10.

Success and Growth

God makes it very clear in the Bible that He wants increase/profit. He expects "fruitfulness." In the parables of Jesus, the greatest recognition and rewards went to His servants with the greatest number of talents; both of the faithful servants doubled their original talents. So whether we look at an individual, an organization, or a business, God's plan for each is to increase and multiply, to have growth and "success." Consider the case of Joshua; God gave a clear strategy to achieve success.[1] He wanted Joshua to reach his fullest potential, to reach his destiny–and to lead Israel (an organization) into its destiny as well.

Having a group of people work together as an organization allows for greater success. If they are indeed "organized," they can do more to achieve success and growth than an individual. One outstanding example of teamwork (with wrong motives) is Nimrod's plan to build a high tower so that the people might become "like God."[2] Amazingly God states that Nimrod's team was capable of doing whatever they put their heart and mind to, as long as they were in unity. He stopped their unity–and thus success–by confusing their language. This resulted in the organization disintegrating into many groups and sub-organizations, and the loss of common purpose.

> *God is still giving out the keys*
> *for success if we will receive*
> *and apply the principles.*

Nimrod and Company were attempting to "do" life their own way, without God. And so He stopped them.

On the other hand, Joshua was very committed to doing things God's way, so God gave Joshua the keys for success. God was so involved in Joshua's success that he continually guided him and answered his prayers. This includes the one incredible time

---

[1] How to achieve success: Joshua 1:2-9.

[2] Nimrod and the Tower of Babel: Gen 11:1-9.

when Joshua "spoke to the sun" and stopped it for one day.[1]
God enabled the Israelites to win the battle that "very long" day.

God is still giving out the keys for success if we will but receive
and apply the principles. And He is still intervening in the ordinary course of events to bring about success and growth for
those who believe. The historical accounts of Nimrod and
Joshua teach the principle that it is very important to have unity
and teamwork to achieve success,
but what a disaster if the focus is
our own selfish goals and self-
exaltation rather than God-given
goals and purpose.

> *God's Way or*
> *Nimrod's Way?*

As we contemplate victory and success, and God's will for these
in our lives and endeavors, it becomes very clear that not all of
us are achieving these things. Let us begin to look at what may
be required to change our situations.

C. What is the Purpose of a Business?

Destiny: Individuals and Groups of Individuals
We submit that every individual has a destiny, a purpose for
which he has been born, and that each one of us is currently involved in the process of working out this destiny. We press on
because of the inner drive toward survival, toward success, toward completing the purpose set before us.

If we accept that individuals
have a destiny, it is not difficult to surmise that a group
of people may also have a

> *Businesses have*
> *Purpose and Destiny!*

group destiny. It is likely that God has a plan, purpose, function,
and mission for the group, whether small and large, particularly
when they come together as a team (business) to accomplish its
purpose and destiny? We believe this is so. Here are some important reasons for the existence of a business.

---

[1] God helped Joshua achieve success: Joshua 10:12-14.

Three Reasons for the Existence of a Business

a. Create wealth that is not only a blessing for the owners and employees but that is used for the expansion of the Kingdom of God.[1]

b. Bring forth creative ideas and inventions that result in products and services that are a blessing to others as well as provide the "equipment" needed for the expansion of the Kingdom of God. The "equipment" includes things such as TV, jet airplanes, internet, etc.

c. Provide a place where quality leaders can raise up mature, productive, and "whole" people who will not only work together as an efficient and effective "team" as a company but they will also take the Kingdom of God out into the world.

D. Primary Causes of Problems

Getting back to problems and solutions, we know God wants us to succeed. If so, then why do we have so many problems? We know He has empowered us to succeed, so why does it seem to be so hard to eliminate them? Is there a primary cause that we might discover and eliminate? Referring back to the story on page 1, how can we discover solutions to those failures that make no sense?

We believe there is always at least one primary cause, maybe more than one. Though not necessarily obvious or easy to discover, it is always present.

> *There is always a primary cause!*

Chronic business problems that are hard to eliminate are evidence that the primary cause has not been dealt with. People tend to work only with the symptoms and not the primary cause. Therefore the problem reasserts itself, perhaps with the same symptoms or maybe with a new set of symptoms.

---

[1] Please note Deuteronomy 8:18.

7

> *Fixing Symptoms is not the same as removing the Cause.*

The primary cause is not being identified because people are not looking in the right place. They do not know where the right place is. Most people (at least in the USA) are not aware of the spiritual realm and the unseen and unknown forces opposing mankind and God's destiny. This hidden yet real opposition is doing its best to prevent any Godly success.

Roots

We like to refer to these primary causes as "roots." Just as a tree's roots are hidden and out of sight, so are the unseen and unknown forces of opposition. Our goal as we serve a business or organization is

> *The primary cause is usually hidden.*

to discover and deal decisively with the roots of the problem, not just the fruit or symptoms.

Another metaphor we can use to describe this phenomenon is an iceberg, where we have the "seen" and the "unseen." As with an iceberg, it is the unseen that is likely the more significant source of influences creating difficult problems. If one deals with the unseen forces or roots creating the problem, even seemingly difficult problems can become simple and easily solved.

The "Seen"
(Natural Forces)
(Symptoms/Fruit)

The "Unseen"
(Spiritual Forces)
(Root Causes)

E. Spiritual Solutions for Spiritual Problems

As stated earlier, our goal is to assist you and your organization become all that God has called you to be. An important part of this is to obtain spiritual solutions for spiritual problems. We

> *Spiritual Solutions attack the Spiritual Roots.*

want to present the five roots/sources of spiritual influences that cause business problems and failure, and to present a procedure for removing these from our organizations (and individual lives). The process we present is comprehensive, covering all five roots/ sources. Normal problem solving, dealing with surface issues and symptoms, will not bring relief to these types of problems. We purpose to recognize and bring spiritual solutions that eliminate the spiritual roots of our problems.

> *This is a compre-hensive approach that includes ALL of the sources.*

F. Difficulty of Changing an Organization

It is a known fact that billions of dollars a year are spent on business consultants. One of the fascinating conclusions from a number of studies is that the advice given usually doesn't do much good, if any. The business consultant comes in, identifies all the problems (it's usually not that hard to do), makes recommendations, suggestions, and lays out a strategy – perhaps even a good one. Then he leaves and the management attempts to implement the plan. However, there is a vital omission. The spiritual roots, the fundamental causes, that affect the attitudes/cooperation of the people, have not been dealt with. And so the consultant's solution is temporary and the "fix" is not permanent because it only dealt with the symptom level and the physical realm rather than the roots in the spiritual realm. Generally speaking, people resist changing their behaviors. Perhaps we could say they are "unable" to change how they function, unless the roots that have them trapped in that behavior are removed.

One book that details the failure to solve business problems is by Anne Schaef and Diane Fassel, *The Addictive Organization*.[1] Essentially, they present the case that dysfunctional people cause dysfunctional organizations and then perpetuate the sickness carried by the company. This is a good presentation of the problem, but the authors do not provide a solution for the "real" roots behind the dysfunctional people and organizations.

---

[1] Please see the Biography section at end of this book for information about this book.

G. Businesses: the "new" Battle Ground

There is much discussion and prayer about "Taking Our Cities for God." In 2001, John Dawson published a book with this title which sparked a great impetus to do this very thing. Since then, many others have written about various aspects of this topic, including Cindy Jacobs and Peter Wagner.[1] Never in history have so many joined prayer networks, read the many books on intercession and spiritual warfare, and gathered into huge stadiums to wage spiritual warfare in unity and agreement. It is an awesome time as there are some entire cities seeing the holiness and power of God displayed in their everyday life.

At the other end of the scale, there are many saints and ministries called to provide healing and deliverance for the individual. Our ministry, Restoring the Foundations, is one of these. We believe in this aspect of God's salvation. We have been greatly privileged and blessed to bring the Lord's healing to individuals since the mid-1980's. Besides our ministry, there are tremendous resources available to every saint to help him progress in his sanctification.

But there is another "in-between" arena emerging. It has been gaining momentum over the last ten to twenty years. It is God in the "market place," frequently referred to as "market place ministry."

> *We desire to help Businesses receive God's Healing and Freedom.*

The usual focus is on helping businesses conduct themselves according to Biblical principles, on mentoring business men and women in wise and sound Christian business practices, on networking and accountability, etc. These focuses are vital and important. But there is an additional important focus needed.

---

[1] Please see the Biography section at end of this book for information about the authors mentioned in this section.

Unless individuals and their businesses first becoming free from negative spiritual forces/roots, imparting Biblical principles and mentoring can have only limited success.

We want to assist businesses with this "new" area. We want to see businesses and other organizations of our cities become as free and unhindered as we have seen individuals become. We believe

> *Taking Cities by starting with Individuals, then Organizations, then Neighborhoods.*

that as the organizations enter into healing and gain their freedom, then taking our cities for God will be expedited. The plan is to progress from the healed individual to the healed organization to healed neighborhoods and then cities. Then we will see fuller success and greater victory in the same way as God promised Joshua.

H. Suitable Businesses

You may ask, "How difficult will it be to apply these principles to my business or organization?" Although we believe that the approach presented in this book is applicable to any size or type of organization, we also know that the ease or difficulty of doing so can vary enormously. New, small, and/or one owner businesses will find it relatively easy. Larger and older organizations will have to do more research and spiritual groundwork. It is not impossible for larger or older organizations to gain freedom, just more difficult.

The important company parameters that determine the degree of difficulty are: years in existence (amount of history), number of influential leaders during this time, number of employees, the business ethic/culture, the number of times the business has changed locations, the amount of land and buildings, and whether public or privately owned. For larger, publicly owned companies, it will definitely be more complex applying the Transforming Your Business approach.

Yet even in large companies, a subsidiary or semi-independent department with committed leadership can apply the Transforming Your Business procedures to cleanse their organization in much the same way that a business within the city can be cleansed even while under the community influences.

Additional important factors are: what fraction of the company employees are Christian and are willing to cooperate with a plan to fulfilling destiny? Are there are employees of other faiths/ religions to consider? Are there labor law issues raised that must be considered? Are there constraints on what one can or can not do publicly and openly? We don't want to give the evil one any opportunity to divert our energies fending off accusations of unfair labor practices.

Yet with God, all things are possible.[1] So if you have a heart's desire to bring transformation to your company, let us encourage you to seek the Lord and find his strategy for your situation. He wants every one of us free, including our organizations.

I. Restoring the Foundations Ministry for Individuals and Business

The organizational ministry approach presented in this book builds on the Restoring the Foundation (RTF) ministry approach for individuals.[2] The important principles and concepts needed for ministry to an organization or business are a direct extension and expansion of the principles and concepts for ministering to a person. It is important to understand these principles and con-

---

[1] Jesus declares this truth in Matthew 19:26.

[2] Books by Chester and Betsy Kylstra that express the full revelation of the Restoring the Foundations ministry are *Restoring the Foundations, second edition*, published by Proclaiming His Word Publishing, January 2000; *An Integrated Approach to Biblical Healing Ministry*, published by Sovereign World, May 2004 (UK and world except for USA and Asia), and *Biblical Healing and Deliverance*, published by Chosen Books, September 2005 (USA and Asia). You may order these books from the author (see Author page at the end of this book), your nearby Christian book store, or from online retailers such as Amazon.com.

cepts so that you will have a base to build on as you read the rest of this book. If you are not already familiar with the RTF ministry, we would encourage you to read Appendix C which summarizes the key aspects of Restoring the Foundations ministry. You may also consider obtaining one of the books mentioned in the footnote for a more in-depth study.

It is an easy step to extend the Restoring the Foundations revelation for ministering to individuals to ministering to an organized group of people; i.e., a business. The only thing that is different is that organizations normally occupy buildings and land. This is a part of their identity and function. And so the spiritual influence resident on the land, with the building(s), and in the geographical area needs to be included in the plan to obtain freedom.

However, before we get into the details of the Transforming Your Business approach, there are some basic things we need to know.

PART ONE

Things We Need to Know

We have presented the premise that the significant causes of problems for an individual or an organization are negative spiritual roots. If we want to get to the bottom of the problems, we must discover and remove the negative spiritual roots.

In Part One we want to look at truths we need to know regarding the spiritual realm before we look in detail at negative spiritual roots.

In Part Two we will apply these concepts and understandings of the spiritual realm to the organizational realm. Then we can understand the spiritual dynamics of organizations and the setup for problems.

In Part Three we will put into practice effective solutions that truly work. We will develop an Action Plan to apply the truth and principles of God's Word to remove the negative spiritual roots underlying the problems affecting our businesses.

In Parts Four and Five we will present supportive information about Principalities and Intercession that will be needed as we develop and implement the Action Plan.

God's Plan: Freedom, Destiny, Fellowship
First, let us remember God's primary plan. He desires fellowship with us as individuals and with us as the human race. He made us in His own likeness and image[1] so that we would have God-like characteristics and could relate to Him. Wrong decisions by Adam and Eve led the human race down the road of

---

[1]   Please see Genesis 1:26-27.

15

rebellion and abandonment, the road to alienation and death.[1] God, knowing that His gift of free-will would lead to rebellion, had already put into motion a plan.[2] In His perfect time, He sent forth His Son, Jesus Christ, to fulfill the righteous requirements of the law.[3] His desire was to redeem the earth and bring restoration and fellowship to as many of the human race as would receive His incredible offer of salvation in their heart.[4]

Satan's Plan: Bondage, Failure, Isolation
On the other hand, the fallen archangel wants just the opposite for you and for me. He so hates God and the human race that he is doing everything possible to tempt us and trap us, to disqualify us as God's instrument in the earth, unable to fulfill our destiny. He is doing his best to alienate man's fellowship with God. He deceives men to even blame God, their only source of help, and thus lose joy and purpose. He uses every opportunity to bring forth his "stealing, killing, and destroying"[5] into our lives.

Part One is designed to help us understand the different ways we give the Devil opportunities. Yes, we can and do participate unknowingly to help Satan destroy us. This hinders and keeps us from God's best, us and the other people we join with in our businesses and organizations. It is imperative that we discover what we have been doing wrong, dig out the roots behind it, and then stop our cooperation with Satan.

---

[1] Please see Genesis 3:1-7.

[2] A number of scriptures combined reveal God's plan. For example, please see Matthew 13:35, John 17:4, Ephesians 1:4, 1 Peter 1:19-20, and Revelation 13:8, 17:8.

[3] Two examples of scriptures showing that Jesus came intending to fulfill the Law are Matthew 5:17-18 and Luke 24:44.

[4] Please see John 3:16.

[5] Please see John 10:10.

I. Fundamental Concepts: The Negative

We will first investigate the primary ways negative spiritual roots are given ground and opportunity to develop, expand, and become evident in individuals and thus in organizations. We will look at the positive Fundamental Concepts later.

A. Sin and Curses

The "short" answer is that negative spiritual roots are given opportunity through sin. Sin has results or consequences. Here is a "longer" answer as well.

> *Sin gives opportunity to negative spiritual forces that are the roots of many problems.*

Sin is the word used to describe transgression, violation, and/or the attempted breaking of the Law of God. Often sin is considered to be of a lower level when the transgression is done knowingly, as in deliberate disobedience, but even unintentional transgression is still sin.

The consequence of sin is many-fold. It is like a pebble dropped into a pond, sending ripples out in all directions. The Biblical word for the consequences of sin is "curse." When God's Law is violated, a curse is released. The curse ripples outward affecting those it touches. Generally, it puts "spiritual pressure" on others to "enter into" or commit the same type of sin. We will expand on the subjects of sin, curses, and consequences throughout this section on negative fundamental concepts.

Giving "Place", "Legal Ground", "Open Doors"

These three words/phrases give us another way of looking at the consequences of sin. We will use them interchangeably throughout this book. In Ephesians, Paul writes:

> *Ephesians 4:26-27 (KJV)*
> *Be ye angry, and sin not: let not the sun go down upon your wrath:* ***Neither give*** <u>***place***</u> ***to the devil.***

When we sin, we give "place" to the devil. The Greek word translated "place" means "an occupied or inhabited space." In other words, when we sin, we open the door, inviting in forces of darkness, and give them a place to take up residence and a habitation. You might ask, "Where is this residence?" The residence is in our lives, in that area given over to that type of sin!

> *Sin gives "place," "legal ground," an "open door" to the enemy.*

We often use the expression "legal ground" to convey this concept of giving "place" to the devil. When we sin, we issue him a "legal ticket," as it were, to come and go as he wishes. We invite him to "tromp" on the ground, bringing ever more defilement into that area of our lives. Not a pleasant thought, is it? Who wants the devil, or any of his henchmen, having free access into our lives to oppress, torment, afflict, hinder, steal, kill, or destroy?

In the Genesis biblical account of Cain and Abel, God speaks to Cain after his faulty sacrifice. He warns Cain that he is about to create a major consequence if he does not straighten out his thinking and his "bad attitude."

> *Genesis 4:6-7*
> *:6 ... "Why are you angry? Why is your face downcast?*
> *:7 If you do what is right, will you not be accepted?* ***But if you do not do what is right, sin is crouching at your door; it desires to have you, but you must master it."***

Tragically, Cain did not "master it," but "sin mastered him." Cain opened wide his front door and invited sin into his "house" as he willfully ignored God's word. He killed Abel and loosed major curses/ripples/consequences into his own life and the lives of his descendants. He provided "Open Doors" into his life and his descendants' lives to the kingdom of darkness

Regardless of which expression we use, "place," "legal ground," or "Open Doors," we as individuals bring our place/legal ground/open door to our organizations. What do you think happens when a number of individuals all bring the same type of "place?" We together provide a **"BIG place"** for higher level negative spiritual forces which promote and amplify the same type of sin. It is no wonder that problems exist in our businesses, not to mention every group to which we belong.

B. Personal Sin, Sins of the Fathers, and Curses

The most well-know portion of God's Law is the Ten Commandments. These set a standard that God considers an absolute, unlike the relativistic ethics so widely accepted today. The first mention of the Ten Commandments in the Bible is in Exodus 20:1-17. Violating any of these Laws/Commandments is clearly sin. The Ten Commandments expose attitudes and actions contrary to the Kingdom of God, against the love and nature of God.

Sins of the Fathers (and Mothers) and the resulting Curses
The second commandment is particularly relevant for us today as we look at the source(s) of negative spiritual roots. It is an expression of God's hatred of idolatry[1] and its deceptive entrapments. When we or our ancestors succumb to this sin, an incredible curse (consequence) is put into motion.[2] This conse-

---

[1] There is an extensive discussion of idolatry in Part Four starting on page 207.

[2] Dealing with the ancestral sins and curses from the second commandment is the first step in Restoring the Foundations ministry, as mentioned on page 316.

quence continues on for generation after generation, as each generation, pressured by the curses, commits and enters into the same sins. Here is the scripture from a modern translation.

> *Exodus 20:4-6 (NIV)*
> *20:4 "You shall not make for yourself an idol in the form of anything in heaven above or on the earth beneath or in the waters below.*
> *20:5 You shall not bow down to them or worship them; for I, the LORD your God, am a jealous God,* **punishing the children for the sin of the fathers to the third and fourth generation** *of those who hate me,*
> *20:6 but showing love to a thousand [generations] of those who love me and keep my commandments.*

The King James Version of the Bible expresses the curse this way.

> *... visiting the* **iniquity** *of the fathers upon the children unto the third and fourth [generation] ...*

Whether the sin/iniquity is "visited" or the children "punished," these are not outcomes anyone would want. The ripples of the curse from the sin of idolatry extend out for three or four generations. The curse actually applies a pressure onto the children to "enter into" the same type of sin as their parents, grandparents and great-grandparents. And once they do, the curse is "re-energized" or "recycled," continuing for another three or four generations. This happens again, and yet again. This is why we see the same types of sin/curse being repeated in family lines for generations. Hence, each individual carrying these ancestral sins/curses brings them into the business/organization with which they are involved.

Personal Sin and Curses
As each generation commits and thus "enters into" the same type of sin as their ancestors, these become personal sin for that generation. When we sin in the same way as our ancestors, we swing wider the doors already open. In addition, each generation has the opportunity to invent new ways of sinning, opening

new doors to a new set of curses. Unfortunately, it seems that in today's world there is an ever increasing array of possibilities. We all have many opportunities to transgress God's Word and Will. When we sin in an entirely new way, we open a new door to a new set of curses. Both kinds of sin (old and new) result in our exposing ourselves to even more pressure from the resulting curses, pressing us further into sin and the domain of darkness.

Sin on the Land
Later we will illustrate how the land itself is polluted and con-taminated by the sin of the people living on the land. How the very land itself remains defiled generation after generation, thus exposing successive generations to the same curses. This is an-other form of ancestral sins and curses that we must deal with in our businesses, since in general; all organizations occupy land and buildings.

C. Ungodly Beliefs: Lies We Have Believed

It is true that we can sin because of the lies we have believed. Unwittingly, we do and we say things that, if we really believed God's truth, we would not do or say. In the Restoring the Foun-dations ministry for individuals, the second problem area we minister to is Ungodly Beliefs. We help individuals realize the lies they have believed; lies about themselves, about others, and about God. We help them exchange those lies for God's truth, changing their thinking and actions from ungodly to Godly.[1]

The primary scripture admonishing us to change our "thinking" is in Romans 12.

> *Romans 12:2 (NIV)*
> *Do not conform any longer to the pattern of this world, but **be transformed by the renewing of your mind**. Then you will be able to test and approve what God's will is–his good, pleasing and perfect will.*

---

[1] We discuss ministering to Ungodly Beliefs for individuals on page 317.

Organizations also have "Ungodly Beliefs." What the leaders (and other influential people) believe will be seen in every aspect of the business. Everything from the business vision, core values, operating procedures, etc., to attitudes about how to treat employees, how to price the produce, etc., will be demonstrated for all to see. The Ungodly Beliefs of the group will be revealed whether they want it to be or not. However, usually they are not aware of the lies believed and accepted as truth. For them, it will seem "normal," not realizing others can see and evaluate.

We will refer to the business or organizational wide belief system as the "**Organizational Culture**." We could also use "Business Culture," "Corporate Culture," "Church Culture," "Civic Club Culture," etc. However, we will use Organizational Culture as the general, all encompassing phrase. This is a very important topic for us as we deal with negative spiritual roots. We will come back to it in Part Two.

D. Soul/Spirit Hurts:
Sinful Responses to Inner Wounds

As the hurtful events of life occur, particularly during our childhood, we add to our sin burden through sinful responses. This is especially true before we hear the gospel and receive the Lord Jesus Christ as Savior. As others press our "buttons," we lash out in anger and frustration, propagating more hurt and sin. We are cooperating with the kingdom of darkness, giving the enemy of our soul even more "place" from which to bring destruction into our lives.

Jesus knew that we would all receive wounds and need healing of them, so that we could stop our sinful responses. The "hot buttons," the "trigger points," all must be eradicated so that we can think Godly thoughts, respond in Godly ways, speak uplifting words,[1] support others rather than taking them down, learn how to respond in Godly love rather than reacting in "hot" recoil. He came to bring healing to each one of us, to heal our "broken hearts," to restore to wholeness and love.

---

[1] Paul directs us to have grace-filled speech in Ephesians 4:29.

Luke 4:18
*The Spirit of the Lord [is] upon me, because he hath anointed me to preach the gospel to the poor; **he hath sent me to heal the brokenhearted**, to preach deliverance to the captives, and recovering of sight to the blind, **to set at liberty them that are bruised**,*

Organizations, too, can have group wounds. These affect all the people, as the Organizational Culture retains the memory of the hurtful event. God desires to heal here also, as a group of people. We will explore this root of negative spiritual problems in Part Two.

E. Demonic Oppression: Demons and Demonic Strongholds

We want to allow for the possibility that you may not be familiar with the concept of demons (or evil spirits). You may have questions about whether they really exist or not, whether they are really dangerous if they do indeed exist, or what we can or can not do about them, etc. Let us just say that we were once totally naive in this area, and so, if this topic is new to you, we are very sympathetic. We did not grow up with demons being our dinner table topic of conversation. Neither did we hear about demons at church. In fact, it was not until we were in our forties that God decided it was time for us to learn about demons.[1] And learn we did. Over the years, we have learned a number of very important things about demons.[2]

A few key things that we have learned is that demons do exist, they are dangerous, they purpose to "steal, kill, and destroy," and they do have power and authority given to them through our sin. However, and much more importantly, we have learned our

---

[1] We write about these experiences in both Betsy's autobiography *Twice Chosen* and in the training book *Restoring the Foundations* (RTF). Please see Resources on page 345 if you are interested in finding out more about these books.

[2] As an indicator of what the Lord has taught us, the chapter on Demonic Oppression in the *Restoring the Foundations* book is 60 pages in length.

authority over them through the finished work of Jesus Christ on the Cross.[1] In ministering to multitudes of people over the last 20 years, we experience time and time again the awesome delivering power of Jesus as we declare His Word with authority.[2] Yes, demons are real, and yes, they are out to kill. However, the good news is as we take back the "place" we have given to them, i.e., as we stop sinning, repent, and apply God's solution to removing them and their influence from our lives, we can stop their destructive destroying work[3] in us and in our businesses.

One Devil, many "devils"

We want to address an issue raised in the Ephesians 4:26-27 passage that we looked at a moment ago (on page 18). Paul states that we are to "give

> *Jesus Christ provides us authority over ALL the power of the demonic.*

no place to the devil." At first glance this may seem rather scary. After all, who would want to give place to the "devil," inviting the devil into his house? Well, not to fear. Let us remind you that Satan, the Devil, is not omnipresent, i.e., he is not present everywhere at the same time. He focuses his presence where he thinks he can do the most damage without being damaged himself. However, remember that he has an army, a large number of fallen angels, who work for him to carry out his strategies.[4] His army is "everywhere present" looking for opportunities, i.e., "place," where they can take up housekeeping and then proceed to use their host for evil while destroying him. Our job is to create a "peace" zone rather than a "place" zone. We want to create a place of peace where Satan's army is excluded.

---

[1] We will discuss the Cross in more detail shortly.

[2] Jesus, with obvious great delight, makes this powerful declaration in Luke 10:19.

[3] John 10:10 is an important verse contrasting the destructive work of the "thief" (devil) and the abundant life-giving work of the Chief Shepherd, Jesus Christ.

[4] His purpose is stated on page 16.

Proceed as if Demons really do exist regardless of what they really are!

One last thought as we continue to introduce this topic of demons. There has been much discussion throughout the centuries by very learned men and

> *Our job is to create a "peace" zone rather than a "place" zone.*

women attempting to define what a demon is and how/where they originated. This discussion will probably continue until the Lord comes back. While we are interested in knowing more about the inhabitants of the kingdom of darkness, for the sake of this book and the desire and purpose of freeing our organizations, we will proceed with our current understanding of Scripture, our experiences and other people's experiences, and declare that demons do exist, they do have power, and that they are out to destroy us. However, we are no longer naïve, we do understand (and receive) our authority and victory, and so we will proceed to remove their influence from our individual lives and from the lives of our organizations regardless of where they came from and what they are.

Definitions

Derek Prince, the British scholar who has studied and lectured widely about the demonic realm, gives an excellent, all-encompassing definition of demons.

> *Demons are invisible spiritual entities with minds, emotions and wills of their own. They are in league with, and under the control of Satan. They are out to do his bidding and to torment the people of God.*

We would say a hearty "Amen" to this definition, and then add a bit more to it.

> *Demons are spiritual entities in Satan's army that oppress, harass, and sometime possess individual humans. They are given their "place," i.e., "legal ground," to oppress by sin and curses.*

Demonic Strongholds

As the Lord began to have us minister to individuals, we discovered that sometimes it was not enough to "just" cast out one demon after another.[1] Rather, we found an entire complex of demons working together. It was not easy to cast out the demons because they supported each other as they resisted us. We learned that they usually had a complex array of legal ground that needed to be "recovered," i.e., taken back legally by applying God's promises. We had to apply what we now call the Integrated Approach to Ministry,[2] i.e., Restoring the Foundations (RTF) ministry, dealing with each of the first three problem areas within the one stronghold, in order to help the person obtain his freedom from the Demonic Stronghold.

> *Demonic Strongholds are a group of demons working together in a complex structural organization within a person's life to steal, kill, and destroy. Their legal ground comes from the Sins of the Fathers and Resulting Curses, the person's Ungodly Beliefs and his sinful responses from Soul/Spirit Hurts.*

Once the concepts of "legal ground" and the interdependence of the four problem areas were grasped, it changed forever how we did ministry. We saw such increased effectiveness and speed of healing and freedom. It has been a great pleasure since we started training teams in 1986 to be a part of an army of equipped saints bringing this ministry to many needing healing and deliverance.

---

[1] In Mark 16:17 Jesus describes the normal life of "believers," which includes casting out demons.

[2] We discuss the Integrated Approach to Ministry for individuals in Appendix C on page 316.

When we deal with a business or other organization, we almost always are dealing with Demonic Strongholds. These are not only afflicting individuals directly, but also entire businesses and organizations.

F. Principalities

As we continue to learn the fundamental concepts relating to negative
spiritual roots of problems, let's continue to move up the scale of complexity. We are referring to the complexity
of the scope of operation or influence
of evil forces. To help us do this, let us

> *Three Levels*
> - *1st Heaven*
> - *2nd Heaven*
> - *3rd Heaven*

conceptualize three levels of spiritual operations. These levels
are: the atmosphere of the earth, the "first heaven,"[1] the spiritual
"space" outside the earth's atmosphere, the "second heaven,"[2]
and the spiritual realm where God dwells, the "third heaven."[3]
These three "heavens" are either directly mentioned in the Bible
or they are implied.

The Bible refers to evil spiritual entities that are in the first and
second heavens. These appear to be more complex, higher level
spiritual entities than (personal) demons. Let's look at Ephesians 6:12.

> *Ephesians 6:12*
> *For we wrestle not against flesh and blood, but against*
> ***principalities***, *against* ***powers***, *against the* ***rulers*** *of the*
> *darkness of this world, against* ***spiritual wickedness*** *in*
> *high [places].*

---

[1]   The First Heaven is the nearby atmosphere. See Ephesians
    2:2, Rev 8:13, 12:1.

[2]   The Second Heaven is near-earth realm. See Rev 9:1 and
    12:7.

[3]   The Third Heaven is "heaven." See 2 Corinthians 12:2.

The word "principality" comes from the word "principle." This means the "principle" thing, the "number one thing." The word "principality" is referring to the "number one" evil spiritual entity in a region. It could be the regional or territorial "Strong Man."[1]

The terms "powers," "rulers," and "spiritual wickedness" likely are referring to different levels or ranks of spiritual entities. However, regardless of whether Paul is trying to convey details about the spiritual structure of the first and second heavens or not, it seems likely that Satan's army consists of different levels of power, authority, and size of regional control. We will use the word "**principality**" as a general term to refer to negative spiritual entities and powers within the first and second heavens.

We have an example in Daniel 10 of a principality in action.[2] A messenger angel needed help from the warring angel Michael before he was able to break through to Daniel. He was being resisted by the regional principality. He stated that he had started his trip the day Daniel started to pray, but that he was "held up" by the prince of the kingdom of Persia for 21 days until Michael showed up. It seems obvious that the prince of Persia was not (is not) a human prince, but a spiritual "principality" over the region, a territorial principality, with authority and power to resist the passage of one of God's angels.

> ***Principalities:*** *A general term covering all levels of Satan's army that operates within the first and second heaven. These demonic forces have "legal right" to oppress, harass, and "engineer" situations to create more evil. They can affect individuals within their domain as well as groups of individuals, i.e., organizations, cities, regions, and nations, depending on their scope of authority.*

---

[1] Please see Matthew 12:29.
[2] Please see Daniel 10:12-13.

As we move from the arena of ministering to individuals to the arena of businesses and organizations, we move from dealing with individual demons and demonic strongholds afflicting a person to higher level entities harassing a group of people. The group might be small, such as a family, to quite large, such as a nation. Likewise, the principalities may be small, lower level entities to ones that are quite large. They are part of a spiritual hierarchy over the region afflicting families, neighborhoods, towns, cities, states, nations.[1] A few extremely large principalities may have the entire world as their region of influence. Perhaps the "Queen of Heaven" is of this nature.[2]

Cyclical Reinforcing
One interesting thing about principalities is the cyclical reinforcing nature of the type of sin the principality fosters. Let's say we have a region where the sin of homosexuality is rampant. What type of principality will be over the region? Right! At least one principality of sexual sin and defilement will be present, with a strong focus on homosexuality. The principality will draw people into the region that are either already engaged in this sin or that are susceptible to entering into it. The sin of the additional people strengthens and builds the principality. Thus it is able to exert even more influence and power, drawing in even more people. This reinforcing continues until confession of sin and repentance begins to clear the land, reversing the cycle, removing authority and influence from the principality.

Pick any type of sin and we can find locations in the world where this sin is prevalent, a place that is "known" for this sin. It's a self-perpetuating, self-multiplying system. As the sin is given place, it leads to more sin which magnifies the principalities that in turn, draw in more people to get them involved. This pattern and the cycle continue.

---

[1] Frank Peretti's novels "Piercing the Darkness" and "This Present Darkness" did much to bring these understandings about principalities into the Christian public awareness.

[2] The Queen of Heaven is mentioned in Jeremiah 7:18, 44:17-19, 25. Also, we briefly discuss this principality in Part Four on Principalities (starting on page 208).

Two Types

There are two types of principalities or spiritual powers that are of interest to us within the context of this book. The first type is the "territo-

> *Two Types of Principalities*
> *- Territorial/Regional*
> *- Group/Organizational*

rial" or "regional" principality. This one has legal ground because of sin on the land, or defilement of the land. This sin/defilement accumulates on the land, providing more and more "place" for the building up of the principality. This is starkly spelled out for us in Leviticus 18.

> *Leviticus 18:24-25*
> *18:24 Do not defile yourselves in any of these(sinful) ways, because this is how the nations that I am going to drive out before you became defiled.*
> *18:25 **Even the land was defiled**; so I punished it for its sin, and the land vomited out its inhabitants.*

The second type is a "group" or "organizational" principality, which has legal ground because of sin attached to the people, either personal or ancestral. When an organization acquires and occupies land and structures, these two types of principalities merge together and exert a combined influence on the business.

Displacing Principalities

One last comment before we move on. From a spiritual warfare standpoint, we do not "cast out" princi-

> *Principalities are removed by "displacing" them.*

palities in the same way we "cast out" demons from an individual. Rather, we remove the legal ground of the principalities, stop or minimize their influence, and refuse to cooperate with them. This causes them to "diminish" in "size." As they become weaken, we "push" them "away," "displacing" them so that we can open up the heavens over the land, the organization, the church, the business.

G. Baggage: Problems in a Suitcase

What word can we use to represent all of these actual or potential open doors, the different ways that we provide legal ground for problem-causing spiritual roots to get established? What word conveys the heavy load(s) of guilt and shame we might be carrying, the defiling and dirty nature of sins and curses, demons and principalities? How about the term; "Baggage?"

Most people would not think of the word "Baggage" as a scriptural term. However, it does communicate the concept we want, even if it is not a King James word.[1] We could use words such as "garbage," "stuff," etc., but "Baggage" seems to do it well.

> **Baggage:** A general term we will use to represent the sum or total accumulation of all sin, curses, demons, principalities, i.e., "evil," already associated with a person, organization, or place, as well as the **potential for future evil.**

One of the meanings given to "Baggage" by Webster is, "*Superfluous or burdensome practices, regulations, ideas, or traits.*" This is indeed how the baggage of sin binds us and hinders us.

Our definition for "Baggage" includes the potential for future evil. Ancestral sins and curses don't always manifest in a person's life until later in life. Sometimes it is not until there is a moment of weakness, or a crisis in a person's life, or some other event, that provides a trigger to release the curse. For example, a trauma of some sort may occur. The person feels overwhelmed, with too much hurt and pain to deal with. The enemy rises up and whispers, "This pain is too great. One drink will make it so much better." That one drink may be all it takes to trigger an ancestral sin and curse of alcoholism. *The enemy has*

---

[1] While the word "baggage" is not in the King James Bible, the word "bag" is, as is "stuff." The concept is clearly the same.

waited for a strategic time. The potential for more sin, more evil, was there all along. It was part of the "Baggage" the person was carrying.

There are three primary types of baggage we will refer to in this book. There is the "personal" baggage that each one of us carries. There is also "group"

Three Types of Baggage
- **Personal**
- **Group/Organizational**
- **Territorial/Regional**

baggage, the combined total of the individuals making up the group or organization. And there is the "territorial" baggage that has accumulated on the land and structures because of the former residents of the land. We will mention a fourth type in Part Two, the "environmental" baggage.

> **Group/Organizational Baggage:** This is the sum total of all sin, curses, demons, principalities, i.e., **evil, associated with the founding fathers** (and mothers) and all those who joined the organization since the beginning, as well as the **potential for future evil.**

> **Territorial/Regional Baggage:** This is the sum total of all sin, curses, demons, principalities, i.e., evil, **associated with a piece of land** and the structures upon it, as well as the **potential for future evil.**

In the following pages, we will use the term "Baggage" as a short hand code word. It will free us from repeating all of the above words for the various types of sins and curses over and over again.

II. Fundamental Concepts: The Positive

In wading through the negative fundamental concepts, we decry with Paul in Romans 7:24, "Oh wretched man that I am! Who shall deliver me from the body of this death?" Our need for deliverance from the negative is exposed. Whether we want to focus on it or not, it is present. So we ask, "How do we eliminate the negative?" Paul answers the question for us in the next verse. "I thank God through Jesus Christ our Lord." The "positive" is Jesus Christ. He is "the" solution. It is important for us to know what He accomplished for all of us on the Cross.

A. The Cross of Christ

The reason God the Father sent Jesus the Christ to earth was to rescue us and show us His divine love. The human race, deceived and trapped by the master deceiver, was utterly lost and without hope. But even before man fell, God already had a solution. He would provide the way, the perfect sacrifice, based on the pattern of sacrifice and substitution He would establish as part of His Law,

> *Jesus provided the Solution*
> *for every Spiritual Problem.*
> *Our Job is to*
> *Appropriate His Provision!*

God's plan was to provide the adequate substitute on our behalf to pay the price for our sins that we were not able to pay. Jesus was that perfect substitute, the perfect sacrifice. As He died on the Cross, Jesus provided a solution for every problem we would face, especially our spiritual problems. Our job is to appropriate His provision.

Matthew 5:17
Do not think that I have come to abolish the Law or the
*Prophets; I have not come to abolish them **but to fulfill***
them.

Here we have an incredible paradox: Jesus Christ fulfilling the requirements of the Law by being that perfect sacrifice, so that we can be free of the consequences coming from that very same Law, because we can not fulfill its righteous requirements. Wow! This is awesome. He said, "I am the Way." He is the only way out from the consequences of sin. As we progress through this book, and as we apply the Action Plan to our businesses, we will be appropriating the finished work of Jesus the Christ on the Cross over and over again. This is God's solution to every problem we may face.

B. Revelation: Gifts of the Holy Spirit

How do we discover what we need to know so that we can recognize and remove negative spiritual roots and their unwanted fruit? Once again God has provided the solution. God wants us to know; He wants us to have "success," to rule and reign with Him. Jesus told His followers before He went to the Cross that after His death and departure from the earth, He would send His Spirit to provide direction, comfort, and revelation for His Church.

John 14:26, 16:7
*14:26 But the Counselor, the **Holy Spirit, whom the***
***Father will send in my name**, will teach you all things*
*and **will remind you of everything** I have said to you.*

16:7 Nevertheless I tell you the truth; It is expedient
for you that I go away: for if I go not away, the Com-
*forter will not come unto you; but if I depart, **I will***
send him unto you.

It is important to learn to hear the voice of the Lord,[1] whether by hearing, seeing, or impression. This is how we receive revelation and operate in the gifts of the Holy Spirit.[2] When we use both the natural knowledge that we can discover through research and the supernatural knowledge that comes from the Holy Spirit, we have what we need to investigate the sources and causes of negative spiritual roots within our business.

C. The Tithe: The Gift of God to Sanctify

When you wonder, "How are we going to get all of the pastors, all of the spiritual leaders of the city into agreement so that the city can be taken for God?" Or the equivalent question, "How am I going to get all of the leaders of my business together, in agreement, so that we can move ahead with God's agenda for us?" Well, here is good news!

We were in this rather large city where we were serving several churches with the Restoring the Foundations ministry. As we talked with the pastors about the city being "taken for God," it became clear that they felt there was much disunity among the various church leaders and pastors. Between the differing denominations, theologies, degree of commitments, salvation (or lack there of), etc., they were quite discouraged. One thing they did agree on was, "We will never get all of these people together in one place, much less together against the devil and his destruction! How can we take our city for God with so many leaders not participating?"

The Lord reminded us of the principle of the tithe. "What is the purpose of the tithe?" What does happen when we tithe 10% of our money, the increase of

> *The Tithe sanctifies the Rest!*

our field? An amazing thing happens. The tithe sanctifies the rest of the money. It sanctifies the other 90%.[3] The Lord said to

---

[1] Please see John 10:1-4.

[2] The gifts of the Holy Spirit are listed in 1 Corinthians 12:3-7.

[3] We invite you to ponder Deuteronomy 14:22 and Luke 11:41.

us, in the same way, "*If a tithe of the Godly leaders of the city will come together in agreement and begin to do the spiritual warfare and intercession, and oversee what takes place, they can sanctify the rest.*"

This excited us. The Lord is saying it only takes 10% of the key spiritual leaders in the city coming together to have sufficient spiritual authority to take the city for God. They can sanctify the rest of the city leaders, saved or unsaved.[1] We don't have to have *everybody* in agreement. The more the better, but a tithe can get the process started, and started well![2]

The Few Sanctify the Many!

So the same thing is true for a business. In a business with several leaders, not all of whom are "born again"[3] or interested in spiritual warfare, those that do have a heart to apply the principles expressed in *Transforming Your Business* can represent/sanctify the others. The only cautions are to respect authority and responsibility boundaries, to not get ahead of the Holy Spirit, to not usurp legitimate authority of those over you and around you. However, who knows, as the mercies and power of God begin to move more and more through the organization, maybe all of the leaders will become serious about spiritual things, will become saved, and will move more into their destiny along with their business.

D. Unity and Agreement

We do want "unity," and yet we want more than just "unity." **Nimrod and company** had unity, but God was not pleased with their purpose to build a tower to heaven.[4] So He confused their language and caused them to scatter. We want unity, but in

---

[1] An example of a believer sanctifying an unbeliever is found in 1 Corinthians 7:14.

[2] We see this principle in operation as Abraham negotiated with God to save the city of Sodom in Genesis 18:23-32.

[3] Jesus discusses being "born again" in John 3:1-7.

[4] Nimrod and Company is discussed on page 5.

God's way, with God's righteousness. We want agreement, God's way, and His purpose for our organization. We want agreement with others in our organization, so that we all will "be on the same page." Otherwise, the leaders of the business will not be able to (fully) put into practice the concepts, insights, and revelation presented in this book. Jesus declared the power of agreement.

> *Matthew 18:19-20*
> *18:19 Again I say unto you, **That if two of you shall agree on earth** as touching any thing that **they shall ask, it shall be done for them** of my Father which is in heaven.*
> *18:20 For where two or three are gathered together in my name, **there am I in the midst of them**.*

In the book of John, we have a number of occasions when Jesus states His unity with the Father. He effectively says, "I

Unity and Agreement "with God" is the key.

only say what I hear the Father saying and I only do what I see the Father doing."[1] Can we come to that point of being so connected with our Father that we could make the same declaration that Jesus made?

The way for leaders to transform their organization is to choose unity and agreement with each other and with God. Intercessory prayer by leaders in agreement can change the spiritual climate throughout a business. Employees begin to change their mindsets not even knowing the prayer is going on. Even the Organizational Culture can change and become more congruent with God's purpose, values, and vision. For example, in the book "Good to Great,"[2] Jim Collins and his team distill the characteristics that allowed 11 companies to make the transition from good to great companies. While Jim was not writing a "spiri-

---

[1] You will find examples of this theme in John 5:19-20, 30; 6:38; 8:28-29, 38; 10:32, 38; 14:31; 15:15.

[2] Please check out the Biography on page 331.

tual" book, he did explain the spiritual principles behind the successful transitions. One of the key ingredients identified is a Organizational Culture that includes humble, yet strong-willed leaders that work together as a team. Being passionate about the company vision, having strong values, and knowing they are "on purpose," they operate in unity and agreement.

Perhaps the crowning Biblical passage concerning unity is Psalm 133. It is an awesome possibility to live where the Lord **commands** the blessing. Is it possible that we could experience this in our businesses and organizations?

> *Psalm 133:1-3 (KJV)*
> *133:1 Behold, **how good and how pleasant [it is] for brethren to dwell together in unity!***
> *133:2 [It is] like the precious ointment upon the head, that ran down upon the beard, [even] Aaron's beard: that went down to the skirts of his garments;*
> *133:3 As the dew of Hermon, [and as the dew] that descended upon the mountains of Zion: **for there the LORD commanded the blessing**, [even] life for ever-more.*

So, why not? Why don't we all come easily come into Biblical unity? It seems so simple conceptually. We must conclude that there must be other forces at work besides God's Spirit!

Kingdom of Darkness
What is this kingdom? In Ephesians Paul writes about two things that influence everyone: "the ways of this world" and "the ruler of the kingdom of the air."[1]

> *Ephesians 2:2*
> *... in which you used to live when you followed **the ways of this world** and of **the ruler of the kingdom of the air**, the spirit who is now at work in those who are disobedient.*

---

[1] Referring back to our discussion on the three heavens (page 27), it appears that Paul is discussing either the first or second heaven, or both.

Let us also consider Second Timothy.

> *2 Timothy 2:25-26*
> *2:25 Those who oppose him he must gently instruct,*
> *in the hope **that God will grant them repentance lead-***
> ***ing them to a knowledge of the truth,***
> *2:26 and **that they will come to their senses** and es-*
> *cape from the trap of the devil, who **has taken them***
> ***captive to do his will.***

These are such power packed passages. Paul is stating that
through repentance and knowledge of the truth, the rebellious
toward God can "come to their senses." This strongly implies
that these people are not "in their senses" when in rebellion and
without the truth. Is it too much to generalize and conclude
then, that none of us are "in our senses" while in rebellion
against God? Is it possible that the "prince of the air" keeps the
world (including those in your business) in such a deceived state
that they are afraid of God, not even interested in finding out
how much He loves them? Not able to make quality decisions
to know and receive the Lord, they cannot hear the Lord's voice
to help guide them through life, to help them function in their
job with creativity and faith, not to mention unity and agreement! Once again, we see the importance of not being naive
about demons and their work of deception and destruction.

E. Binding and Loosing

In order to minimize or
eliminate the influence
of the "prince of the air,"
we need to discover the
legal ground and recover

> *We can "bind" the enemy,*
> *hindering his work.*

it. Until that is accomplished, however, we can "bind" the evil
spirits affecting us. Jesus makes a startling statement in Matthew 18:18 about our ability to bring the authority of heaven to
earth to "bind" and restrict the activity of the kingdom of darkness, as well as to "loose" the purposes of God.

Matthew 18:18
*I tell you the truth, **whatever you bind on earth will be bound in heaven**, and whatever you loose on earth will be loosed in heaven.*

In this passage, the Greek meaning behind word "bind" is:

to constrain, as to tie with a rope; to muzzle, as to keep an ox from eating.

Thus Jesus has delegated to us the authority to "tie," as with a rope, the prince of the power of the air to stop his functioning. When it comes to your business, this sounds like a good thing to do; it sounds like a good assignment for the Intercessors.

"Binding" is a powerful weapon in the hands of the Intercessors. When they come into agreement and unity, they can use their authority to bind the prince

> *We can "bind" the prince so people can "come to their senses."*

of the power of the air and his works in the organization. This begins to reduce the ability of the principalities over the organization, as well as the individual demons, to cloud people's minds. The power to deceive and hold captive each person's mind can be bound and stopped. This allows each person to think for himself without this outside interference. Who wants to stay captive to do the will of the devil, or the principalities affecting the organization, or influencing demons? What a repugnant thought! Who in his right mind would not want to know God, be an heir, and operate in His wisdom?

F. Intercession

You might be asking, "What is intercession?" and "Who are the Intercessors?"

Intercession is pleading the cause of another. It is to act as a mediator on behalf of another.

This is what Jesus Christ does for us before God the Father. As the Bible states in Hebrews:

> *Hebrews 7:25 (NIV)*
> *Therefore he is able to save completely those who come to God through him, because **he always lives to intercede for them**.*

In the same way that Jesus intercedes for us, we can stand in for another and plead his cause. This must be possible and it must be important, or else in Jeremiah, God would not be chiding the nation of Israel that they had no Intercessors to petition on their behalf.

> *Jeremiah 30:13*
> *There **is no one to plead your cause, no remedy for your sore, no healing for you**.*

Whoever stands in for another to plead their cause is an Intercessor. This must include the leaders. It can also include those especially gifted by God to bring this type of prayer/petition before the throne of God. In fact, it is a good idea to have intercessors in key positions within your company. We will take up the topic of Intercession and Intercessors in detail in Part Five, being a vital part of successful implementing of the Action Plan. However, for now, let's see what we can do to "plead the cause" of the business leaders and the ones living on the land before we arrived on the scene.

G. Identification Repentance

There is plenty of scriptural support for Identification Repentance through Intercession. As we discussed above using Jeremiah 30:13 as one example, many times God asks the question, "Is there no one to pray for you?" God is looking for leaders that will identify with and "stand in" for the people and the land. Here is another example of His cry from Ezekiel:[1]

---

[1] You may find other examples of Identification Repentance at Daniel 9:3-19, Nehemiah 1:4-10, Isaiah 21,

> *Ezekiel 22:30*
> *And I sought for a man among them, that should **make up** the hedge, and **stand in** the gap before me for the land, that I should not destroy it: but I found none.*

We as leaders can "stand in" and intercede for the entire organization. We can accomplish "Identification Repentance" to represent the people and the land before the Lord, functioning as priest and intercessor. This is vitally necessary if we are going to remove the negative spiritual roots of problems from our organizations.

When we decide to free our business from accumulated sins and curses, we might be the founders; in which case we lead the ministry repenting for our own sin and what we brought into the foundations of the organization.

Or we might be the current leaders/owners of an ongoing business. In this case, we want to "stand in" for, i.e., intercede for, the founders and all leaders that have preceded us. We are effectively identifying with them, confessing and repenting for their sins and ours, as we and others in the organization bring our petition before the throne of God.

> *"Identification Repentance" is how we "stand in" for others*

Of course, we must also identify with the former residents of the land and the corruption they brought upon the land through their sin. As owners/renters/leasers/etc., we now have legal and spiritual authority over the land and the structures. It is our job to bring all of the accumulated sin and curses, i.e., Baggage, to the Cross so that it can be cleansed from the land. God's heart is redemption. He wants us and the land restored and removed out of the domain of Satan.

42

Let us remind you that it is not necessary for every leader to agree with or participate in the Identification Repentance. As we mentioned earlier on page 35, if at least a "tithe" of the leaders are in unity and agreement, they can begin to change the spiritual climate and future of the business.

There are many books available discussing this important arena of "Identification Repentance," as well as "Intercession." We have a number of them listed in the Bibliography on page 331. Cindy Jacobs and Peter Wagner are two well-known authors on this subject, while John Dawson first used the phrase "Identification Repentance" in his book *Taking Our Cities for God*, released in 2001. Dutch Sheets is the author of a very clear, straightforward book on Intercession that is highly recommended.

H. Occupying versus Possessing

Before we leave these thoughts of Intercession and Identification Repentance (only for a short time), we want to stress the difference between Occupying and Possessing. The difference is very important as we seek to cleanse the land of defilement and displace the principalities from the land.

You see, a person (or Leadership Team) with limited authority will not impress the principalities on the land. It will take a person (or a team) that has authority over the land. Ideally, this will be a person with civil, legal authority (either owns or rents/leases the land) and with spiritual authority (is submitted to and under the authority of the Lord Jesus Christ). He must be in charge of, responsible for, and **on** the land before he will gain the attention and obedience of the spiritual entities over the land. His authority must be higher than that of the spiritual entity.

Jesus discusses this difference in John, chapter 10, as He contrasts the good shepherd versus the thief and hireling. The good shepherd "possessed" the sheep, took ownership, while the hireling "occupied," worked a job, until it was no longer beneficial to him. It basically is the difference between "taking responsibility for," "owning," "caring for," "making it a part of oneself," versus not caring and not taking responsibility.

Occupying can mean "having control of," such as an occupying army, but the occupying troops are more apt to use and abuse the land than care for it. "Squatters" would be in the same category, with their "squatter's rights," but when the real owner comes to possess the land, the squatters can be easily displaced.

The word "steward" carries with it the concept of responsibility and care. If the earth is the Lord's and the fullness thereof,[1] then we all are called as stewards to carry out God's command given in Genesis one.[2] There God delegated authority and responsibility to Adam and Eve to have dominion over the earth, to rule it, and to care for it. As our business obtains land and structures, it behooves us to not view them as something to be used and wasted, but as gifts from the Lord to be cared for and cherished. As we do this, the land will be blessed and not cursed, it will produce and not be barren.

Actually, in a very real sense, God calls us to "marry" the land. He wants us to have a covenant relationship with the land, much as a husband enters into a covenant with his wife. In fact, the word "husband" originated as one with fields and flocks, as the one who is the caretaker of them. As our company obtains land and structures, and we decide to cleanse the business using the Transforming Your Business process, we will include a commitment to "possess" the land in the Action Plan. And so the land will be fruitful and productive.

> *Isaiah 62:4-5 (NIV)*
> *No longer will they call you **Deserted**, or name your land **Desolate**. But you will be called Hephzibah, and your land Beulah; for the LORD will take delight in you, and **your land will be married**.*
> *As a young man marries a maiden, **so will your sons marry you**; as a bridegroom rejoices over his bride, so will your God rejoice over you.*

---

[1] David expressed this truth in Psalm 24:1. Paul quotes David in 1 Corinthians 10:26.

[2] The verse is Genesis 1:28.

I. Supernatural Thoughts

As we conclude this section on positive fundamental concepts, we are so grateful that we are alive on this side of the Cross. Because of what Jesus Christ did for us, we have access to God and the mind of Christ. We can know His thoughts, we can think like God. We can discern situations and make decisions using heavenly wisdom. We can operate in the supernatural realm as the Holy Spirit manifests His gifts within and through us. We can know what we need to know to "get the devil out of our businesses," to set our businesses free and to accomplish God's purposes.

If this all seems too good to be true, here are some passages from Ephesians, 1 Corinthians, and James to illustrate these points.

> *Ephesians 3:10-12 (NIV)*
> *3:10 His intent was that now, **through the church, the manifold wisdom of God should be made known to the rulers and authorities in the heavenly realms,***
> *3:11 **according to his eternal purpose** which he accomplished in Christ Jesus our Lord.*
> *3:12 In him and through faith in him we may approach God with freedom and confidence.*

God wants to use us to make known to the demonic principalities His manifold wisdom. He wants us to have the supernatural knowledge we need to free ourselves and our businesses. This is according to His eternal purpose. Wow! We can not get more support than this! Can you imagine the look of surprise on the face of a principality when we start displacing it from our land!

> *1 Corinthians 2:9-15 (NAS)*
>
> *2:9 but just as it is written, "Things which eye has not seen and ear has not heard, and which have not entered the heart of man,* **all that God has prepared for those who love him.** *"*
>
> *2:10* **For to us God revealed them through the Spirit;** *...*
>
> *2:12 ... that* **we might know the things freely given to us** *by God,*
>
> *2:13 which things* **we also speak,** *not in words taught by human wisdom, but in those taught by the Spirit,* **combining spiritual thoughts with spiritual words.**
>
> *2:15 ...* **he who is spiritual appraises (discerns) all things;** *yet he himself is appraised by no man.*
>
> *2:16 ... But we have* **the mind of Christ.**
>
> *James 1:5*
>
> **If any of you lacks wisdom, he should ask God,** *who* **gives generously to all** *without finding fault,* **and it will be given to him.**

These passages further reinforce God's determination to give us everything we need to demonstrate His wisdom, glory, power, goodness, love, and superiority.

We will discuss these passages and concepts more in Part Three, the Action Plan, as we prepare the Intercessors for their role in bringing freedom. We will be seeking knowledge and wisdom "from above" regarding the negative spiritual roots of spiritual problems, knowledge we could not gain from natural sources. We will be seeking God's strategy for implementing the Action Plan, to bring our entire organization into healing and freedom so that we can operate in Kingdom principles, fulfilling purpose and destiny.

But wait. There is another step we can take.

J. Putting God in Charge

Do you remember a bumper sticker that first appeared during World War Two? It read, "God is my co-pilot." We remember thinking when we first read it, "My, isn't that sweet. Having God in the co-pilot's seat helping the pilot is such a nice idea!"

Yes, it is a good idea to have God's help. However, over the years we have learned that there is a better way. Rather than letting God help us, it is much better if we put God in charge and we help Him. This is the place "co-laboring with him."[1] It is the place of "Sonship." The best arrangement for us is "God and son." Choosing to put God in the pilot's seat and our self in the co-pilot's seat as the helper is the wise decision. We want to have Him lead us as we learn to manage and operate the "family" business.

It is interesting that Jesus stated in Luke, "I must be about My Father's business!"[2] At age twelve He was already clear about Who was in charge and what His role was. We see this attitude carried on during His ministry as He only did what He saw the Father doing and He only said what He heard the Father saying.[3]

In Romans we have an incredible verse:

> *Romans 8:14*
> *For as many as are **led by the Spirit of God**, they are the **sons of God**.*

What if we as business leaders dedicated our businesses to the Lord and put Him in charge of leading the business. What if we functioned as "sons" of God and only did what we saw the Father doing and we only said what we heard the Father saying? What if the Intercessors and Leaders were all "sons" of God,

---

[1] First Corinthians 3:9 expresses this truth.

[2] These words are in Luke 2:49.

[3] We discussed this point in the section on Unity and Agreement on page 37.

listening for His guidance? Is this too far out? There are many who have done this already.

Let us share just a couple of stories from the many examples available of men and women who put God in the "pilot's seat" and became His co-pilots. The results are astounding.

Ralph Doudera in his book, *Wealth Conundrum,*[1] shares the process and conversations with God that moved him from being the owner of "his" business to being the steward of "God's" business. Ralph got rid of his over-stressed and emotional roller-coaster life and gained the joy of watching the Lord multiply the business beyond his wildest dreams.

Way back in the 1950's, Dr. R. Stanley Tam was likewise convicted by God to legally convey full title of his company to God. He wrote a book, *God Owns My Business*, about the process God took him through. His story is one of failure to success, of rags to riches. At first Stanley failed, as had several other companies, as he tried to create never-before developed plastic products. However, once he obeyed God and turned ownership over to the Lord, the problems were solved. Today, United States Plastic, States Smelting, Industrial Safety, and Tamco stand as major testimonies to the grace of God and the benefits of His ownership.

Both of these men have demonstrated the first purpose for the existence of a business (page 7), as they have been used to transfer millions of dollars into the Kingdom of God. Is this what God wants for you and your business?

If you have ownership authority in your business, we encourage you to seriously think and pray about putting God in charge of your business. If you have management authority over a subsidiary or a semi-isolated department, you may have the spiritual authority put God in charge of that unit, even if you cannot transfer the legal title to Him. It is important that you do not

---

[1] Please see the Bibliography for information about these two books.

usury legitimate authority from those over you and add new problems to your existing ones.

However, regardless of the level of authority you may have or where you are in the company structure, you can always draw on the principle of the tithe (see page 35). This gives you the basis to bring together a group of "sons of God" to represent the Kingdom of God in your business. As you follow the leading of the Holy Spirit, anything is possible as God is invited into the management and operation of your part of the company.

If you are wondering, "Just how does one put God in charge of my business?" we will include some of the initial steps in the Action Plan of Part Three.

However, it is "interesting" that as *Transforming Your Business* was being finalized and prepared for release, the Lord was already revealing to our friend and associate, Dr. Carle Hunt, the contents of a companion book. The title given the book by the Lord is, *Leading a Transformed Business.* It will expound further on many of the concepts and principles introduced in *Transforming Your Business*, including how to put God in charge of the business. The book will also lay out the details of the importance of hearing God's voice with immediate obedience, purity of heart, the significance of anointing, revelation, impartation, the staffing of Intercessors and how to lead them, carrying out ongoing vigilance cleansing and alertness, and many other subjects important in leading "God's" transformed business.

We look forward to presenting this new book for your use in becoming all you can in the Kingdom of God.

But for now, let's learn about the Spiritual Dynamics of Organizations, the next step on the road to an Action Plan.

PART TWO

Spiritual Dynamics of Organizations

Every organization (business, church, club, etc.) consists of both the individuals of the organization and the location/structures occupied by the organization. As discussed in Part One, we need to consider the personal and group Baggage carried by the people and the territorial Baggage "accumulated" on the land and buildings. Each type of Baggage contains the negative spiritual roots of ancestral sins and curses. The personal Baggage includes the ancestral sins and curses from the individual's personal family line, while the territorial Baggage contains the sins and curses from the former residents on the land. We also need to consider the personal and group Ungodly Beliefs, or Organizational Culture. Sinful responses to the hurts within the individuals and the organization also contribute to the Baggage. The hurts need to be healed and the sinful behavioral patterns changed. As the Baggage is repented of, cleansed, and reduced, the "place" given to the group and territorial principalities can be recovered, the demons cast out and the principalities displaced.

In Part Two, we will look at two different aspects of spiritual dynamics. The first aspect is the cause and effect phenomena known as sowing and reaping. Sins produce curses, which in turn, leads to more sin. This dynamic ripples down through the generations and accumulates on the land. We will look at these spiritual roots and God's solution to these sources of problems.

The second aspect of spiritual dynamic is the interaction over time of the three primary components of an organization: the people, the land/structures, and the interface between these and the rest of the world. We consider what has happened along the "time line" during the life of an organization. What significant things have happened in the spiritual realm as a business is created and then at each significant event in its existence?

As we combine the basic "Things We Need to Know" from Part One with this material in Part Two, we will gain additional insights. We will then be prepared for Part Three where we develop an Action Plan to begin removing the negative spiritual roots of spiritual problems from our organizations and our personal lives.

Cause and Effect Phenomena

One of the most fundamental laws of the universe is the law of Sowing and Reaping.[1] When a seed is

> *Most Important Law:*
> *Sowing and Reaping*

planted (released), the built-in mechanisms start a sequence of actions which leads to a harvest. As these actions occur, energy is absorbed from the sun (energy source) and nutrients are drawn from the soil as building material. Thus a tiny seed can become a huge oak tree, a corn plant, or a fruit tree. Each seed produces after its own kind, yielding more seeds in the process. The Cause (seed, root) results in an Effect (harvest, fruit). This same phenomena occurs in the spiritual realm. Spiritual seed reproduces after its own kind just as natural seed reproduces after its kind.[2] Bad spiritual seed results in a bad spiritual harvest. A bad spiritual harvest is another name for "problems." Let's look at the sources of bad spiritual seed.

> *A "bad spiritual harvest" is*
> *another name for "problems!"*

---

[1] Please see Genesis 1:11-25, where God declared that everything reproduced after its own kind.

[2] Please see Galatians 6:7-8. We choose whether we sow to corruption or we sow to life.

I. Negative Spiritual Roots of Spiritual Problems

As we have said more than once, we want to deal with the negative spiritual roots leading to problems so that we can obtain complete freedom. What are these roots, and from where do they come? We planted the "seeds" for this discussion in Part One; now let's get into the specifics.

A. Spiritual Inheritance: Biological/Spiritual Authorities

> Sins of the <u>Founding</u> Fathers and resulting Curses (SOFFCs)

The second commandment (on page 19) states that a curse is activated by the sins of idolatry and disobedience. This curse is released onto the children, for three or four generations. The curse's residual is a heart tendency within the children to sin in the same ways that their forefathers sinned.

Thus, when several people come together to create a business/organization, each brings his family sin patterns and tendencies (i.e., Baggage) with him. When the sin patterns from each person are combined as a whole, these form the "**Sins of the <u>Founding</u> Fathers (and mothers) and resulting Curses**" (SOFFCs) sin pattern for the new organization. As these people come together within an official legal structure, they create a starting point, a "birthing," of the organization that sets the context of the entire business for the rest of its existence. This is completely analogous to the birthing of a baby, who carries within itself the complete DNA, both physical and spiritual, of its ancestors.

For example, let's say four couples decide to start a business. Each person commits to their part. Perhaps this includes the amount of time each one will put in, the money each will contribute to get things going, personal equipment and skills dedicated to the success of the organization. But, what else does each one contribute? That's right. Each one also brings his particular ancestral sins and curses to the mix; his "Baggage." He brings his family's "familiar" spirits (demons) as well as the ones he has given place to in his own life. Each one's "Baggage" contributes synergistically to the group/organizational "Baggage," the "startup Baggage" of the organization.

However, it is even more complex than just one's biological forefathers. Both scripturally and experientially we see the evidence that other authority figures in our lives contribute to the pressure to enter into, or commit, the same type of sins as our ancestors/spiritual authorities. Besides our parents and other ancestors, our spiritual inheritance can come from step-parents, teachers, coaches, pastors, and others that are influential in our lives. These important people can impart encouragement or discouragement into our lives, blessings or curses. We carry this impartation with us into our businesses.

For example, have you ever been shamed or put down by a teacher or coach? If so, it is likely that this wound is still being carried on the inside of you, as part of your Baggage. The ripples of the past sin are continuing whether you (or I) like it or not, just as the children of Israel bore the punishment of their fathers.

> *Lamentations 5:7 (NIV)*
> *Our fathers sinned and are no more, and **we bear their punishment.***

B. Spiritual Inheritance: Land and Structures

Sins of the <u>Resident</u> Fathers and resulting Curses (**SORFCs**)

When the group creating the new organization select land and buildings to house their new business, generally there is no consideration given to questions such as, "Who was on this land before us? What did they do? What Godly and ungodly activities took place on this land and in these buildings? What spiritual forces were released or strengthened? What influences will they have on us and our organization?" Or perhaps the most important question, "What can we do to remove these influences?"

Though very few would think about such questions (and much less try to answer), the effects of the former sins, as well as the righteousness on the land, brings a "spiritual" inheritance to the group. "Resident" ancestors affect the land. All of the former inhabitants of the land, from the beginning of time, have contributed to the current "sin burden," i.e., the Baggage, on the land. This area is the "**Sins of the <u>Resident</u> Fathers and resulting Curses**" (SORFCs).

We can see an example of this phenomenon with God's promise to Abraham in Genesis.[1] God promised He would give the land of Canaan to Abraham's seed, but not until the iniquity of the Amorites had reached its fullness.[2]

> *Genesis 15:16*
> *But in the fourth generation they shall come hither again: for the **iniquity of the Amorites [is] not yet full**.*

It is clear that the sin of the Amorites was accumulating. Their "Baggage" was compounding against them, until the day that the scales tipped and the Israelites, Abraham's descendants, were given title deed to the land.

---

[1] This promise is repeated a number of times. Please see Genesis 13:15, 17, 15:7, 18.

[2] Abram's seed would have to wait for four hundred years, or four generations, and go through much hardship, before the promise would be fulfilled. Please see Genesis 15:13 and 16.

In Leviticus 18 the Bible makes it very clear that the land accumulates the sins of the inhabitants and becomes defiled.

Leviticus 18:24-29
18:24 "'Do not defile yourselves in any of these ways, because this is how the nations that I am going to drive out before you became defiled.
18:25 Even the land was defiled; so I punished it for its sin, and the land vomited out its inhabitants.
18:26 But you must keep my decrees and my laws. The native-born and the aliens living among you must not do any of these detestable things,
18:27 for all these things were done by the people who lived in the **land before you, and the land became defiled.**

> **The Land "vomited" out its inhabitants**

18:28 And if you **defile the land, it will vomit you out** *as it vomited out the nations that were before you.*
18:29 "'Everyone who does any of these detestable things--such persons must be cut off from their people.

This passage contains very strong language. Imagine the land "vomiting out" its inhabitants. Imagine God "punishing" the land for the sins of the people.

When the land is defiled, how does God punish the land? One way is by becoming unfruitful, by barrenness. There are a number of "chilling" passages in the Bible that give this impression.

Here are several verses from Deuteronomy 28. Other passages are listed in the footnote.[1]

> *Deuteronomy 28:18, 38-40, 42*
> *28:18 The fruit of your womb will be cursed, and the crops of your land, and the calves of your herds and the lambs of your flocks.*
>
> *28:38 You will sow much seed in the field but you will harvest little, because locusts will devour it.*
> *28:39 You will plant vineyards and cultivate them but you will not drink the wine or gather the grapes, because worms will eat them.*
> *28:40 You will have olive trees throughout your country but you will not use the oil, because the olives will drop off.*
>
> *28:42 Swarms of locusts will take over all your trees and the crops of your land.*

Not a pretty picture, is it? It sounds like a lot of work with very little payoff. Not the kind of business that we want to be involved with, is it? And yet many of us are. Why? Because we don't understand the accumulation of sin and curses upon the land and how this stops the fruitfulness of the land. In modern day terms, the Israelite's agricultural business operated at a loss.

Imagine this promising new multi-million dollar business moving into its sparkling new buildings on a tract of land that was a "good buy." Unknowingly to the new owners, the land has been defiled. Over the ensuing months and years the curses on the land "pressure" the new owners, the employees, and the business toward and into the same type(s) of sin that

> *How can a promising new Business fail? It can if the land "vomits" it out!*

---

[1] Scriptures describing unproductive land are: Isaiah 24:1, 3, 5-6. Also please read Deuteronomy 29:22-24, 27-28, Isaiah 24:1-6, Jeremiah 44:22, and Romans 8:22.

produced the defilement. As they succumb to the defiling sin patterns, giving "place," the business and the people become defiled. The curses cause the business to have continual problems, never realizing their original promise or real potential. Rather, it continues to lose money until they are forced to sell the facilities and leave. Truly, the land has "vomited" out its occupants and has become even more unfruitful (i.e., unproductive)!

With our transient society, we have little or no knowledge of what has gone on before we arrive on the scene. Yes, we may be able to obtain some recorded history, but it takes real digging to learn about the sin patterns. And even with the best of records dating back 100-200 years, these kinds of things are rarely recorded in the legal records of the land. There is a lot of history (from the dawn of time to now) that we do not know by natural means.

How dependant we are on the grace gifts of the Holy Spirit (page 34) to show us what we need to know of the "happening" in the past. God desires to redeem the land and all who dwell in it. He is eager to find a people who will work with Him to cleanse the land. He wants to reveal information about the things that have defiled the land; the things we must spiritually cleanse to rid the land and structures of the resident father's sins and curses. He wants to work with us to restore the land.

As we prepare an Action Plan to free the land and the organization, we need to keep in mind that every group that moves onto a piece of ground, that occupies the structures, receives a spiritual inheritance from all those that have gone before. To this they add their own spiritual Baggage, including their belief systems and attitudes of mind, i.e., their "Organizational Culture."

C. Spiritual Organizational Culture: Attitudes and Beliefs

Mind Sets, Ungodly Beliefs (UGBs), Thought Patterns, Attitudes, Core Values, Ethics

The third area of "open doors" is very broad. Everything having to do with the thinking and thought process; i.e., business mind set, heart attitude, ethics, business practices, employee-management policies, etc.; all are included in this category. The term "Organizational Culture" will be used to refer to this arena that provides an open door to spiritual forces, both good and evil, as each business develops its own culture, its own way of doing things and its own system of expectations.

Webster defines culture as:

> *The totality of socially transmitted behavior patterns, arts, beliefs, institutions, and all other products of human work and thought.*

This definition also applies to subsets of society, such as religious culture, business culture, etc. So we will apply this word and definition to an individual business. We will specifically focus on the belief aspect of the word "culture," since all other things, i.e., behavior patterns, ethics, work, etc. come out of the belief system.

We suspect that most businesses are not really aware of their Organizational Culture. They didn't plan it or design it. Rather, it just "is." It developed and grew without any purpose or control. They do not realize that they have created their very own microcosm, with their own culture, distinct and different from other businesses and organizations.

Of course, there is nothing wrong with being different. Different is not the issue. The issue is the likelihood that some or most of the Organizational Culture has been put in place through the

Ungodly Beliefs and attitudes[1] of the founders/leaders. Without realizing it, the ethics, standards, core values, integrity, and character of the originators of the business permeate the atmosphere of the organization, affecting each person there as well as those who interact with the business.

> ## *Organizational Culture*
> *Includes attitudes, mind sets, ethics, business practices, belief systems, core values, and character attributes accepted as "normal" within the organization. "This is the way we do business!" and "This is who we are!"*

These interactions are part of Principle #3 of the Principles of Principalities,[2] the "Spiritual Magnet." Employees, vendors, customers; all will be such as to "fit" with each other, with the Organizational Culture of the business, to whatever degree it is Godly or ungodly.

If the Organizational Culture consists of Godly attitudes and practices, then the business is set to be blessed and prosper. However, if it consists mostly of ungodly, unrighteous attitudes and practices, the business is set to merge in with the regional principalities and the curses on the land, adding to them and being increasingly influenced by them. This will cause problems; "spiritual problems."

---

[1] You may refer to page 317 in Appendix C for a discussion about Ungodly Beliefs.

[2] You may glance ahead to Principle #3, "Spiritual Magnet," on page 69.

Here are some scriptures showing God's dislike for group think-ing/attitudes that are ungodly.

> *Genesis 6:5 The LORD saw how great man's wicked-ness on the earth had become, and that every inclina-tion of the thoughts of his heart was only evil all the time.*

And so God sent a flood to remove the wickedness of mankind from the earth. Mankind's collective thoughts were "only evil all the time." Here is another verse describing the general thoughts of all of the people in the organization/city of Jerusa-lem.

> *Jeremiah 4:14 O Jerusalem, wash the evil from your heart and be saved. How long will **you harbor wicked thoughts?***

In Exodus the Lord judges the entire nation of Israelites as "stiff-necked," i.e., stubborn and uncooperative. Is it safe to say that this is not the type of Organizational Culture we want to culti-vate?

> *Exodus 32:9 "I have seen these people," the LORD said to Moses, "and **they are a stiff-necked people.***"

It would be better if our organizations let go of all evil thoughts and begin to think God's thoughts! That would get rid of wick-edness, "stiff-neckedness," and lack of cooperation.

> *Isaiah 55:7-9 (NIV)*
> *55:7 Let the wicked forsake his way and the **evil man his thoughts. Let him turn to the LORD**, and he will have mercy on him, and to our God, for he will freely pardon.*
> *55:8 "**For my thoughts are not your thoughts**, nei-ther are your ways my ways," declares the LORD.*
> *55:9 "As the heavens are higher than the earth, so are my ways higher than your ways and **my thoughts than your thoughts.***"

Isaiah 55 would seem to discourage us about thinking God's thoughts. His thoughts are too high. What are we going to do? Hang on, we will find the solution in the next section.

Meanwhile, to help you become more attuned to ungodly Organizational Culture attitudes and mindsets, here are a few to examine. We have also included a number of examples in the Action Plan in Appendix A, starting on page 278. These are divided into a number of groups: employees, vendors, customers, etc. In case you disagree with us as to whether these beliefs are ungodly, remember that the standard of what is Godly or ungodly, truth or lie, comes from the Bible. As Jesus declared in John 14:6, "*I am the way, **the truth**, and the life:...*" Jesus is our standard of truth.

Examples of Ungodly Organizational Culture Statements

> – Strife and division are normal. It is just the way it is.
> – Creativity will always be stifled. There is no place to share new ideas where they will be heard and appreciated.
> – I have to be guarded at all times. Anything I say will likely be misunderstood and/or used against me.
> – No one appreciates all of the hard work I do or the leadership I provide.
> – Our company will never get ahead. We just go from one crisis to the next.

Note that we **are not saying** that these statements are untrue in the sense that the people believing them may have had these experiences. They may indeed reflect the "facts" of their life. Rather, we **are saying** that these are lies in the sense that God has a higher call and purpose for us and our businesses. He has a better way, a higher way, a way that allows His truth to come forth as our experiences. Part of the process of getting free from the entrapment of these lies is to choose God's way **without** denying the facts of our past.

> *We have Two choices:*
> *- Continue based on our*
> * past experiences. Or,*
> *- Choose a new path by*
> * believing God's Truth.*

The Organizational Culture is an extremely important arena of spiritual warfare, particularly as we consider the Group and Territorial Principalities. One of the key ways we cooperate with them is to be in agreement with them and their lies. Believing lies, expecting difficulties, operating out of fears, responding out of hurts, are just what they want. They do not want us agreeing with God, expecting His blessings, protection, creativity, insights, favor, open doors, and prosperity to overtake us. Renewing our individual minds and then our corporate "mind" is an extremely important part of the Action Plan. We must transform our Organizational Culture in order to transform our business.[1] This will also prepare us to receive healing for our organizational wounds.

D. Spiritual Organizational Hurts/Losses

Soul/Spirit Hurts (SSHs), Losses

When we consider an organization with its many people, the wounds they have are very important to the functioning of the business. Each person is responding out of his own hurts. Each one is making decisions and interacting with the other people (and the customers) based on his belief system with its many lies and expectations of more hurt. Fear and shame motivate many of them, causing them to shrink back from taking a risk, even a reasonable risk. It is a wonder that we and our organizations make any progress at all!

---

[1] In Romans 12:2 (page 21), Paul calls us to "renew" our minds so that we can think "God" thoughts and know His Will.

Let's take it one step further. What happens when the organization itself suffers a wound? Are the people within the organization affected? Is there any residual effect from the losses and strife? How about the lost contract, lawsuits, the feud between two departments, one or more of the employees being ostracized? Should we be concerned about or do anything about these things?

Obviously, we feel the answer is "Yes," or we would not be writing this section. We believe the organization carries these wounds[1] and that they have a continuing influence on the Organizational Culture, which in turn affects the people. The ability to clearly hear God's voice about decisions and to have the faith to implement the decisions is diminished as the wounds accumulate. Fear and shame begin to have more effect on decisions, particularly on risk taking, than faith and logic. People begin to "play it safe," rather than risk failure and possibly suffer more hurt. The prevailing climate of the business erodes, changing from confident expectancy to a cautious defense of the known, the "tried and true." Everyone is affected, even the new people, who did not directly experience the hurt or loss.

---

[1] The concept of the organization having its own spiritual awareness/atmosphere separate and apart from the individuals seems well supported from an experiential point of view. Tom Marshall expresses these ideas well in his book on "Understanding Leadership." (see Bibliography.)

Here are several verses about corporate hurt. Israel had a corporate hurt. The entire nation was carrying the wound.

> *Jeremiah 6:14, 30:10-19 (Speaking of Israel as a nation)*
> *6:14 They dress the **wound of my people** as though it were not serious. 'Peace, peace,' they say, when there is no peace.*
>
> *30:12 "This is what the LORD says: "**Your wound is incurable, your injury beyond healing**.*
> *30:13 There is no one to plead your cause, **no remedy for your sore, no healing for you**.*
>
> *30:15 **Why do you cry out over your wound, your pain that has no cure**? Because of your great guilt and many sins I have done these things to you.'"*
>
> *Micah 1:9 (Speaking of Israel as a nation)*
> *For **her wound is incurable**; ...*

> • *We want to turn things around before God Himself causes our wounds.*
> • *We want to insure that we have intercessors to plead our cause.*
> • *We want to insure that we have God's remedy for our wounds.*

Israel's sin had grown so great that God Himself would bring the wounding. This is a very serious situation, one to avoid no matter what. We want to insure that what we are doing with our lives and our organizations are not stirring God's wrath.

As we bring Transforming Your Business ministry to an organization, it is important to expose all of the hurts, loses, factions, division, strife, etc., that have happened. We want to look at every possible sin that may have setup the company to experience these woundings. We also want to discover any ongoing sinful reactions because of the wounding. The effects of these will be permeating the environment of the business. The Lord desires to heal these and to bring His unity and purpose back into the organization.

E. Spiritual Organizational Oppression/Principalities

Evil/Negative Spiritual Forces, Demonic Oppression

In Part One we discussed at some length the various levels of negative spiritual forces. We feel that understanding demons, demonic strongholds, and principalities[1] are fundamental realities we need to know. So we will not repeat that information here. (You may review these on pages 23 to 31.)

> *Let's remove all legal ground provided to demons, demonic strongholds, and principalities.*

Rather, we want to emphasize that the first four areas we have just discussed, besides being sources themselves of negative spiritual roots of problems, all provide "legal ground" to demons, demonic strongholds, and principalities. These include: the Sins of the Founding Fathers and resulting Curses (SOFFCs), the Sins of the Resident Fathers and resulting Curses (SORFCs), the Organizational Culture, and the Organizational Hurts and Losses. They open the door and invite into our businesses and organizations higher level spiritual beings and their influence. These spiritual entities then multiply, amplify, and exacerbate what might already be a tough situation into an even worst predicament. Problems that might have been solved by ordinary means become unsolvable. The owners, business consultants, and others try to help, but they don't have the required world view. They are not adequately familiar with the spiritual realm. They are not attuned to the concept of evil and

---

[1] You may refer back to pages 23, 26, and 27 for these topics.

the enemy of our soul who is out to "steal, kill, and destroy."[1]
And even if they have some awareness in this area, it is unlikely
that they know of God's provision of healing and freedom for
both individuals and organizations. We will bring these understandings into play as we develop an Action Plan for the business in Part Three.

---

[1] Please read John 10:10.

II. Seven Principles of Principalities

Before we begin presenting God's solution for these five types of negative spiritual roots, we want to present a "summary" look at the spiritual dynamics of the combination of people, land, buildings, and evil entities. This can be expressed as seven principles to help bring understanding of the multifaceted interactions. We will see just how self-reinforcing and destructive these spiritual entities are when given an opportunity (place) as they work to expand the kingdom of darkness within a business and region.

As you consider these seven principles, let us encourage you to ask the Holy Spirit to show you whether any of these are in operation in your business.

To aid communications, we've given each principle a "nickname" as shown in the box. At the end of this section we have included a picture of the principalities and business spiritual interactions. The number in the box is also on the picture so that you can see where each principle is at work.

Principles of Principalities
Brief Descriptors

1 – *"Territorial/Regional"*
    Principalities
2 – *"Group/Organizational"*
    Principalities
3 - *Spiritual Magnet*
4 – *Leader's Leverage*
5 – *Employee's Reinforcement*
6 - *Internal Multiplication*
7 - *External Interactions*

---

1. Territorial/Regional Principalities

They were there all the time waiting for you.

The land and structures that an organization occupies will already have "in place" established territorial/regional principalities from the defiling of the land by the former inhabitants, i.e., from the "Baggage" on the land. These will be a subset of the larger principalities over the city and/or region.

2. Group/Organizational Principalities

A match made in "heaven"

Each founding father (and mother, leader or group of leaders) of the organization brings his own "Baggage." This Baggage combines and interacts, creating the "group/organizational Baggage, which provides an initial "place" for the group/organizational principalities to form and establish. Usually this Baggage matches surprisingly well with the "home-town" territorial principalities already resident. As the founding fathers' personal/group principalities combine/fuse with the home-town principalities, there is an enhancement and magnification of the principalities. They are stronger, more influential, and more destructive. They have renewed power and ability to strategize to carry out their destructive work. Needless to say, the new business probably has no awareness of the forces that are mobilizing to thwart its hopes and dreams.

3. Spiritual Magnet

You are with your own kind!

The group Baggage "draws" others who have similar Baggage and/or who have the potential/susceptibility to "enter into" the same types of sin and curses. Thus new members of the group generally are also a good match with the existing members and the organizational principalities. Each new member brings/contributes his Baggage to the group Baggage. This includes his personal ancestral sins, curses, and demons. Perhaps this dynamic is the basis for the saying, "Birds of a feather flock together."

This problem will diminish as a business and its leaders go through its own cleansing. The "draw" of undesirable employees will lessen. Rather, employees who bring a positive contribution to the holiness and righteousness of the business will appear. And they too can be taken through the healing and cleansing process to reduce even further their "Baggage."

The personal application of the Restoring the Foundations ministry approach (discussed starting on page 316) provides an awesome opportunity for cleansing. The Holy Spirit guides the ministers to help the person become aware of, deal with, and close many "Open Doors," certainly the more important ones. As the organization helps its members go through this ministry, the members will become more Christ like and less like the founding leader(s); at least less like the founding leaders used to be.

4. Leader's Leverage

As a Leader, you have more Influence than you realize

The more authority/responsibility a person has within the organization, the more his Baggage contributes to and influences the organization's Baggage and principalities. The founders/officers/top leaders have the most influence, affecting everyone in the organization. Of course they have their legitimate authority to make decisions and set direction, however, they also enable positive and negative spiritual forces throughout the organization. Whatever sin is present and ongoing in the leaders will generally also be manifesting in individuals making up the organization. If the leaders are trapped in pornography, we would expect to find a large fraction of the entire company afflicted by this sin.

For example, we were invited into a difficult church situation to bring God's healing to the congregation after major sin had been exposed. It had come to light that two of the leaders were involved in adultery. As we ministered to the people in the organization, we discovered that nearly every one was caught up in one form or another of sexual sin. The leader's sin had opened the door, and the people had "given place" to the same principalities strengthened by the leaders.

Let's take another example of a person moving up into the leadership structure of the organization. As he is given more authority and responsibility, the more his Baggage contributes to and influences the organizational Baggage. This increased organizational Baggage, then, reaches out and increases its influence on the rest of the company, pressuring them to enter into the same type of sin. The highest level leader, of course, has the most influence. Whether the organizational principalities are getting stronger or weaker depends mostly on the leadership and what they are doing, or not doing, to remove the legal ground given to the principalities by themselves and others.

Several often observed sins among an organization's leadership include sexual sin, illegitimate control, making decisions for others (living their life), rejection and abandonment of certain members, and pride. All of these point to a leader, whether president or pastor, needing personal ministry such as Restoring the Foundations ministry.

5. Employee's Reinforcement

Leaders are encouraged, either for good or for evil.

In a similar manner, the employees of the business, with their combined spiritual influence coming from their combined Baggage, exert a pressure on the leadership to conform to the member's sins and curses. While each individual employee may not have much influence himself, the combined influence of all of the employees can equal or exceed that of the leaders. Without even realizing it, leadership can be influenced to embrace and support "shady" dealing and other forms of deception, all the while justifying it as normal and legal. This area is ripe with self-deception and rationalization. In other words, each part of the organization is pressuring the other parts in the direction of the corporate-wide sin and curses. The corporate principalities, of course, are enjoying every minute of their success.

Once healing and freedom begins to come into the organization, this mutual influencing between leaders and employees will operate in the opposite direction. It will begin to promote godliness because of the positive reinforcement.

6. Internal Multiplication

Everyone is magnifying everyone else, including you.

The internal interactions between the leaders and employees of a business, as described in the previous two principles, will be such as to **multiply** the amount of group "Baggage" and thus give more "place" to the organizational principalities. This is a cyclical, multiplying effect between the employees and the leaders. There are additional multiplying effects between the employees and the principalities, and between the leaders and the principalities. This all reinforces and multiplies the sin and curses. This is another example of the law of sowing and reaping in operation, as each group sows seeds reaped by the other, with each round of sowing producing a bigger harvest.

7. External Interactions

Birds of a feather flock together.

The customers/clients/others, i.e., those "outside" of the organization that interact with the organization will tend to be from that portion of the general population that has similar types of Baggage and principalities as the organization. This is part of the Environmental "Baggage" (discussed in section 4). For example, if the leaders of the organization believe everyone is out to "get them," and that they have to count every penny, the people they deal with will probably have the same penny-pinching tendencies. If they "shave" every order, delivering less than promised, their customers will probably be cheating them as well. On the other hand, if the business believes in the "blessing-blessing" model, doing its best to make sure that the customers are always satisfied, they will generally have customers that want to bless them back.

If a business is run by a "bunch of thieves" and they are cheating left and right, breaking every law that they think they can get away with, continuing to push everything to the limits, it is likely that the business will have principalities of thieving and robbery. Their employees with steal from the business, and their vendors and customers will likely also be thieves. The leaders will continually wonder why they keep losing everything. They are releasing curses of stealing. So the curses from these sins, plus the strategic work of the principalities, will cause them to be stolen from. The enemy has been given that right, the Open Door, to steal from them. Or we might have a business with a group of people that aren't themselves necessarily stealing, but their ancestors did and they passed the ancestral curse on to the current leaders. This situation has a different root, but the same principality will be present carrying out curses of stealing, loss, defeat, and failure.

8. Summary

We can illustrate the seven principles with the following picture. We have two types of principalities over the business; the Territorial/Regional ones and the Group/Organizational ones (principles #1 and #2). (You can decide which principality type is black and which is white.) Then the business/organization draws to itself others of like nature (#3). The leaders and employees reinforce and magnify each other's sin and sin tendencies (#4, #5, and #6). And lastly, the businesses customers and vendors will also have similar Baggage (#7).

We can also summarize the Seven Principles of Principalities using the three-way attractions that are in effect. These attractions are the result of the negative spiritual roots attempting to produce more fruit; bad fruit. First, note in the figure on the next page that the people are drawn both by the organizational culture and principalities, and by the land's curses and principalities. Second, the organizational culture and principalities are given "place" by the people, causing the principalities to be drawn to the people. In addition, the organizational principalities are drawn to land with similar sin and curses, since the land is carrying the curses from the past sins. In like manner the land

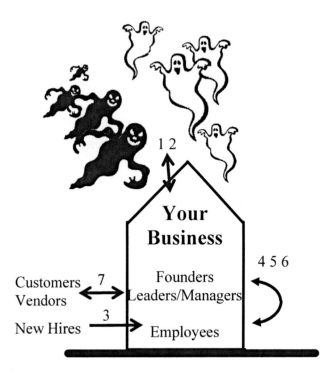

is being drawn to the organization and to the people. Thus each part attracts the other two parts, as sins of like nature draw people, land, and organizations with sins of like nature.

Thus, when an organization decides to obtain land and buildings, it appears that there is more at work than just pure logic and economics in finding and then choosing what to buy or rent. It is possible that spiritual wickedness in high places is engineering a match so that sin can be multiplied, so that people and organizations are blocked, or at least hindered, in reaching and fulfilling their purpose and destiny?

We can take comfort in the fact that God is not surprised by the attempts of the enemy to destroy purpose and destiny. Once we decide to stop cooperating with the enemy and to cooperate with God, He will cause Romans 8:28 to swing into action and *"cause all things to work together for good."* In the end, the enemy loses.

It is with relief that we now switch from discussing the different ways sins and curses have destructive impact on our lives and organizations and move on into God's solution to these negative spiritual roots of spiritual problems. But first: ...

What about the "puzzle" we shared on page 1? You re-member; the story about the two Bible colleges and churches splitting because of the very similar sinful behav-ior? Is it still a puzzle to you, or does it make "sense" now? Invisible forces coming from negative spiritual roots were at work. In fact, until someone, or a group of "some ones," with spiritual authority does something about the five negative spiritual roots on the land and buildings, the invisible forces will continue to exert their destructive influ-ence. So let's learn God's solution so we can help our-selves and others get free of these forces!

III. Spiritual Solutions for Spiritual Problems

The five negative spiritual root causes (discussion beginning on page 53) are not without solutions. As presented in Part One, the solutions all come from the provision God the Father has given us through His Son, Jesus Christ and His sacrifice (and completed work) on the Cross. It is time to learn the specifics of this incredible provision. In Part Three we will apply these specifics as we implement the Action Plan.

It is important to note as we start this section that we have written it from the point of view of a Leader considering whether to apply the Transforming Your Business procedure to his business/organization. It is written assuming the reader has the legal and spiritual authority to execute the Action Plan of Part Three, including all of its ministry steps.

If you do not have this level of authority, let us encourage you to read on anyhow, but with the viewpoint of one who can be God's "plant" to gather a representative "tithe" group to begin to the process of bringing God into your organization in a fuller way. Our strong caution to you is that you ask the Holy Spirit to keep you very aware of your boundaries,[1] knowing what is legitimate for you to do and what is not. After all, you don't want to open new doors for additional oppression by principalities! Then begin to do what is within your scope of authority and responsibility.

---

[1] We have much to say about boundaries in Part Four. Even though that discussion is focused on Intercessors, the principles are applicable to everyone.

A. Solution for Sins of the Founding Fathers and the Resident Fathers

Freedom from Ancestral and Resident Sins and Curses

As we prepare to implement the solution for negative spiritual roots, we will combine the **Sins of the Founding Fathers and resulting Curses** (SOFFCs) and **Sins of the Resident Fathers and resulting Curses** (SORRCs). We will use the same process of freedom for both of these roots. The only difference between these two is the source of the root, i.e., ancestors or the inhabitants of the land/structures.

Part Three will explain how to discover the specific sins and resulting curses affecting us and our business from the SOFFCs and SORFCs. For now, let us learn God's solutions.

Confession

The first mention of God's pattern for freedom from the Sins of the Founding Fathers and Resident Fathers is in Leviticus 26:40. The pattern is confession. God gives us His conditions under which He will reestablish His covenant with us. The condition is to confess our own sin and the sins of our ancestors.

> *Confess means to acknowledge, to take responsibility for, something God is holding against us. It is the opposite of "blame-shifting" and "denial." We agree with God that we have broken His Law and that the consequence is just. We deliberately realign ourselves with the Kingdom of God by our own free will.*

As long as we blame-shift and deny our part in the sin, we only cover it, making it difficult for God to forgive us and take us back under His covering. We have learned that it is wise to be quick to confess our part and to forgive others for their part.

> *Leviticus 26:40-42   (KJV)*
>
> *26:40* ***If they shall confess their iniquity, and the iniquity of their fathers***, *with their trespass which they trespassed against me, and that also they have walked contrary unto me;*
>
> *26:41 And [that] I also have walked contrary unto them, and have brought them into the land of their enemies;* ***if then their uncircumcised hearts be humbled***, *and they* ***then accept of the punishment of their iniquity:***
>
> *26:42* ***Then will I remember my covenant*** *with Jacob, and also my covenant with Isaac, and also my covenant with Abraham will I remember; and* ***I will remember the land.***

We are so blessed to be on this side of the Cross because Jesus Christ already bore and fully received the punishment we would otherwise be receiving. All we have to do is to humble ourselves,[1] confess our iniquity and the iniquity of our ancestors, and appropriate the truth that Jesus has already borne our punishment.

There are a number of applications of the Leviticus 26 pattern in the Bible. Notable examples are in Nehemiah 1 and 9, Ezra 9, and Daniel 9. We also see this pattern 1 Kings, when Solomon is praying to God during the dedication of the temple.

---

[1]   Please see Psalm 51:17 and Micah 6:8.

1 Kings 8:33-50
*8:47 and **if** they (Israel) have **a change of heart** in the land where they are held captive, and **repent** and plead with you in the land of their conquerors and say, '**We have sinned, we have done wrong, we have acted wickedly';***
*8:48 and **if** they turn back to you with all their heart and soul in the land of their enemies who took them captive, and pray to you toward the land you gave their fathers, toward the city you have chosen and the temple I have built for your Name;*
*8:49 **Then** from heaven, your dwelling place, hear their prayer and their plea, and uphold their cause.*
*8:50 And **forgive your people**, who have sinned against you; **forgive all the offenses** they have committed against you, and cause their conquerors to show them mercy;*

One very important and well-known verse encompasses confession, forgiveness, Identification Repentance, and the land is:

II Chronicles 7:14
7:14 If my people, which are called by my name, shall humble themselves, and pray, and seek my face, and turn from their wicked ways; then will I hear from heaven, and will forgive their sin, and will heal their land.

We very much desire for the Lord to heal the land.

The principle of confession is continued in the New Testament. One of the most significant verses is 1 John 1:9.

1 John 1:9 (KJV)
***If we confess our sins**, he is faithful and just to forgive us [our] sins, and to cleanse us from all unrighteousness.*

> *It is important to note the little word "if" in God's promises.*

Please notice the conditional "if" in 1 John as well as in the above 1st Kings passage. The condition indicated by the "if" must be satisfied before God can or will do His part of fulfilling the promise. Our part is to "confess," to be "humbled," and then the Lord, who is *faithful* and *just*, will *forgive* and *cleanse* us. In the Leviticus passage, He declares that He will remember His covenant with the patriarchs and the land. We feel this means He will re-establish His promises and provision for us, including our relationship with Him.

Forgiveness: Of Others
After confession, the next step is forgiveness. We start with forgiveness of others. God states in the Bible that He will not forgive us until we forgive others. One passage expressing this truth is:

> *Mark 11:25 (NIV)*
> *And when you stand praying, __if you hold anything__ __against anyone, forgive him, so that your Father in__ __heaven may forgive you your sins__.*

We need to release others of whatever we are holding against them, both individually and corporately. This provision is for our sake, that we not be bound to the other person or organization, holding us back and keeping us trapped. The Lord particularly does not want us trapped in anger and bitterness, two very common results of unforgiveness.

Forgiveness: Asking for Ourselves--Repentance
After we forgive others, we are positioned to ask the Lord to forgive us. In Bible terms, this is called "repentance." The word means to "turn around," as in turning around and going a new direction. In this case, God wants us to go His direction, the way of holiness and righteousness. Again, we want to do this both individually and corporately.

Forgiveness: Of Self

When we are ministering to an individual, sometimes it is important to also have the individual forgive himself. He may be more upset with himself than anyone else for involvement with the sin.

When we consider an organization, in addition to the Leaders forgiving themselves, there may be situations where the business has been "its own worst enemy." Poor decisions may have set the organization up for defeat and failure. If so, the Action Plan should include forgiveness and release of the Leadership and all others involved in the decisions and resulting wounds to the organization.

> ## We Appropriate by Faith!

Appropriation

Once we have confessed and accomplished the necessary forgiving, we are positioned to stop the effects of the curses coming from the ancestral sins, both biological and from the land. One powerful scripture showing us the way is Galatians 3:13.

> *Galatians 3:13-14*
> *3:13 **Christ redeemed us from the curse of the law by becoming a curse for us**, for it is written: "Cursed is everyone who is hung on a tree."*
> *3:14 He redeemed us in order that the blessing given to Abraham might come to the Gentiles through Christ Jesus, so that by faith we might receive the promise of the Spirit.*

> ## Jesus Provided.
> ## We Appropriate.

Our part is to "appropriate" by "faith" the power of the Cross into our lives and our organizations. Jesus Christ has provided it, but we have to believe Him and receive it, as we discussed on page 68. As we have ministered to many individuals, it is an awesome thing to observe them being released from family curses, as well as word curses, as they appropriate the provision of the Cross. Sometimes we see their countenance change in a matter of minutes. Frequently we receive excited reports describing the newfound freedom being experienced. One man reported feeling a heavy weight going off his shoulders and he actually began to walk more upright. Others were released from the success-failure cycle. The list of possible curses is a very long list. However, the good news is that regardless of how long the list is, the provision of Jesus Christ is more than enough to break the power of every curse.

As the business Leaders "stand in" for, i.e., intercede for, all past leaders with confession and Identification Repentance, the spiritual dynamics of a family, group, organization, or business can change from oppression and hindrance to encouragement and freedom. The "ups" and "downs" of the success-failure cycle can be traded in for the steady growth of a blessed organization rather than a cursed one. **All it takes is for the Leader(s) to appropriate the power and authority of God on behalf of the business. All it takes is for the Leaders and the individuals of the business to take responsibility for their own sin, their family's sin, the business's sin, and the land's sin through confession and Identification Repentance. All it takes is for the Leaders to stand in the power and authority that Jesus Christ delegated to the church[1] (and the business) and break the power of the sins and curses coming down the family lines, both biologically and spiritually, both in the business and on the land.**

The Land
After applying the ministry to free the land from the sins and curses, there is one more step that we can and should do to fully free the land from all barrenness. In Part One we discussed the principles of Possession (page 43) and "marrying" the land. As we appropriate the Finished Work of Christ on the Cross, we want to receive the gift of the land and structures and commit to be the Godly steward of them. We will formally accept the land and "possess" it, take responsibility for it, commit to care for it,

---

[1] Jesus does this in Matthew 28:18 as He commissions the disciples to go make disciples.

and declare blessing upon it. We then will have every right to expect productivity and fruitfulness as we "live" on the land, whatever our product or service may be.

Once we apply this Solution to the organization and to the land, we will have completed the first two rounds of freedom. Once we have properly prepared, this part of the overall Action Plan can be completed quickly. Next is to further our gains by helping our organization change its attitudes and expectations to align more and more with God's way of thinking.

B. Solution for the Organizational Culture

Acquiring Godly mind sets

The challenge of changing an entire Organization!
Starting on page 59, we discussed how the Organizational Culture contributed to the negative spiritual roots of spiritual problems. We presented scriptures showing how much God detests wicked and ungodly thinking. For those of us wanting to please God, this should motivate us to change. However, changing ourselves is one thing, changing an entire organization is another thing. Since businesses are made up of all types of people with all types of backgrounds, it may seem impossible to change an entire organization. How can we help everyone in our business begin to think Godly thoughts, perceive the world through God's eyes, and develop Godly habits and behaviors, so that our business has a Godly Organizational Culture? We would like the entire belief system of the business to include **expectations, judgments, ethics, core values, morals, operating practices, employee agreements, customer policies, etc.,** that are Biblically based and Holy Spirit empowered.

Ingredients of a Godly Organizational Culture

Paul apparently thinks this is possible. He encouraged the church at Philippi to have a corporate attitude of being like-minded, of being one in spirit and purpose. Do you suppose he would expect us to also do this?

Philippians 2:2
*... make my joy complete by being **like-minded**, hav-ing the same love, **being one in spirit and purpose.***

We believe that an organization can do this if we go about it God's way. We want to use Godly principles to help ourselves as leaders and the employees of our business change our think-ing patterns. We want to help everyone develop a desire and a commitment to begin to think as God thinks. We have the promise in First Corinthians:

1 Corinthians 2:16
*... But we have **the mind of Christ.***

We can move toward this condition as we work with the Holy Spirit to renew our minds. The most impactful scripture that points the way to obtain the mind of Christ is:

Romans 12:2 (NIV)
*Do not conform any longer to the pattern of this world, but **be transformed by the renewing of your mind**. Then you will be able to test and approve what God's will is--his good, pleasing and perfect will.*

We can have our minds renewed a number of ways. Reading scripture is one very good way. Sitting with a Restoring the Foundations minister trained to discern the lies within our heart is another way. However we do it, the important thing is that we do it, exposing and exchanging one lie at a time for God's truth.

An Example of Godly Core Values
On the Trane company website (www.trane.com), we found a wonderful example of Godly core values; published for all to see. Trane publishes their core values which they clearly expect all who apply for their Graduate Engineer Training Program to adopt and follow. The values are:

In the spirit of creating a solid foundation of interdependence within the program, we have embraced the following seven principles in preparing the Account Manager for the Trane distribution organization:

1. Always act in the long-term best interest of our customers
2. Be a leader
3. Treat others fairly and with dignity and respect
4. Be a good team member
5. Adopt and project a positive attitude
6. Commitment to a life long self-development attitude
7. Be the trusted advisor to the customer

Trane has been a leader in its field for a long time. Clearly the founders and leaders of this company chose Godly core values to guide their company from the beginning.

Spiritual Solution
Just as we go through a "legal" process with an individual to cancel agreements with ungodly thinking, we want to follow a similar process with an organization, one very much like the process for the SOFFCs and SORFCs. Once Leaders have come into unity and agreement, having identified the ungodly aspects of the Organizational Culture and prepared the employees, we are prepared for a "formal" time of Identification Repentance. We are ready to go through a "legal" process of canceling our agreement/covenant with the enemy and his lies, and establishing a new Organizational Culture based on God and His Word. We will implement this process in Part Three.

Confession
The first part of this procedure is essentially the same as we discussed for the Sins of the Founding and Resident Fathers and resulting Curses (page 77). Only in this case, rather than dealing with the curses from the ancestors violating the second commandment, we are confessing our sins of believing and acting upon our personal Ungodly Beliefs and the ungodly aspects of our Organizational Culture. We confess for ourselves and for those who came before us (Identification Repentance), both for the founding leaders and those living on the land.[1]

---

[1] Once again we are applying Leviticus 26:40.

Forgiveness

Next we forgive all of the former leaders (and any others) for their contribution to the ungodly Organizational Culture. For complete cleansing, every aspect of the corporate values, ethics, practices, etc., that is not in alignment with the Word of God must be confessed and forgiven. *Now is not the time to discount or minimize the importance of past sins.* While we are not interested in blame shifting or criticizing past leaders, or pointing out their faults and sins, we are interested in acknowledging the beliefs and actions that displeased God by violating His Word and that brought curses upon the organization. Since none of us are without sin, we are all guilty.[1] We are not interested in judging previous leaders but in removing the consequences of their sin and our sin from the organization and from the land. We want to remove all "place" that has been given to demonic spirits and principalities.

> *God's pattern is to confess and His requirement is to forgive.*

Once the forgiveness of past leaders and all others is accomplished, we are positioned for the next step: to ask God to forgive us. As the leaders of the business, we must be willing to turn away from any aspect of the Organizational Culture that is ungodly and **commit to a pathway of righteousness, a pathway of doing things according to Biblical principles, guided by the presence and wisdom of God brought to us by the Holy Spirit**.

The last step of forgiveness is to consider whether we need to forgive ourselves for any or all of the same ungodly things for which we just asked God to forgive us. We can forgive ourselves because God has forgiven us. We forgive ourselves as individuals, and then, once we are ready, we can do this as an organization.

---

[1]   Please note Romans 3:23.

Appropriation

After the confession and forgiveness steps, we are ready to cancel our individual and corporate agreements/covenants with the enemy. Each and every (important) way we have believed in a lie, we have had a covenant with the kingdom of darkness. Essentially, we have given Satan a legal right to entrap us and hold us captive to do his will,[1] both individually and corporately. We want to cancel these covenants in a similar way that we would cancel a civil contract. We are taking back "legal ground,"[2] and so we need to do a "legal transaction" to break our agreements/covenants/contracts with the devil.[3] This can be done for the business as the Leaders continue to appropriate the power and authority of God to apply the Cross to each and every ungodly aspect of the Organizational Culture.

Establishing New Truths

Once we have legally separated ourselves from the ungodly aspects of the Organizational Culture, we are ready to receive and commit to Godly principles and truths. For each area of ungodliness, we ask the question, "God, what do You say about this situation? How do You want us to think and act as a company?" As we listen and contemplate the written word of God, the Holy Spirit works with us to creatively formulate new **beliefs, expectations, ethics, values, morals, operating practices, employee agreements, customer policies, etc**. We want approaches and practices that express God's heart rather than the lies.

---

[1] We are referring back to page 39 and 2 Timothy 2:25-6.

[2] Please note again Ephesians 4:26-27.

[3] Sometimes Satan is referred to as a "legalist." He is a legalist in the sense that he holds God to His Word. The Accuser insists that God allow sin to have its outworking, including providing an "open door," i.e., "legal ground" for him to oppress us. Meanwhile, God is trying to get our attention so that we will cooperate with Him. He wants us to satisfy the conditions of His conditional promises so that He can move from His Justice Seat to His Mercy Seat and bring the freedom and deliverance of the Lord Jesus Christ into our lives. Let's choose to cooperate with the Lord and do our part to help Him set us free.

> *Replacing ungodly aspects of the Organizational Culture is easy--Find out what God says is His truth about our core values and practices and come into agreement with Him!*

Examples of Godly Organizational Culture Statements
Here are some examples of Godly truths that we might use to replace the ungodly lies in the previous examples on page 62.

> 1. Strife and division are normal. It is just the way it is.
> **Godly**
> As I receive God's healing, and as this business is healed, unity and agreement will become the norm. This is God's way, the peace that passes all understanding.

It is amazing how easily we accept our situations, particularly our growing up years, as "normal," no matter how weird, extreme, abusive, or ungodly they may be. And so we carry these expectations of "normal" into our business situations.

Expectations are powerful.[1] Ungodly expectations "reach out" into our surroundings and work with the ancestral curses, family demons and territorial principalities to bring continued difficulties and destruction into our lives. As we repent and break our agreements with the lies we have believed, as we and our businesses are healed of an ungodly culture, our expectations begin to change. They change because we are bringing our belief systems into alignment with God's thinking. We begin to experience unity, agreement, and walking in God's way. Let us assure you; having a Godly Organizational Culture is better than the "former" life.

---

[1] In Mark 11:22-24, Jesus lays out this principle of believing (expecting), speaking, and receiving.

> 2. Creativity will always be stifled. There is no place to share new ideas where they will be heard and appreciated.
>
> **Godly**
>
> As God touches and changes our business, others, especially leaders, will be able to receive new ideas and see them for the gifts that they are, the very lifeblood of our organization.

A Godly Belief that frees creativity in a business will be good for both individuals and the organization. After all, God is the "Creator!" God desires to pour His creativity into all of us that we might demonstrate His goodness and glory here on the earth as blessings and prosperity overtake us.

> 3. I have to be guarded at all times. Anything I say will likely be misunderstood and/or used against me.
>
> **Godly**
>
> As God heals me, I will be able to trust others and expect their good intentions toward me. If anyone does happen to be untrustworthy, the Holy Spirit will help me discern this and adjust accordingly.

In many ways, the trust issue is at the heart of all our wounds and Ungodly Beliefs. The hurts we experience while young cause us to retreat to the inside, protecting ourselves from further hurt from others. We project this mistrust onto God, expecting Him to mistreat and abuse us as well. Yet He wants to heal us and enable us to walk a fruitful and productive life in harmony with others. When we as a business team become able to feel safe with our cohorts, there is probably no limit to what we can do.

> 4. No one appreciates all of the hard work I do, or the leadership I provide.
>
> **Godly**
>
> God has equipped me and appointed me to this position. His grace enables me to work hard when necessary and to rest when appropriate. His Voice guides me as I lead others. Whatever appreciation I receive from others is an added blessing from Him.

The gifts of the Holy Spirit[1] are for the blessing and building up of others. God desires and expects His Leaders to draw on supernatural abilities and gifts to be His instruments to bring forth His will here on the earth. This includes you being a Godly Leader of your company. There is no room for "pity-parties" or other self-focused energy and time wasters. This only assists the devil in his work. If this is a belief you have been struggling with, you have a strong indicator that there are Open Doors of oppression against you and your family line. Let us encourage you to take a serious look to see if you would benefit receiving ministry in this area.[2]

> 5. Our company will never get ahead. We just go from one crisis to the next.
>
> **Godly**
>
> As we remove the negative spiritual roots in the five problem areas that are holding us back, the Lord's blessings will begin to overtake us. As we align with His Will for us and our company, favor and grace will go before us, opening doors and guiding the way. Thank you, Lord, that we are moving ahead, no longer going from "crisis to crisis," but from "glory to glory!"

---

[1]   The Gifts of the Holy Spirit are listed in 1 Corinthians 12:7-11.

[2]   Please become serious about seeking help, such as receiving Restoring the Foundations ministry through the Healing House Network, to take care of the Open Doors and major strongholds in your life.

God has designed all living organisms to grow. Lack of growth, or difficult growth, indicate Open Doors for the enemy to hinder or block God's purpose and destiny for the organization. It is past time to remove these negative spiritual roots and move ahead.

As the Leaders and Intercessors receive revelation about the ungodly aspects of their Organizational Culture, as they formulate Godly expressions to replace the ungodly parts, as they prepare to legally transition the business from the old culture to the new culture, there comes a time when it is necessary to involve the entire company. This brings forth the question, "How do we get everyone on board to accept and live the new Organizational Culture?" This is a great topic for Part Three, where we will implement God's solution to remove the roots of an ungodly Organizational Culture and replace it with God's culture.

C. Solution for Organizational Hurts/Losses

Positioning ourselves to receive healing

Jesus outdoes Himself in this area when we are doing individual Restoring the Foundations ministry. He loves to come and heal hurts, even ones we do not know we have. Yet the usual is to put up walls, guard our hurts, trying to shield them from being exposed or hurt again. We shout, "Don't touch that hurt. I'm just fine!", even though all sorts of nasty "Baggage" is attached to the hurt. We make decisions without even being aware how much they are affected by our hurts. It is truly a joy to be a part of Jesus Christ healing the "broken hearted."[1]

God wants to heal the wounds of our business/organization just as much as He wants to heal individuals. We can see this in the many scriptures that show Him crying out for corporate Israel to turn from its wicked ways and come back to Him. However, to whatever degree Israel's spiritual adultery grieved God, He always came back to the promise and desire to restore Israel.

---

[1] Please see Luke 4:18, where Jesus reads chapter 61 from the scroll of Isaiah.

Jeremiah 30:17-30:19

30:17 'But I will restore you to health and heal your wounds,' declares the LORD, 'because you are called an outcast, Zion for whom no one cares.'

30:18 This is what the LORD says: I will restore the fortunes of Jacob's tents and have compassion on his dwellings; the city will be rebuilt on her ruins, and the palace will stand in its proper place.

30:19 From them will come songs of thanksgiving and the sound of rejoicing. I will add to their numbers, and they will not be decreased; I will bring them honor, and they will not be disdained.

God is promising restoration to the nation, to Jerusalem (the city), and to the palace. He will bring joy, multiplication, and respect once again. He wants to bring healing to "the organization."

In the New Testament, we see Jesus weeping over the city of Jerusalem.

Luke 19:41-44 (NIV)

19:41 As he approached Jerusalem and saw the city, he wept over it

19:42 and said, "If you, even you, had only known on this day what would bring you peace —but now it is hidden from your eyes.

19:43 The days will come upon you when your enemies will build an embankment against you and encircle you and hem you in on every side.

19:44 They will dash you to the ground, you and the children within your walls. They will not leave one stone on another, because you did not recognize the time of God's coming to you."

This is a case where God wanted to heal Jerusalem so that it would have peace, but it did not recognize His coming. This is amazing when we consider that the religious Leaders were waiting for the coming of the promised one. Yet when He came, they did not recognize or receive Him. It is scripture such as this that causes us to cry out to God, "Don't let us miss the day of your visitation!" As businesses and organizations on this side of the Cross, every day is available as a day of His visitation. All we have to do is to invite Him and welcome Him. Let's do this and receive our healing.

Receiving Healing

We receive healing for our corporate wounds in much the same way we do as individuals. We prepare by gathering information on all of the significant events that caused hurt and pain to the organization. When we are ready, we then go through the same initial steps that we did for ancestral sins and curses and for our ungodly Organizational Culture. As an organization, we will confess, forgive, repent, and forgive ourselves. We will do this for each wound. This will satisfy the conditions of God's conditional promises and sets the stage for the Lord to come with His healing.

From this point on, the procedure is different. We have positioned ourselves, both as individuals and as an organization, to receive God's healing. However, unlike breaking curses and changing our Organizational Culture, there is really nothing more we can do. We cannot heal ourselves or our businesses. Rather, we must pray and ask God to heal our wounds. It is time to invite and welcome into our midst the Lord of Glory. The Leaders and the Intercessors will have prepared the way. They have the lists of significant woundings. When the time is right, we as the entire business can gather and present ourselves before the Lord and ask for healing, both individually and corporately. When we ask, He is faithful to come and heal. We will do this as part of the Action Plan.

> *Lord Jesus, we invite You to come visit us. Thank You for bringing Your healing!*

D. Solution for the
Organizational Oppression/Principalities

Deliver us from evil influences

Now comes the fun part. We have applied God's solution: (1) to sins and curses which bring sorrows, (2) to an ungodly Organizational Culture which brings torment, and (3) to Organizational Hurts/Losses which bring pain, confusion and isolation. We have diminished and done our best to eliminate all legal ground given to the enemy. We are now ready to cast out the demons, disassemble the strongholds, and displace the principalities that have used that legal ground against us. It's time for "D" day.[1]

When we attempt to comprehend what Jesus went through on our behalf, it is beyond imagination. His "passion" was beyond anything any other human has ever experienced. So we imagine that it must be particularly satisfying to Him when we continue to complete His victory by diminishing the enemy and his ability to steal, kill, and destroy.[2] We know that we experience deep gratitude every time we help another person gain freedom from the clutches of demons. Think what the Lord must feel! First John 3:8 seems particularly relevant at this point.

> *1 John 3:8*
> *... For this purpose the Son of God was manifested,*
> *that **he might destroy the works of the devil**.*

This was one of the reasons Jesus came to the earth. He was sent to destroy the works of the devil. After the apparent defeat at the Cross, He rose again and defeated death, hell, and the grave.[3] Colossians makes it clear.

---

[1] "D day" stands for Deliverance Day!

[2] We continue to remind you of John 10:10, where Jesus declares the extreme difference between what the thief does and what He does.

[3] Jesus speaking as recorded in Revelation 1:18.

Colossians 2:15 (NIV)
*And **having disarmed the powers and authorities**, he made a public spectacle of them, triumphing over them **by the cross**.*

The KJV has "**having spoiled principalities and powers**." The defeat at the Cross became the victory over every single part of Satan and his army. Every demon, every power, every principality; all triumphed over by the Cross.

He then delegated His victory to us.[1] Just as God delivered the inhabitants of Canaan into the hands of the Israelites, Jesus has delivered the demons and principalities into our hands. Our job is to drive them out just as the Israelites were to drive out the Canaanites.

Exodus 23:31
... for I will deliver the inhabitants of the land into your hand; and thou shalt drive them out before thee.

Here are a couple of passages specifically addressing the destruction of principalities over organizations (cities).

Proverbs 21:22 (NIV)
A wise man attacks the city of the mighty and pulls down the stronghold in which they trust.

Amos 5:9 (NIV)
He flashes destruction on the stronghold and brings the fortified city to ruin,

We are ready to be "wise men." We are ready to pull down the strongholds and principalities that have been hindering God's plan for our lives and businesses.

This is one job that is fun. It is fun to remove oppression and become free. It is fun to be successful and accomplish what God

---

[1] In Matthew 28:18, Jesus delegates all authority in heaven and on earth to His disciples.

has gifted and called us to do. It is fun to do our part to advance the kingdom of God and redeem another piece of the earth. The verse in Ephesians is so true:

> *Ephesians 2:10 (NIV)*
> *For we are God's workmanship,* **created in Christ Jesus to do good works,** *which God prepared in advance for us to do.*

God has prepared "good works," shall we say "fun works," for us to do. So let's do the "fun works."

Enforcing Victory

This part seems simple after completing the ministry for the first four negative spiritual roots of problems. All confession, humbling, and forgiveness has been done. The major curses have been broken. We are on the way to establishing a new Organizational Culture, one that pleases God. We have prayed for and received healing for the major wounds. In other words, much "place" has been recovered from the enemy. This greatly eases the effort required to cast out demons and strongholds, and to remove/displace the principalities. In fact, without the application of the Integrated Approach to ministry to recapture the "land," we may have little, if any, success in reducing the influence of the enemy over our business.

We like to say that we have changed the status of the enemy from being a "squatter" to a "trespasser." A squatter has legal rights to the land because of continuous occupancy. In the case of demons and principalities, the initial "place" was given because of sin. Then the demons occupied for a long time, acquiring "squatter's rights." However, once the actual owner reasserts his rights to the land, the squatter becomes a "trespasser." He no longer can claim rights. He may still be on the land, but at any time the rightful owner can ask the sheriff (Holy Spirit) to escort the illegal alien away. As the rightful owners of our businesses, we are going to work with the Holy Spirit to remove the demons and demonic strongholds, and dismiss, displace, and pushback the principalities.

This operation requires that we know who we are in Christ,[1] that we submit ourselves to God,[2] and that we receive (appropriate) and apply the authority that has been delegated to us.[3] If we have transferred the title of the business over to God (see page 47), then we are even better positioned as His stewards to bring the Kingdom of God into greater manifestation within and over the business.

As we prepare to engage the enemy, we expect that the Leadership and Intercessors are continuing in unity and agreement. By this point in the implementation of the Action Plan, it should be easy to remain in unity and agreement.

As we engage in this operation, we are not planning to pray in the normal sense. We are not addressing the

> *The elements of enforcing Christ's Victory.*

Lord. Rather, as the representative of the Lord Jesus Christ, we are addressing demons, groups of demons ensconced in strongholds, and principalities. We are addressing **Principalities, Powers, Rulers of Darkness, Spiritual Wickedness in high places**.[4] We are demanding that the enemy "listen up" to what we are saying. We do not request, rather we command the enemy to obey. In the process, we command the demons and strongholds to be turned over to the Lord Jesus Christ and go where He sends them.

---

[1] Ephesians 2:6 is one of many scriptures that express our legal position "in Christ." This passage shows our "legal position" at the right hand of God.

[2] We are implementing James 4:7. We are submitting to God, resisting the devil, and commanding him to flee!

[3] Receiving by faith the authority delegated to us by Jesus, as expressed in Matthew 28:18.

[4] This list comes from Ephesians 6:12.

We then begin to enforce the victory obtained at the Cross.

- We command demons afflicting the individuals within the business to leave.
- We command demons operating within the business to leave.
- We command strongholds to be disassembled and torn down, and the demons to leave.
- We command principalities to loose their grip from the land, structures, and the people.
- We command principalities to remove themselves from their former legal ground.
- We command principalities to disconnect from each and every access opening to the business.
- We command principalities to withdraw from us and from the company's land and buildings.
- We command principalities to draw back from above us, leaving an open heaven over us.
- We continue to launch mighty spiritual weapons against the enemy until he is pushed back and displaced from our land, from the "place" where we have authority.

Once we sense that the victory is enforced and that the heavenly atmosphere has cleared, we can rejoice and thank the Lord for His provision. We will also discern whether the enemy has already planned a counterattack and begin to put it in place. If so, we will come against the counterattack and dismantle it before it can form.

Even while rejoicing and enjoying our new freedom, however, we will not be naive and assume that it is all over forever. As we read in Luke 4:13, we know the devil will withdraw waiting for a more opportune time.[1] So we now move into an ongoing "Watchman" operation. We will have sensitive, discerning Intercessors located at strategic positions throughout the company, trained to be alert to any signs of attempted "re-infestation," whether by subtle means or outright attack. We have won our freedom and we are not going to give it back!

---

[1] The devil makes this statement after failing to defeat Jesus in the wilderness (NIV).

IV. Organizational Dynamics: Birth and Ongoing

As we pause a moment and think about what we have learned, we actually have covered quite a bit of ground (yes, pun intended, "Legal Ground!"). We have looked at the five primary sources, or spiritual roots, that generate problems. We then looked at the five spiritual solutions to these problems. Each one is founded upon the finished work of Jesus Christ on the Cross. His finished work is the fulfillment of all scripture (God's promises). As we awaken to truth and appropriate by faith what He did for us, we are strengthened and empowered to attack and remove the negative spiritual roots from our personal lives and the 'life" of our business.

Now let's change our viewpoint from a "problem/solution" orientation to the "time line" of an organization orientation. Let's look at the dynamics of a business as it is "birthed," grows, and then matures. We want to see how serious issues emerge and continue along the time line. We want to discover what we as leaders can do to anticipate and thus solve/eliminate the problems and their effects before they occur.

A. Context of the Beginning (Birth) of the Business

How excited everyone is when a new baby is born. The parents, grandparents, and close friends gather around and welcome the new life into the world. Every toe and finger is checked, and the baby is pronounced, "Healthy and in good shape." Everyone must be satisfied that this baby has all the necessary "moving parts," that everything needed to face life and succeed is in place.

It is the same when a new business is created. Effectively a new birth has occurred. If a corporation is being formed, legally it is a "new birth," as the state recognizes and validates the existence of a new "legal entity."

Unfortunately, neither the new parents nor the founders of the new business comprehend nor consider the spiritual roots that already exist. Even when all the "parts" are working well, negative spiritual forces are already swirling around the new born plotting failure and defeat.

"X" marks the spot on the time line when the business is created. Just as the birth process is hazardous to the future health of the baby, the time of creation of the organization is significant to its future health.

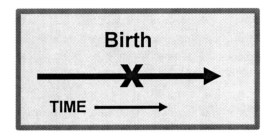

1. Birth Fusion

At the time of the birth, the Territorial/Regional Principalities already on the land combine with the Group/Organizational Principalities brought by the founders. It is as if a nuclear "fusion" device has exploded, as the two different groups of principalities "fuse" together and become one. The business now has its own unique principalities.

Just as each baby is unique, with its very own DNA, so is every organization. Each one has its own genetic makeup, including its principalities. The number of principalities and their relative strength or importance of influence is uniquely set by this combining of what was already on the land waiting for the new organization and what the founders brought with them.

We want to remind you of the definitions (on page 31) of the Group/Organizational Baggage and the Territorial/Regional Baggage. These are what are being brought together as the two sets of principalities are being fused. The process is not, unfortunately, just additive; it is multiplicative. It is a synergy process where the whole is greater than the sum of its parts. The new business does not start with zero Baggage, just as a new baby does not start with zero inheritance. Rather, the spiritual DNA, both good and bad, is there right from the beginning. (The circle with its shaded area represents the Baggage.)

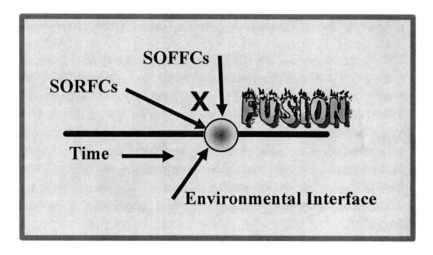

2. Environmental Interface

What we inherit from the Surroundings (Interface), i.e., Boundary Effects.

We also want to mention an additional factor that comes into play at the birth of the organization and continues thereafter. Just as no man is an island unto himself, a business does not stand alone. The surroundings beyond the legal boundary of the land occupied by the business also impact and influence the business. This is the "Environmental Interface" or "Boundary Effect." The same five sources of negative spiritual roots are outside our fence, affecting everyone in the world. Their Baggage, of course, affects them. It also "reaches" through our boundary and affects us. Thus the "Environmental Baggage" is defined as that component of "their" baggage that affects our business.

> **Environmental Baggage:** This is the sum total of all sin, curses, demons, principalities, i.e., evil, **pressing on the organization from the outsides (surroundings)**, and that have access into the organization, i.e., influence, as well as the **potential for future evil.**

For example, what if we think about locating our new business in a part of town where the rent is really low. Hum, that sounds good. We visit there and find everything really depressed. There are iron grates on all of the store windows and houses, the street is littered with trash, and the people are walking around with heads down, not able to look you in the eye. We decide that we have certainly found a unique culture, but it is going to have unique operational problems for our business. The rent might look very attractive but is the total cost of doing business worth it?

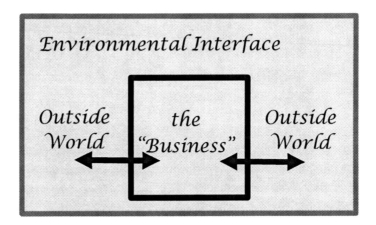

How about a high tax area? Or better yet, a tax haven? Probably we need to look at all the factors in these decisions. What negative spiritual roots will be lurking just beyond our front door, if we choose to locate in either one of these places? We might be planning to implement an Action Plan for our organization, but what kind of ongoing spiritual warfare is going to be needed to deal with the Environmental Interface? Let's consider the type of things that make up the Environmental Interface.

Environmental Interface

1 - Region: Values, Ethics, Appearance
2 - Relationships
3 - Authority Figures (pastors, mafia)
4 - Competitors
5 - Government/Regulatory Agencies
6 - States/Nations (import/export)

In each of these Environmental Interface areas, we must win the spiritual battle just as we do within our organization. We want and need **favor** with those outside our boundaries if we are to have success. If we do not know there is a battle, if we do not understand and deal with the five negative spiritual roots of problems beyond our borders, we will likely continually struggle to achieve success as we deal with those outside of our boundary. Which would you rather have, "Favor" or "Struggle?" The Bible says that God grants favor to His (obedient) kids. Among other things, Jesus came:

> *Luke 4:19 (NIV)*
> *... To proclaim the year of the Lord's favor.*

Another wonderful promise is in Isaiah:

> *Isaiah 49:8*
> *This is what the LORD says: "In the **time of my favor**
> I will answer you, and in the day of salvation **I will
> help you**; I will keep you and will make you to be a
> covenant for the people, **to restore the land** and to re-
> assign its desolate inheritances,"*

103

As we remove the negative spiritual roots from our business and prevent the negative influence via the Environmental Interface, we can ask the Lord for His time of favor.[1]

B. Context of the Ongoing Business

Once the baby survives the birthing process, it begins to grow and mature, as does the business. The other three negative spiritual roots immediately begin to grow and develop as well. The Organizational Culture begins to develop as attitudes about "how to do business" spread among the personnel. While it may take a while for significant hurts to occur, the potential for hurt and loss is established. And the fusion of the Group and Territorial Principalities begins to bring oppression into those areas of wounding that are Open Doors. All these negative spiritual roots exert an unwanted pressure on the newly formed business.

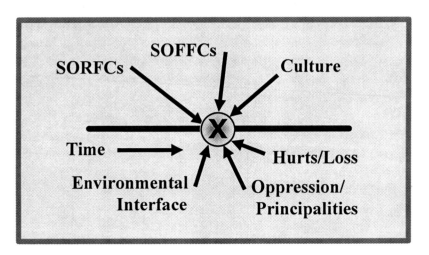

And so time passes. The new (baby) organization moves along the time line. It grows, expands, tries things, reaches out into the surrounding world. And "Oh, yes," it accumulates more Baggage with each passing day, as represented by the expanding circle of Baggage. Hopefully it is also accumulating blessings and productivity.

---

[1] Other significant passages about favor are: Psalms 5:12, Proverbs 12:2, 19:12, Isaiah 61:2.

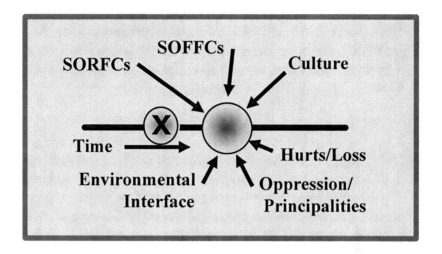

1. Ignorant of the Need for an Action Plan

When the leaders of an organization do not understand the impact of the negative spiritual roots (of problems), the corporate Baggage just continues to grow over time. Problems add up and begin to reinforce one another. The inability to solve the issues becomes more overwhelming to the leaders and department heads. It is understandable that after a while no one really tries anymore. "What is the use? Whatever I do won't be effective anyhow." And so another brick is placed on the wall of the ungodly Organizational Culture. The accumulating Baggage might look like this next figure.

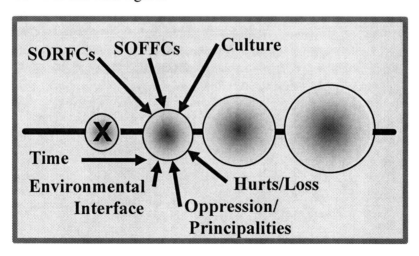

Not a pretty sight, is it? This picture could represent the increase of defilement on the land, the building up of hurts in a marriage, the disharmony within a department, as well as the increased Baggage for the business as a whole.

2. Aware of and Applying the Action Plan

But what if .....? What if the leaders knew how to develop and implement the Action Plan discussed in Part Three? Rather than allowing the Baggage to grow, they would apply God's solution(s) to pull up and out the negative spiritual roots and then continue to exercise diligence to keep the organization cleansed. The amount of Baggage can be dramatically reduced with Identification Repentance, improving the Organizational Culture, keeping Organizational Hurts healed, and displacing the principalities.

To illustrate, let's use this chart to show the possibilities. Let's say that sometime in the past a group obedient to the Lord humbled themselves and did Identification Repentance, with the resultant cleansing of the land. However, they did not continue and the Baggage began accumulating again. Then a new business acquires the land and puts an Action Plan into operation. Again the amount of Baggage is dramatically reduced. This time, however, the spiritual warfare is continued. The business remains sensitive to attacks from the enemy and the re-accumulation of Baggage. The Leaders and Intercessors periodically go through the cleansing process to insure that there is no significant buildup of Baggage. The business has expanded the Kingdom of God and occupied another piece of the earth.

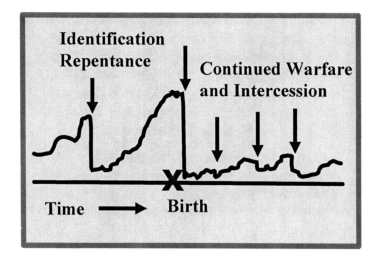

Here is another view of the Baggage on the land and over the organization with ongoing spiritual warfare.

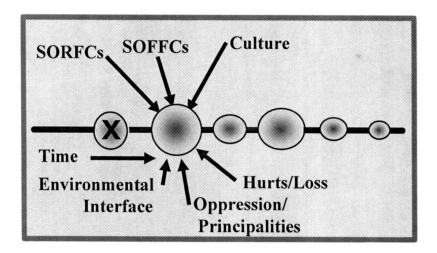

The Baggage has been dramatically reduced and then is kept under control at a minimum level. This is what we desire to accomplish in Transforming Your Business. We want to minimize the Total Baggage carried by the organization so that the business is minimally hindered in accomplishing God's purpose. Let's move on into Part Three and learn how to do this!

Total Baggage: This is the sum total of all sin, curses, demons, and principalities, i.e., evil, associated with the group/organization, the land/structures owned/occupied by the organization, and the influence from the Environmental Interface, as well as the potential for future evil.

Thus it is the sum total of the **personal**, **group/organizational**, **environmental**, and **territorial/regional baggage**.

PART THREE

Action Plan for Transforming Your Business

We are ready to develop an Action Plan to eradicate negative spiritual roots that create spiritual problems hindering and attempting to destroy your business or organization. We will take the "Things We Need To Know" and the "Spiritual Dynamics of Organizations" and move forward to build upon these. This is what we have been working toward! It is this implementation of an Action Plan that will set a business free and propel it into the destiny and purposes of God.

Book's Point of View
Let us stress again that we are writing from the point of view of a Leader (or a number of Leaders) considering whether or not to apply the Transforming Your Business ministry approach to his business. It is written as if you the reader have the authority and responsibility to make decisions and execute them, if not for the entire business at least for your domain within the business.

However, if you are not a Leader with the authority and influence to directly affect the business, we assume you are a child of God[1] with His delegated authority to take the Kingdom of God wherever you go, even as you enter the marketplace to work. Thus you have an indirect ability to affect the business. The caution for you is to not overstep your bounds of authority and anointing. Please read the section on boundaries in Part Five (page 229) before you begin any part of the Transforming Your Business process.

---

[1] If this is not true, let us strongly encourage you to reread the Warning page just before page 1. If you have gotten this far through the book and not yet received the Lord Jesus Christ as your Lord and Savior, it is imperative that you do so now.

Key Ingredients for Transformation

The key ingredients to effectively transform your business or organization are these:

a. Allow the Holy Spirit to impart a Vision for Transforming Your Business. Make a decision to transform your business. Achieve unity and agreement among the Leadership Team. All of these are serious prayer issues and deserve serious consideration.

b. Develop the structure, gather the information, and plan the implementation of the Action Plan.

    Conduct the research and do the spiritual intercession to gather information to fill in the details of the Action Plan. (Determine the negative spiritual roots of current and future problems.)

    Plan the details of how to implement the Action Plan

    Designate the team to implement the Action Plan.

    Use the Action Plan in Appendix A as a starting point template. (You may copy Appendix A or download it from the web site **www.TransformingYourBusiness.org** as a WORD document.)

c. Implement the Action Plan

    Conduct the ministry to the business to remove the negative spiritual roots and recover the legal ground. (Confess, forgive, repent, break, remove, renew Organizational Culture, seek corporate healing, displace/remove Principalities)

d. Ongoing Organizational Transformation

    Continue with ongoing healing, diligent vigilance, spiritual warfare, and Intercession.

The Action Plan for your business is a carefully constructed Holy Spirit cooperative plan. God has been preparing the Church for these times. He has given much revelation and experience in these matters. We have applied the Restoring the Foundations principles to individuals, now it is time for a broader application. We are now ready to launch into the details of the Action Plan. The sooner we prepare the plan, the sooner we will get the devil's bony fingers out of your affairs!

Preemptive Strikes
There is one other important thing you want to be aware of since you have chosen to read this book. **It is likely that the intensity of the warfare in and around your company has already begun to heat up**. While Satan can not see the future, he does know who God's chosen are and what their gifts/potential are. Satan has had his agents listening in on your Leadership meetings; he has not liked what he is hearing. He knows what you have been reading. He knows what you are planning. He will commission attacks designed to dismiss, dislodge, discourage, distract, and defeat the possibility of the Leadership going ahead with a Transforming Your Business Action Plan. Your job is to anticipate these attacks and stand together with the Intercessors to defuse and stop them before they get started or entrenched. We'll explain how to do this in Part Five (on page 249).

> *Don't let fear coming from the devil keep you from God's faithfulness!*

I. Leadership Team

We have continually emphasized the importance of the Leadership Team in bringing about a successful implementation of the Transforming Your Business process. They must be a "team" in every sense of the word or the process will falter and perhaps fail. They must understand the importance of vision, knowledge, conviction, commitment, attitude, will, unity and agreement. As a team they must determine the "cost" of the transformation and be willing to continue the process even when it gets tough. They should understand just how much all of the negative spiritual roots are intertwined. That is, each root is supported by, and supports, the others. As each Leader absorbs, embraces, and commits to do his part, the team will have "good success."[1]

The only exception to having the entire Leadership Team working together is if a sub-group of Leaders decide to commit to function as a "tithe" for the other "unaware" Leaders in order to begin the healing and cleansing process.[2] And if there is no one on the Leadership team prepared to lead the Transforming Your Business process, then you the reader will need to see what portion of the business you can impact as you bring your authority and the Kingdom of God into your domain.

1. Impartation: Vision, Knowledge

One of the important functions of a Leader is to impart vision, purpose, and destiny into the people he is leading. Without imparting vision (as the founders came together), it is likely that the business would not have been birthed. Imparting vision is an ongoing activity of Leaders so that the people know: what they are a part of; where they are going; how they are going to get there; and why they should go.

This is again the time for imparting vision. As you consider applying the Transforming Your Business process to your business, it is a time for the Leaders and employees to grab hold of the possibilities, the vision of what "might be" as the hindrances and bondages over the business are removed.

Here are three relevant scriptures from the Bible regarding the need for vision (and knowledge).

---

[1] We are emphasizing God's setting up Joshua for success (in Joshua 1:8). God wants to do the same for each one of us.

[2] We discussed the provision of the Tithe on page 35.

Prov 29:18 (KJV) Where [there is] no vision, the people perish: ...

Isaiah 5:13 (KJV) Therefore my people are gone into captivity, because [they have] no knowledge: ...

Hosea 4:6 (KJV) My people are destroyed for lack of knowledge: ...

Lack of vision and knowledge results in being waylaid and frustrated, being captured, destroyed, and/or killed. In our day there is a lack of knowledge regarding the existence of negative spiritual roots, much less on how to remove them. And so people are in captivity, destroyed, and even killed. However, we do not need to be ignorant. God has revealed the needed knowledge and we must use it to establish vision in the people for change, for freedom and deliverance. The alternative is not acceptable or pretty.

We must caution you, however. Hell's number one effectual ploy and play is to have you dismiss this as too "out there" and even "laughable." If you embrace the revelation expressed in this book, he will do all he can to make this seem overwhelming. He will help you decide to not "engage" by "putting your head in the sand" or running. This is why we have broken the process down into little pieces and made it very easy to implement. This is why we are publishing this word and revelation that you may catch and run with the vision. For success in this day and season, for fulfilling your destiny, Transforming Your Business is actually the number one job for you as a Leader.

2. Commitment: Attitude and Will

If at all possible, it is very important that each Leader in your business acquire the knowledge contained in this book. It is important to become convicted that applying the Action Plan for Transforming Your Business is not only worth doing, but that it is vital for fulfilling the call of God on his life, on his family, as well as on the corporate destiny. Once convicted, it is equally important that he adopt an attitude of commitment and a "setting of his will" to carry out the process to completion, no matter what. It is time to "count the cost,"[1] becoming convicted in his heart that God is wanting him to make a quality decision to succeed. That he is going to press in and press on to the end regardless of the spiritual warfare, economic difficulties, upset employees, lost customers and venders, etc. It must be decided that cleaning out the Baggage and pursuing God and His destiny is more important and has far more eternal value than what is happening in the temporal.

It requires this level of commitment to defeat Satan. It must be established right from the beginning. Half-hearted unity and partial agreement among the Leaders will just encourage Satan to keep fighting. He knows that a house divided cannot stand.[2] If there is even one little crack in the commitment or unity of the Leaders to carry through, he will do his best to exploit it. However, when Satan knows that the Leaders have made a firm commitment, that there is no turning back, and that they have the knowledge and vision to succeed, he will give up quickly and go find someone else without vision and knowledge that he can torment and defeat.

3. Settle: Unity and Agreement

We may have already made our point about the importance and necessity of unity and agreement among the Leaders. In case you want to refresh your memory, the earlier discussions are on pages 6 and 36. In addition, you can check the index for pages where unity and agreement are discussed.

> *Jesus expresses the power of unity and agreement in Matthew 18:19.*

All discussions of "whether we should do this or not," should be concluded as part of the "due diligence" in deciding to do the Transforming Your Business Action Plan. As the Leaders read this book and discuss how it applies to their situation, the many different ramifications need to be identified and analyzed. The

---

[1] Jesus discusses "counting the cost" of the entire project before commencing in Luke 14:28-31.

[2] Jesus shares this principle in Matthew 12:25-26.

real question to be settled is whether God is calling them to heal their company and land, to cast off the shackles of oppression, and to move ahead in their calling and destiny.

Once the decision is made to move ahead, there will be many times when the Leaders will be seen and heard by the employees (and others). Regardless of who is speaking, the people need to hear a united voice of commitment, strategy, and sure victory. As knowledge is being conveyed and vision imparted, the hearers should be given a consistent, united stance from the Leaders as they move from the implementation of the Action Plan to the ongoing maintenance portion. The commitment, conviction, unity, and agreement among the Leaders should be worn like a cloak for all to see. This is a time for going forward in step knowing the victory is assured.

4. Willing: to "Humble" Themselves

Part of God's solution to Sins of the Founding Fathers and Resident Fathers includes the pattern of confession as expressed in Leviticus 26:40. This is discussed on page 78. Confession (and forgiveness) by its very nature requires us to "humble" ourselves; however, Leviticus 26:41 has an explicit condition of "if then their uncircumcised hearts be humbled." God is asking for a heart that is truly sorry, repentant, eager to change, and given to Him. It implies that we stop looking to ourselves as the strong ones with all the answers and we look to Him. The book of James has a passage that makes this very clear.

> *James 4:6-7*
> *4:6 But he giveth more grace. Wherefore he saith, God resisteth the proud, but **giveth grace unto the humble**.*
> *4:7 **Submit yourselves therefore to God**. Resist the devil, and he will flee from you.*

We humble ourselves when we submit to God. This is not nearly as difficult as it might initially sound. God so orders all things that when we **do** what He says and asks, we end up blessed far more than what it may cost us initially. Jesus certainly is our example.

Humbling ourselves results in far more grace, enabling us to forgive and receive forgiveness. We are given the authority to cause the devil to flee from us. We acquire power and authority to cancel ungodly (spiritual) contracts and displace principalities. Not a bad deal, really, for a little "humble" pie.[1] And most important of all, God is not resisting us in our "proudness."

Perhaps you haven't thought about the fact that God Himself may be "resisting" you in the attitude of "proudness." Be assured, it is best to be on God's side, aligned with Him, than on our "own" side, aligned against God. We will not win when we fight against God!

Leader's Most Important Decision

The decision the Leaders must make is to be willing to confess their sins and the sins of all former Leaders of the business.

They must be willing to "stand in" for all former inhabitants of the land/structures. Through "Identification Repentance" they will confess the sins of the previous Leaders and residents

> *Once this Decision is made, everything else is "downhill!"*

of the land. Once this decision is made and all of the Leaders are in unity and agreement, the most difficult part is over.

Depending on the situation (discussed in the planning section), the Leaders will lead the employees of the business in either private or public confession, forgiveness, and repentance (thus humbling themselves). This comes during the second company meeting, the Action Meeting(s).

---

[1] Jesus discusses the benefits of "humbling" in Matthew 18:4, 23:12, and in the parallel passages in Luke 14:11, 18:14. Two other significant references are Philippines 2:8 and Colossians 3:12.

116

5. Putting God in Charge

In Part One (page 47) we discussed the potential results of making the ultimate transformation: putting God in charge of the business. While we know that this is the only reasonable way to operate a business (or a life), we must leave this decision with the Leadership Team. Putting God in charge will produce a radical change (for the better) in the business. The Leadership Team has to determine if it is ready for such a major change. It has to determine if it has the desire, authority, will, and power to make this decision and carry it out.

If the Leadership Team does not have the authority, or if you the reader are not a part of the Leadership Team, the principle of the tithe can still be applied to begin to bring the presence of the Kingdom of God into the company. Applying your authority to bind the enemy and loose the presence of God will in itself begin the transformation of the business.

We will include an optional step in the Action Plan that you use if the Leadership Team chooses to put God in charge by transferring ownership of the business into the Lord's capable hands.

6. Receiving Personal Restoring the Foundations Ministry

One last thing before we go into the Action Plan itself. It is important to immediately begin laying the axe to the negative spiritual roots of the personal "Baggage" brought into the

Two-fold Return on Investment right from the beginning!

business by the founders, owners, and other key Leaders. It is important for several reasons. First, the Restoring the Foundations ministry will help them in their own personal and family lives. Second, it will reduce the ability of the enemy to interfere in the affairs of the Leaders and through them the business (Principles of Principalities # 2 and #4). And third, as the Leaders walk in newfound freedom and ability to hear the voice of the Lord, their job performance should increase significantly.

117

We recommend that as soon as the decision is made to commence with Transforming Your Business that the key Leadership (and their spouses) begin to receive their personal Restoring the Foundations (RTF) ministry from qualified team members of the Healing House Network. Depending on the number of Leaders, it could take several months before each one (including spouse) is able to schedule a week of ministry with a Healing House Network team.[1]

Another approach would be to schedule a retreat for the Leaders (and spouses) with a number of Healing House Network teams. Everyone would be ministered to during the same time period. This would have the added benefit of everyone experiencing healing and freedom at the same time. It would empower team building, increase accountability, and help them focus on the coming spiritual warfare.

Either of these approaches could be strengthened by having a seminar for the Leaders based on the Restoring the Foundations revelation and understandings before they received their personal RTF ministry. The Leaders would see the ministry demonstrated and experience God's healing touch in a group setting. Then when they arrived for their personal ministry, they would be primed for maximum receiving of the Lord's healing and freedom. This would have the added benefit of beginning to train the Leaders in the basics of RTF ministry, preparing them to be "Helpers" during the Action Meeting(s).

They will also be equipped to continue to work with the Holy Spirit in: their personal sanctification process, building stronger confidence and boldness, being better prepared to withstand any attacks of the enemy, being able to cover and protect the company Intercessors, and praying with more fervency and faith.[2]

---

[1] You may call the Healing House Network office at 800-291-4706 to discuss the best ministry team for each Leader and spouse and schedule an appointment.

[2] Please note James 5:16.

All of the things we have been discussing; commitment, unity, agreement, etc., will be easier to "walk in" for each Leader after his ministry. We believe you will find this a firm foundation and good return on the investment made. And we haven't even ministered to the business yet!

II. Developing the Action Plan

The decision has been made. The die is cast and there is no turning back. You are determined and declaring, "The access Satan now has to exert significant influence in my company is drawing to a close." What do we do now?

A. Development Team

The first task of the Leadership Team is to select the Development Team and commission them: i.e., authorize and empower them to successfully accomplish the job. Set a time line and a budget. If necessary, relieve members from other duties that can either wait or that may be eliminated as the business becomes free and healed.

The Development Team will develop the Action Plan. They will be charged with gathering the necessary information and then using it to formulate the plan. Their work will set the foundation for the Implementation Team to build on as they carry out the steps needed for Transforming Your Business.

Identify Skills/Gifts Needed and Select Team
As you consider those to be appointed on this team, let us suggest a combination of one or more of the company Leaders, then other committed staff gifted with the needed skills. An additional consideration is to plan on having at least one, better yet two, team members who also serve on the Implementation Team. This will provide "carry over" and better communication of the knowledge gained, lessons learned, and reasoning behind the Action Plan.

We suggest that the skills/gifts listed in the box are the minimum essential ones needed by the Development Team. Your business may require additional skill sets/gifts. For example, you might consider whether you want an

> ## Development Team
> - Leader/Oversight
> - Prophetic Intercessor(s)
> - Researcher(s)
> - Strategist
> - Implementer

"outside" consultant who is trained in Transforming Your Business ministry to be either an "on call" advisor to the team or to be a member of the team.

How Many People?
"How many people should be on the Development Team?" One factor is the size of the business. Another guideline is, "Who has the largest stake in the contents and outcome of the Action Plan?" Within these guidelines, we submit that the smallest team possible is the best.[1] It is difficult enough to get busy people together. We suggest your asking the Intercessors to help select those most capable, the most involved and dedicated, and the ones most able to fulfill one or more of the listed skill sets and giftings. This should provide you with the best list of candidates.

1. Leader/Oversight
The Leadership Team needs to provide leadership to the Development Team as well as have at least one representative on it. Whether additional Leaders should be active members of the Development Team will depend on the size of the business. The more active Leaders there are, the more they can not do their "regular" job.

---

[1] One of Parkinson's Laws is: The amount of time, effort, and expense required to make a decision is inversely proportional to the number of people involved. (See Biographic for information about his book.)

2. Prophetic Intercessor(s)

Try to have at least one Prophetic Intercessor on both the Development Team and the Implementation Team. This position is a critical one. It should only be filled after much prayer and listening to the Lord. This person (and thus the family) will be a prime target as the business presses to move forward. Ideally this person (and family) will have already received *Restoring the Foundation* ministry (or the equivalent). Their main safeguard from attacks of the enemy will be a proper attitude of heart. They should have a humble heart, an attitude to serve, and be eager and willing to submit to the vision, covering, and Leadership of the company. In other words, this person should not be particularly susceptible to the hazards discussed in Part Five on Intercessors and spiritual warfare (page 226). At any sign of influence by any demons or any of the principalities discussed in Part Four, particularly the occult ones, they should desire and ask for immediate help to deal with any "Open Doors." They must be willing to be protected by the Leadership while standing in this front line position.

This person must have a keen gift of discernment (yet not be judgmental) and be able to hear the voice of the Lord clearly. They should be one that eagerly seeks relationship with the Lord and is solid in his Christian walk.

This person is also the natural candidate to oversee and lead the company Intercessors in spiritual warfare. This further increases the importance that this person being among the initial Leaders to receive the thorough form of the *Restoring the Foundations* ministry. They must be helped to have every Open Door closed and personal Baggage reduced as much as possible.

If there is no one to occupy this position, nor any one that can be raised up for it, there may be a necessity to bring in an outside Intercessor consultant. More is said about this topic, including the possibility of hiring a new staff Intercessor, on page 239.

3. Researcher(s)

There is a lot of information to gather, both natural and spiritual. Having at least one person on the team who loves details, dusty books, digging, and organizing is essential. While this person can also be one who is able to obtain spiritual revelation, their primary work will be done among the natural things of this world.

4. Strategist

At least one of the team members should be a strategist, a planner. One who sees patterns in the midst of chaos. This person shifts through the data as it is collected, both natural and spiritual, to seek the roots of the negative spiritual problems. They will work with the Implementer to devise plans that will obtain maximum benefit as the gathered information is applied to obtain God's solutions.

5. Implementer

The Implementer will be on the team to insure all of the details of the Action Plan are covered. This person's gifts will include coordination, handling details, organizing meetings, and also intercession. They should be able to *communicate well* with the employees and help prepare them for the changes in the business.

Your Development Team

Again, you may need additional skill sets and/or special people on the Development Team. The point is to have all that you need but no more. Applying the Transforming Your Business process to your business may be a significant investment. There is no point in making it larger than necessary.

B. Action Plan: Overview

To give you a "jump start" on developing an Action Plan, we have included an Action Plan template in Appendix A. To make it even easier for you, we have placed a downloadable WORD document file containing the Action Plan template on the **www.TransformingYourBusiness.org** web site.

The Development Team's job is to expand the template and fill in the details. From this gathering and compilation of data, they will prepare plans for transforming the company. If you haven't yet perused Appendix A, we invite you to do so.

The Action Plan has two primary phases, the Development phase and the Implementation phase. The Development phase has two parts, the Information Gathering and Ministry Planning sub-phases. These phases are followed by the Ongoing Transformation phase, a maintenance activity to not lose ground or fall back into the old ways.

Here is a simple time line schedule showing the sequencing of each phase.

Time Line Schedule

ACTION PLAN (AP)	Phase I Develop	Phase II Implement	Phase III Ongoing
Select Development Team	■■■■■■	■■■■■■	■■■■■■
Release Intercessors	■■■■■■	■■■■■■	■■■■■■
Minister RTF to Leaders	■■■■		
AP: Development			
Information Gathering	■■■■■■		
Ministry Planning	■■■■■		
AP: Implementation		■■■■■■	
Ongoing Transformation			■■■■■■

Information Gathering
The first (sub) phase of the Action Plan is essentially a business interview/assessment. The template provides space to compile the past and present characteristics of the company, structures, and the land. It gathers crucial information needed for the implementation of the Transforming Your Business process to remove the negative spiritual roots and their effects. The Development Team is responsible for gathering the necessary data.

Ministry Planning
The Development Team will also conduct the second (sub) phase which is to plan the details for implementing the Action Plan. This will include recommending the members of the Implementation Team. These may or may not include one or more members of the Development Team.

Implementation
The Implementation phase has as its main focus two (or more) organizational-wide meetings. The first, the "Preparation" meeting, the appropriate employees of the business will be informed of the decision and intent to transform the business, the scriptural basis to be used, and the main elements of the Action Plan.

The second meeting is the "Action Meeting." In this meeting the Leaders will begin to apply God's solution to the primary negative patterns/spiritual roots affecting the business. The Leaders of the Implementation Team will lead the organization through the ministry process as the business declares war and begins to recover legal ground from the enemy. This is the company "Baggage reducing" time. It will likely require more than one Action Meeting to work through the most important primary negative patterns and the associated spiritual roots.

Ongoing Transformation
After the completion of the Implementation phase, the business will enter an "Ongoing Transformation" phase. This is an important maintenance posture to insure the doors stay closed and to contain and stop all attempted future attacks before they can influence and contaminate.

C. Action Plan Sub-Phase: Information Gathering

Let's look at the Action Plan template and become familiar with its main elements. What do we need to do and how do we go about accomplishing it?[1]

Contact Information

The first part of the Action Plan template includes contact information for the person in charge of developing the Action Plan. This may be you, or it may not be. However, before the business is finished with the Transforming Your Business process, there may be a number of people with whom it will be appropriate to share the Action Plan. Having your contact information here may help them find you at a critical time. This will be especially true if you involve a Transforming Your Business consultant to help you develop and/or carry through the Action Plan.

1. Organization Information

It is likely that others will be reading this Action Plan who are not familiar with your business. It will help set the context of the ministry by providing the basics and the nature of the organization; i.e., name, location, vision and mission statement as well as primary products and/or services.

2. Current Leaders/Principals

Who are the people in charge? Who has the authority and responsibility to "run" the business? Who has impact and influence? Who are the ones that should come into unity and agreement in order to present a united front to the world and the spiritual realm? This is the place to identify these people, as well as their willingness to participate in the Transforming Your Business process, particularly the "humbling," Identification Repentance, and self-examination activities.

---

[1] You probably have some of the information needed for the Action Plan already available in other company documents. Copies of these may be included with the basic Action Plan.

3. Historical Baseline Data

It is time to record some baseline data about the business. We want to know what has been going on in the past (and currently) so that we can observe the changes in the future. We believe that the future metrics will be much better than the current/past. We expect the business to change for the better as the negative spiritual roots behind company limitations and bad patterns are eliminated. It is important to obtain some objective business metrics on performance, marketing/sales, employees, customers, vendors, and anything else of relevance for you. It is important that you select key parameters that are significant and meaning-ful for you and your business. Of course, the "tell all" metric will be the "bottom line." We would expect it to initially have a change in trend to "good" growth, then later to "explosive" growth. If this doesn't happen, or only partially happens, then we know that there are additional negative spiritual roots to be discovered and eliminated.

4. "Beginnings" Information

Where, when, and why did the business start? By now it should be very clear that we put a major importance on the origins and birth event of the company. If the company is now in a different location from its origins, it may be worthwhile to expand the spiritual mapping activity to include all previous locations of the business.

5. Previous Leaders/Principals

We are sure, as with all of the current Leaders, that the previous Leaders were men and women of vision, quality, productivity, and commitment. As with us, they were probably people that were "in process." While on the one hand we do not have a right to malign their character, it is important to acknowledge before the Lord (i.e., confess) their contribution to the Baggage of the organization. After all, they are the ancestors of the organization. The pattern of Leviticus 26:40[1] is to state the facts of their contribution. It is not to "blame shift" nor to infer motives, hidden agendas, or "hearsay." As Joe Friday used to say on the old TV show Dragnet, "Just the facts, ma'am, just the facts."[2]

6. Organizational Patterns: Fruit

This section begins to get us into the "fruit" of the matter. What are the characteristics that define and describe the business? Be "real" here and state both the good and the bad, and if present, the ugly. The information presented here will be used to help "back track" from the "bad" fruit to the negative spiritual roots feeding and producing these patterns.

It is sometimes difficult for the people involved to be able to identify their own "stuff." We all think that our lives and the things affecting us are "normal." As you begin to fill out this section, pray and ask the Holy Spirit to reveal to you the fruit that is ungodly and the roots producing it. Give Him permission to reveal those hidden things to the Intercessors and others you trust.

You might consider bringing in a trained Transforming Your Business ministry consultant to help analysis the "fruit." He is trained to recognize bad fruit and to trace back to the roots producing it.

7. Historical Spiritual Mapping
Sins of the Founding Fathers and resulting Curses
Sins of the Resident Fathers and resulting Curses

Let us continue to dig deeper into the foundations of the business. The Development Team members will be busy extracting information. You will know you have selected the right team

---

[1] You may refer back to the discussion on Leviticus 26:40 on page 78.

[2] Please see Biography for biographic book about Jack Webb (i.e., Joe Friday).

members when you see how fulfilled they are as they exercise their gifting. All the members are looking for answers to the question, "What are the sources/roots of the Organizational Patterns/fruits, particularly the ungodly ones?" They are Spiritual Mapping to find the answers to this question.

George Otis, jr., popularized the phrase "Spiritual Mapping."[1] It means to discover the historical activities on a particular piece of land, especially the sins that have accumulated from the past residents. We have broadened the meaning slightly to include the founding fathers as well. We are asking the team to "map" all past sins and curses whether brought to the organization by the founding fathers and previous Leaders, or brought by the previous residents on the land.

Expect to find that many of the former Leaders and the residents on the land all brought the same or similar sins and curses. Expect also that the Principles of Principalities (from page 68) to draw in Leaders that had Baggage in harmony with the Baggage of the founders. Likewise, expect a match and reinforcement from the Baggage on the land as the organization was drawn to the current (and previous) location. These are important correlations to notice and document.

Search through the historical data for the known, natural knowledge about the founders/previous Leaders and the residents on the land. Libraries are good places to start this exercise, both for their books and for contacts with long-time residents who may know information not written or kept in governmental records. Usually their memories will give more clues to past sin than the written record.

Since the records only go back so far, since they are incomplete, and since records generally don't contain information about the negative "stuff," the only truly reliable source of information about past sins and curses is the Holy Spirit.

---

[1] Please see Biography for books by George Otis, Jr.

8. Revelational Spiritual Mapping
Sins of the Founding Fathers and resulting Curses
Sins of the Resident Fathers and resulting Curses

The second part of Spiritual Mapping, the "real" spiritual mapping, is to ask for revelation from the Holy Spirit about the sins and curses of the past that are affecting the present and future. Add to the "natural knowledge" listed on the Patterns page and the Historical Spiritual Mapping page. You want to have an explanation for the negative Patterns/fruit, i.e., what are the negative spiritual roots that produce the Patterns. You want knowledge from the supernatural, i.e., knowledge that we could not obtain except through the Holy Spirit's revelation.

Fortunately, it is "the Father's good pleasure to give you (us) the kingdom."[1] So we don't have to beg for this information. He wants us to know everything needed to insure complete cleansing. His desire and end is for us to redeem the land into the Kingdom of God, to again have dominion over the affairs on the land. So as you are "filling in" the Action Plan, ask the Intercessors and others to seek the Lord and ask the question stated earlier, "What are the sources/roots of these organizational Patterns/fruits, particularly the ungodly ones?" Besides the company Intercessors, it is good to ask other intercessory/prayer groups and networks to help us seek the Father and discover **everything** that needs to be known to bring complete freedom and victory.

It has been our experience that God gives each seeker a piece of the information we need. It is as if He is forcing us to work together as a team, a team with common vision and purpose, in order to obtain a view of the entire picture.

---

[1] This wonderful promise is found in Luke 12:32.

9. Organizational Sins and Curses Groups:
Open Doors/Roots

Now begin to organize the gathered information into groups and sub-groups of associated sins and curses. Organize everything learned about patterns whether from history or from revelation. You will be going for the "bottom of the barrel" regarding the sources of the sins and curses affecting and manifesting within the company. As you look at the Organizational Patterns and accomplish the Spiritual Mapping, you will be able to note the individual sin and curse items within each group, i.e., each Open Door. As this is being done, you will see the primary patterns of groups and sub-groups of associated sins and curses. This information will be very helpful as you plan the strategy to implement the Action Plan for freedom from curses and from the oppression by principalities.

You can use the information in Part Four about "Common Principalities" to help identify and understand the principalities that are "behind" the observed patterns. The historical and revelation data will make more sense in light of the spiritual entities operating over the land and through the people.

10. Ungodly Organizational Culture:
Attitudes and Beliefs

Beliefs, Expectations, Ethics, Procedures, Practices

In this section of the Action Plan there are listed a number of ungodly attitudes/beliefs organized by leaders, employees, customers, etc. These are designed to help you get started as you pray about the Organizational Culture within your business. How many of the listed ones can you see operating within your organization? Check off each one you find so that it can be replaced with the truth. We also hope and expect that the listed beliefs will act as a springboard to heighten your sensitivity to other attitudes present among the people of your company. Use the blank lines to include additional ungodly cultural attitudes that you know (or are relatively confident) are present.

Additional things you can do to discover sources include: looking at the company policy manual, looking into the employee manual, consider the statement of vision, the mission, the ethics, etc. The Leaders and Intercessors can continue to inquire of the Holy Spirit to reveal all ungodly attitudes of mind and heart, and operation within the company.

This area is important to clean up. There should be no agreements/contracts with negative spiritual powers that enable distractions, hindrances, slow downs or stopping of God's direction and purpose for our business (see page 66). Be diligent about searching out and acknowledging any ungodly ways of doing business, or treating our employees, customers, or vendors poorly. It is time to exchange them for God's kingdom ways.

11. Organizational Hurts/Losses

Fractures, Divisions, Rebellion, Anger, etc.

What has happened in the past that has wounded the company? Look for hurts and losses that are carried by the corporate memory of the company. If the business is young, there may not be any (significant) wounds. On the other hand, a multi-generation family owned business may have many hurts and wounds. List the ones known; the ones that others in the company know, and ask the Holy Spirit to reveal any other wounds needing healing.

12. Organizational Oppression/Principalities

It is to be expected that the list of possible principalities over the people and over the land/structures will look very similar to the Open Doors groupings of Sins of the Founding and Resident Fathers in section IX of the Action Plan. There is no need to re-write these groupings. Rather, you may use section XII, Organizational Oppression /Principalities (page 286), to list any additional known or suspected principalities.

As you consider what principalities may be influencing the business, we want to again refer you to Part Four. Reading about the characteristics of the various Common Principalities will enable you to better discern or spot their presence. If there is one or more "uncommon" principalities operating over your property as well, expect the Holy Spirit to reveal what is needed.

13. Final Comments and Summary

You can include here any other facts, history, insights, prophetic words, etc., that have not been noted elsewhere that may be relevant as you prepare to implement the Action Plan.

D. Action Plan Sub-Phase: Ministry Planning

The Development Team will use the gathered information to plan the strategy for Transforming Your Business. Please refer to the second part of the Action Plan template, Ministry Planning, starting on page 288. Keep in mind that we are working toward two meeting types, the "Preparation Meeting" and the "Action Meeting," where the implementation will really begin.

Primary Patterns/Themes

As the Development Team begins the planning phase, they will be looking for the primary negative patterns or themes operating within the business. When these patterns/themes are identified and catalogued, the most important ones will be used to organize the data and will be the "framework" to guide the ministry. The goal is to eliminate each of the five negative spiritual roots behind each pattern/theme.

Here are some examples: is there a prevailing attitude of abandonment, evidenced by people not able to be a part of a team? Or perhaps it seems everyone is fearful and therefore unwilling to "step out" and take even a reasonable risk. Is there an atmosphere of possessiveness, with everyone guarding their territory? How about passivity? Are people able to take initiative and figure out new approaches? Or do they just wait to be told what to do?

Pre-Ministry Planning and Implementation

As the Development Team begins the planning process, and as different people with a variety of skills, giftings and anointings become involved, it may become important to prepare for and supplement the Action Plan ministry with practical actions. For example, there are marketplace ministries providing revelation wisdom in Change Management, Process Improvement, Core Values Assessment, Communication Skills, Inspirational and Core Values Emails, etc. One or more of these may be a "gap" in your business that needs filling by one of God's ordained ministers. Let us again refer you to the Ministry Resources pages at the back of this book for possible help.

1. Planning to Select and Release the Development Team

This planning will be done and the team released immediately by the Leadership Team, using the suggestions discussed starting on page 119.

2. Planning to Select and Release the Intercessors

As the Development Team begins to function, one of the most important immediate tasks, if not THE most important task, is to plan how to select and release the Intercessors. This may or may not be easy. To help the Leadership Team determine how big an effort will be required and what approaches might be used, we have included Part Five "Intercession—Spiritual Mapping." These Part will also stress the importance of the Intercessors to the success of implementing the Action Plan.

The following questions are ones that the Development Team might ponder as they plan how to find, raise up, select, and release the Intercessors.

- Who are the Intercessors within the company?
- What is their level of maturity?
- Is there at least one Intercessor who is suitable to train, equip, and lead the Intercessors, i.e., be the Prophetic Intercessor on the Development and Implementation Teams?

- If there is not at least one suitable Intercessor within the company, should the business search for and contract with one or more well-recognized Intercessors for a season?
- If there is not at least one suitable Intercessor within the company, should the business search for and hire a well-recognized Intercessor consultant/trainer as an employee of the company?
- Should the company buy books and pay other expenses for the Intercessors or should the Intercessors pay their own expenses?
- Should the company have the Intercessors practice, train, and intercede during regular business hours or in the evening?
- Who are the appropriate Leaders to directly oversee and cover the Intercessors?

3. Planning to Select and Release the Implementation Team

It will probably be obvious who should be on the Implementation Team. Thus it should be easy to select this team. We suggest that there are just three main positions/skill sets/giftings needed, so this may be a small team. However, the Development Team will consider what is needed for your company in planning for the Implementation Team, including the possibility of using a trained Transforming Your Business ministry consultant as an advisor or as a permanent member of the team.

> *Implementation Team*
> - *Public Leader(s)*
> - *Prophetic Intercessor(s)*
> - *Implementer*

Public Leader
At least one person should represent the primary owners/founders/board/officers of the business. This person will have the authority, responsibility, charisma, and confidence to represent all of the Leaders in leading the meetings, insuring the

Intercessors are in place and functioning, covering the Intercessors, authorizing the necessary expenditures, and overseeing the ministry for employees.

Prophetic Intercessor
As with the Development Team, having at least one Prophetic Intercessor on the team is important, if at all possible. All that was written about this position for the Development Team (page 121) is also relevant for the Implementation Team. If no one is readily available, one or more of the business Leadership Team will have to fill this gap until the right person is found.

Implementer
The same person filling this position on the Development Team can continue this task for the Implementation Team. Having the same person will certainly help the continuity of developing and then implementing the Action Plan.

Releasing the Team
With the exception of the Intercessor, this team will not go into action until it is time to implement the Action Plan. However, identifying the team members early will allow them to be aware of the work of the Development Team and be ready to "implement" when the time comes.

4. Planning for Healing Ministry for Appropriate Leadership and Intercessor Families

We discussed the importance of the Leadership Team (page 117) and the Intercessors (and their spouses) (page 241) receiving their personal Restoring the Foundations ministry even as the Development Team is getting started. It may take some time to schedule each person with a Healing House Network team. Starting immediately will help the company benefit from Leaders that are more healed and free and will position them to be actively involved in the spiritual warfare.

5. Planning for Ministry to Sins of the Founding/Resident Fathers and resulting Curses – "Open Doors"

As the information begins coming in from the Spiritual Mapping and other research, it is time to begin to identify the principal patterns/themes/relationships in the data. We will organize the data around each pattern as we prepare to minister to the five negative spiritual roots behind and supporting the patterns/themes. Let's start by focusing on the first two roots; the Sins of the Founding Fathers and resulting Curses (SOFFCs), and the Sins of the Resident Fathers and resulting Curses (SORFCs).

We have presented God's Solution for these two roots in Part Two, starting on page 77. Now it is time to develop a specific plan for your business. The Development Team has the data; let's organize it for maximum effectiveness in removing the effects of the sins and curses.

As the Development Team looks at and prays through the collected information, they can begin to identify the 3-6 most significant negative patterns/themes affecting the business. Generally speaking, a person or an organization will not be equally oppressed by every possible sin and curse. Rather, there will be several arenas of weakness or sin tendencies that seem stronger and more influential than the others. For example, abandonment might be a primary problem, or perhaps shame, or bitterness, or control. Maybe the primary pattern is the Control-Rebellion-Rejection Stronghold.[1] How about fears? Whichever pattern or patterns emerge from the information, we can identify the more significant ones (negative fruit) and trace them back to their roots. These patterns and their negative spiritual roots will form the basis for the Action Plan.

---

[1] This is a commonly occurring major super-stronghold discussed in *Restoring the Foundation* by Chester and Betsy Kylstra. Please see the Resource page at end of this book.

With each primary pattern of negative spiritual fruit, there will be several roots that are supportive or associated with it. Look for these associated groups of sins and curses so they can be eliminated along with the primary. For example, abandonment usually gives "place to" and is supported by rejection, rebellion, and sometimes passivity. Bitterness will have anger, depression, and maybe violence. You will minister to these primary patterns and their associated roots as a "unit."

What to do if you have more than 3-6 primary negative Patterns/Themes?

If you feel there are more than 3-6 primary negative influential patterns, we would suggest you pick the 3-6 patterns that you feel are the most important. Use these for the first round of ministry, and save the others for a future time of ministry. After the first round is completed, allow a time of settling into the newly gained freedom. Trying to change too many things too quickly can be overwhelming for the people and Leaders.

We will use the "Organizational Sins and Curses Groups: Open Doors" pages (starting on page 266) as work sheets to collect and organize the information. You may print out a clean set of pages from the Action Plan Template (Appendix A) and begin to mark on them the primary patterns/themes. One way to help keep the information organized is to assign a number to each unit of primary and associated patterns/roots. Then we assign a letter to each associated pattern/root.

To make it even easier to see the associations, transfer the primary and associated patterns/roots groups to another piece of paper. There could be 3-6 boxes of units of primary and associated patterns/roots. Sometimes we use a different color highliter pen to mark each box.

As an example, we show "abandonment" as the primary pattern/root in the following figure. We might decide to minister to this primary pattern/root and its associated patterns/roots first, so we would assign a "1" to the primary and the associated patterns/roots. We have associated with "abandonment" the sub-groups "rejection," "rebellion," and "passivity." We number the groups from "A" to "D" in the order that we plan to minister to them. We determine the best order of ministry as we pray and ask the Holy Spirit.

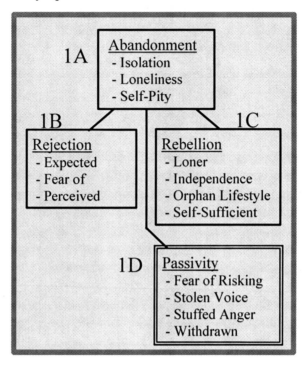

Note that the "passivity" sub-group has a double line border. We used the double line to note that this is a "customized" sub-group that we created. It does not appear in the Open Doors list in the Action Plan Template. We did this to illustrate that you can create your own groups and sub-groups that "fit" for your business. The Open Doors list is there for you as a starting point. Please do not be restricted by it.

Assume that your team now has 3-6 primary groups, each one with several supportive/associated sub-groups, each one numbered in the order of importance/planned ministry. This will give a total number of 12 to 36 groups and sub-groups for the ministry. The ministry process (God's solution) described on page 77 will be applied to each of these units of groups and sub-groups.

The next figure shows another example with "control" as the primary pattern/theme. This example has four sub-groups or associated patterns/roots, each identified with a letter. The number "2" shows that this unit of primary and associated patterns/ roots will be ministered to after we finish with the "abandonment" unit.

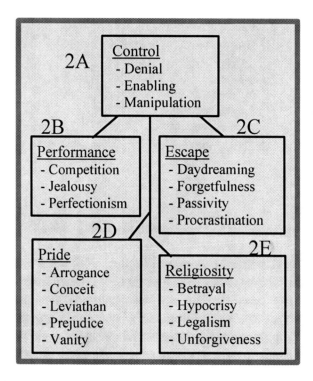

With each primary and its associated patterns/roots, we have listed the active/operating individual sin/curse Open Door (as found by the research team). For example, the "performance" pattern/sub-group includes "competition," "jealousy," and "perfectionism." We might have from 3 to 12 items with each group/sub-group. The Open Doors pages will help you think/pray about what is operating in your company.

Another way to present this information is shown in the next figure. It uses a simple "outline" organization. You may use whichever approach you desire.

Ministry Target: Abandonment

1A Abandonment
- Isolation
- Loneliness
- Self-Pity
- 1B Rejection
  - Expected
  - Fear of
  - Perceived
- 1C Rebellion
  - Loner
  - Independence
  - Orphan Lifestyle
  - Self-Sufficient
- 1D Passivity
  - Fear of Risking
  - Stolen Voice
  - Stuffed Anger
  - Withdrawn

Once the plan is developed, schedule the Action Meeting where you will minister to these patterns/roots. There will be confession, forgiving, breaking, and removing the effect of each item, each sub-group, and each group contained within one primary pattern and its associated roots. When you have gone through all of these, you should experience a clearer atmosphere over the business.

6. Planning to "Marry" the Land

It would be good if the Leadership Team and the Development Team, along with the Intercessors, would inquire of the Lord regarding "Marrying" the Land, as we discussed on pages 44 and 82. If everyone is in agreement, this can be included as part of one of the Action Meetings, usually the first one.

7. Planning for Ministry to
Ungodly Organizational Culture

– Attitudes and Beliefs

Planning to change the Organizational Culture has several significant aspects.

Identify the ungodly Organizational Culture

We have listed in the Action Plan template a large number of Organizational Culture beliefs and attitudes that might be operating within the business (starting on page 278). As the Development Team researches the prevailing "atmosphere" within and without the company, they will select the listed items that apply and also write in additional ones that are specific to the company. We will minister to this negative spiritual root area as well, using God's solution as presented on page 83 in Part Two.

Determine Primary Patterns/Themes

The Development Team's list may be extensive, as they identify items that are a part of the ungodly Organizational Culture. It may be too long for the first Action Meeting. Therefore, select the most important 5 to 10 ungodly aspects of the Organizational Culture that align with the same primary patterns/roots/groups developed from the analysis of the fathers and curses. For example, if "abandonment" is one of the primary patterns, select from the ungodly Organizational Culture list one or more Ungodly Beliefs that support and help hold in place "abandonment." Assume you discover on the list the following three prevailing company attitudes.

- *I may be part of this company, but nobody is looking out for me. Anytime I need something I will have to get it on my own.*

- *I am just another cog in the wheels of this company. Anytime they want to get rid of me, they will do it.*

- *The leadership is too busy to care about my problems.*

141

While these three Ungodly Beliefs appear to be very simple, imagine the effect on teamwork and "esprit de corps" these might have. They align with and help hold in place ancestral sins/curses of "abandonment," "isolation," and the "orphan life-style." It is effectual to eliminate these from your business.

Discover God's Truth

God's truth will counter the established negative patterns/roots. In this process of determining God's truth, the Leaders and Intercessors will renew and expand an ability to hear God's truth (Godly Beliefs) for their every need. He will reveal specific truths to replace the current ungodly attitudes and beliefs.

We always start out by asking the question, "Father God, what do You say is the truth to counter this lie we have believed?" If we have learned to hear God's voice, that still small voice will answer us. As we work together as a team, the Holy Spirit will consolidate our "thoughts" into God's truth. Perhaps having a trained Transforming Your Business consultant[1] available can speed the process and/or provide the training for the Development Team to become proficient at discerning God's truth.

For the above three Ungodly Beliefs regarding abandonment, He may align with truth such as:

- *My managers and supervisors are there for me. They are "servant leaders." Their job and their heart is to insure that I have everything I need, both to do my job and for my own personal growth.*

- *Just as the church has many parts and interactions, so does this company. God will insure that each one of us, including me, is in our right place. Since I have committed to be in the center of God's will for me, only He can move me; only He can open or shut doors that affect my life.*

---

[1] We have included a Ministry Resources page at the back of this book to assist you in finding the type of help you want.

- God has placed me in a business/family that cares about one another. While the leadership is busy, they are busy taking care of everyone including me. They have my best interest in their hearts. As they work to accomplish God's purposes and plans for this company, all of us are being cared for.

Consequences of introducing God's Truth

God will show His strategy for introducing and imparting the truths of the "new and improved" Organizational Culture. It is one thing for the Leaders to decide to change the Organizational Culture; it is another thing to have the employees decide they want to change their attitudes and core values. It is vital to have His strategy. It is more than just changing the company: the individuals are being asked to change their very lives and thus family culture. It is unlikely that everyone will want to do this. At least, they will not want to unless the Intercessors have bound the prince of the power of the air over the business and asked for God's grace to overtake each one.

Yet this is even more far reaching as the customers and vendors will also be impacted. They will experience spiritual forces either moving them closer to or further away from the business. While interceding for the company, the customers and vendors should also be included. For those that are interconnected because of Principle #7 of the Principles of Principalities (on page 72), perhaps the Intercession will enable the Holy Spirit to give them an opportunity to choose righteousness.

As stated often, it is important to release the leaders and Intercessors early in the process to help the people of the organization become free. They can begin to

> *Step One: Restrict ability of the enemy to maneuver and blind.*

reduce the ability of the enemy to use the "legal ground" that he now occupies. They have authority to *bind and restrict the ability of the principalities to influence the hearts and minds of the people* (on page 40). The Leaders and Intercessors can remove the pressure from the people so that they do not stay "out of their senses,"[1] but they are allowed to have a more "sane" response as the Action Plan is presented to the company. This will help the members of the organization choose to change toward godliness. As part of the Intercession and warfare, they can be given a "clear" atmosphere over their minds, at least for a season. However, their final decision is up to them.

The same is true for the customers and vendors. They will experience a new spiritual atmosphere when they enter our place of business. They may like it and want to change, or they may not like it and decide to go elsewhere with their business. For those that don't want to change, as hard as it is to think about losing employees, customers, or vendors, it will be better without any mutual reinforcing of evil spirits and destructive business activities. This process of re-aligning and establishing new relationships with new employees, customers, and even suppliers is another area in which hearing from the Lord will bring peace even if it appears "things are falling apart."

Preparation Meeting: Defining Organizational Culture
Once the Development Team has finished their work and the Action Plan is ready, the Implementation Team will share at a **"Preparation Meeting"** the company's intension to apply the principles in *Transforming Your Business* to the business. They will include that one of the areas of challenge and change will be thought processes and perceptions, and that the business will be looking at current ways of thinking with a plan to change to God's way of thinking and perceiving situations.

Action Meeting(s): Presenting God's Truth
At the Action Meeting(s), the Leaders will lead the organization through the ministry process to remove one primary negative pattern/theme at a time. For example, the primary pattern of "abandonment" may be selected. First the sins/curses groups will be removed, as discussed in the previous section. Then the ungodly aspects of the Organizational Culture that match or align with the same pattern of "abandonment" will be presented, ministered to, and replaced with new Godly aspects.

---

[1] Please refer back to 2 Timothy 2:25-26 on page 39.

The ministry process will include the legal process of *confession, forgiveness, breaking agreement, and canceling the effect* of each ungodly Organizational Culture aspect. Then the new Godly belief/attitude will be *presented, declared and legally accepted.* The Organizational Culture will legally change one ungodly item at a time, until all of the items associated with the primary pattern/associated roots are dealt with.

Help each participant by handing out sheets with the primary patterns/themes and the related Organizational Culture items. The employees will be able to take these with them for continued study and prayer. The Leaders will encourage the employees to review often and mediate on one or more of the new beliefs/attitudes throughout the week.

Renewing Our Mind(s)
How can the renewing of the mind be facilitated within the business context? This takes time. First, as mentioned above, each attendee can be given a copy of the new Godly Organizational Culture beliefs/attitudes. Then, the Development Team can devise a "Renewing Our Minds" campaign. The new business culture must be held in front of the people until it is imprinted into their hearts and minds. These truths need to be displayed everywhere so that the company is immersed in a cloud of truth. How can this be done? The best way is to hear God's strategy for introducing and imparting these truths. This will happen through His Word, in personal prayer time, and through the Intercession times. He will insure that His approach is grasped if He is listened to. Your approach will likely be unique for your organization.

However, to help you get started, here are a few ways to help the employees renew their minds.

- Posters with the new Godly beliefs and attitudes could be placed in the work areas.
- Daily or weekly Bible/prayer meetings could be held for the employees (that want to come). During the prayer time, ask the Holy Spirit to work the new Organizational Culture into each one's heart.
- During department meetings the new Organizational Culture can be discussed. The meeting could end with a prayer asking the Holy Spirit to plant the new aspects of the Organizational Culture into each one's heart and bring forth a new harvest.
- Leadership can ask each employee to be sensitive to any ungodly Organizational Culture activity. These can be brought to the Development Team for later use. This will help sensitize everyone to the presence of lies and how they are affecting the business.

Cooperating and working with the Holy Spirit will bring forth many creative ideas to help change the business. The Holy Spirit will also provide grace to each employee to help him decide to make the effort to change. The speed at which the Organizational Culture becomes the "new" Organizational Culture will be a function of the willingness of the people.[1]

8. Planning for Ministry to
Organizational and Individual Hurts/Losses

After ministry for the Sins of the Founding/Resident Fathers and for the new Organizational Culture, it is time to minister to the negative spiritual roots of Organizational Hurts/Losses. The procedure for receiving the Lord's healing was discussed in Part Two on page 93.

---

[1]   The passage in 2 Corinthians 7:1 seems very relevant here. Leaders and Intercessors: pray that everyone decide to "cleanse ourselves from all defilement of flesh and spirit."

There is not any significant planning needed for this ministry beyond the Information Gathering activity. However, we want to select several significant hurts/losses that align with the primary patterns/roots being ministered to. These can be selected from the list on page 285 of hurts and wounds, disappointments and losses.

In the Action Meeting(s), the Leader will select and minister to the negative spiritual roots of one pattern/theme at a time. For example, if the pattern/theme of "abandonment" is being ministered to, then they will want to ask the Lord to bring healing to this area. This will be done by the Leader as he leads the attendees through the ministry process. The attendee's job will be easy; they will just follow the instructions, relax and listen for the voice of the Lord to bring healing of the hurts and restoration of the losses. As the individuals receive healing, the business will be receiving healing as well, plus recovering legal ground.

9. Planning for Ministry to Organizational Oppression/Principalities

The work and plans up to this point have the purpose of removing legal ground from the Group and Territorial Principalities, as well as the demons and strongholds afflicting the individuals within the company. We are now ready to plan for the actual ministry time.

We discussed God's solution for dealing with demons, demonic strongholds, and principalities on page 94. We are going to apply His solution to remove and displace the principalities from the business.

Since there is a strong correlation between the Sins of the Founding Fathers, the Sins of the Resident Fathers, the resulting Curses, and the Group and Territorial Principalities over the business, use the same work sheets of groups and sub-groups of sins/curses we developed earlier (starting on page 137) for renouncing and displacing the principalities. If the Development Team has discovered additional principalities, these will be listed on page 286. Add these names to copies of the primary patterns groups/sub-groups work sheets.

Casting out Demons and Strongholds

During the Action Meeting(s), continue working with the same pattern/theme throughout the ministry time. So, sticking with the "abandonment" example, cast out demons and strongholds of abandonment, rejection, rebellion, and passivity, as well as the individual demons within the groups and sub-groups.

Displacing and Removing Principalities

Once the deliverance ministry is completed, the Leader will lead the attack to displace and remove the principalities over the business, still sticking to the same primary pattern/theme. Following the example, come against the principalities of abandonment, rejection, rebellion, and passivity, along with all the individual "sub-principalities." Command them to "back off," opening up the heaven over the business. Command them to continue further, displacing them beyond the boundaries of the land/structures "possessed" by the company.

10. Planning to Put God in Charge
- Transfer Title of Business to God

An important decision for the Leadership Team is whether to transfer the business to God's ownership or not. We discussed the foundations of this decision on pages 47 and 117. If the decision is to put God in charge, the actual mechanics of how to do this and to what extent needs to be planned depending on how far God wants to take this in the civil and legal areas.

For example, Stanley Tam had legal documents prepared making God the 51% owner of his business, and then later created agreements that put **all** of the company's profits into a foundation committed to evangelism and spreading the Gospel of the Kingdom.

Obviously, if you are functioning as a tithe of the company to begin to bring God's presence and blessing into the business, it is likely that you do not have the legal and spiritual authority to give the business to God. This can come later as His atmosphere permeates every part of the company and the Leadership changes.

11. Planning for First Meeting: "Preparation Meeting"

This meeting should be upbeat, faith-filled, positive, and expectant, with excitement in our hearts at the prospect of new-found freedom and prosperity. It should be easy to have this attitude, since what could be better than cooperating with God to accomplish our purpose and destiny?

Know that rumors and miscommunications will be circulating throughout the businesses ever since the Leaders committed to move ahead with the Action Plan. Or more accurately, the rumors and miscommunications will circulate to harm if the Intercessors are not active to bind the principalities and prevent their interference.

What Leaders should be publicly Involved?

This is the first public meeting for the Implementation Team. The business Leader member of the team will lead the meeting. The Development Team will decide which Leaders, if any, of the business should be "public" and present with the Leader of the meeting. If appropriate, this would demonstrate agreement and unity to the rest of the company.

What should be done publicly?

The Development Team will plan what to include and what not include in the public Preparation and Action Meetings. Depending on who is invited, and when and where the meetings are held, *there may be some parts of the spiritual warfare that should not be done publicly.* On the one hand, the more of the company involved with the warfare, the better the results and benefit to everyone. On the other hand, if having certain people present will hinder or disrupt the agreement and faith levels, perhaps it will be better for certain portions of the Action Plan to be done by a smaller group of Leaders and Intercessors. Each Development Team will have to determine what is best for their particular situation and plan accordingly.

Who should Attend?
A major decision for the Development Team is who to include for the two meetings. Should just the Leaders meet, should some or all of the employees who are Christians also be invited, or should every person in the company come?

If those wanting to cleanse the business are just a "tithe" of the Leadership and some of the employees, then the decision is easy. These are the ones to meet and conduct the Preparation and Action Meetings. However, if all of the Leaders are involved and committed, then it is feasible to also include some or all of the Christian employees. Whether the rest of the company is also invited will depend on the overall company culture and the leading of the Holy Spirit. If you are using a Transforming Your Business consultant and/or outside Intercessor it would be appropriate for them to also be present.

No one should feel forced to attend these meetings. There is not reason to put at risk the employees, and their families, who are not Christians. In fact, the Leadership and Intercessors should insure that they are protected and shielded from the increased spiritual warfare.

Do not put the Leaders (current and previous) at risk as they confess and forgive others of their sins, and as they ask forgiveness for their own sins. Possible hazards include misunderstanding of the spiritual significance of what is happening by the employees, particularly the ones not yet born again. There could also be rumors and gossip, perhaps even attempted blackmail. Clearly Holy Spirit wisdom is needed in selecting who should be present.

Depending on the size of the business, either written or verbal invitations can be extended to those selected to attend. It is important to maintain a list of those invited so that attendance can be noted at the meetings.

Where and When to Meet?

If just the Leaders are meeting, one of the private meeting rooms should suffice. As more people are involved, obviously larger rooms are needed. The issue is really one of public versus private meetings. Again, if there are employees that would be put at risk by their knowing about the meetings, then perhaps an evening meeting would be better since this would be "after hours" and only those attending the meeting would be present in the business facilities.

Handouts and Overheads

HO

OH

It will be helpful to have handouts with the agenda for the Preparation Meeting and the location, date and time of the Action Meeting. Also, to facilitate everyone being able to pray in unity and agreement, and to do the ministry steps together, we suggest using a computer and projector to display the text on an overhead screen. Please "copy and paste" the prayers and significant information, such as the vision statement, into a power point type presentation.[1]

Agenda for the Preparation Meeting

The agenda for the Preparation Meeting is fairly standard regardless of the decisions made about "what, who, where, and when." We have put the agenda and its contents in the Implementation section, starting on page 159. The Development Team will plan the details the agenda.

12. Planning for Second Meeting: the "Action Meeting"

With the Preparation Meeting accomplished, probably **ALL** of the employees of the company now know that something is going on, even if they were not invited. So schedule the Action Meeting as soon as possible after the Preparation Meeting.

---

[1] To help you recognize when we are talking about "Hand-Outs" or "OverHeads," we will place a "side note" with either the letters "HO" or "OH" in the margin.

The campaign to remove negative patterns/theme and their spiritual roots from the business is now ready for the official launch. Plan it well and execute it superbly. Keep in mind that it will probably take several Action Meetings to actually remove the 3-6 primary negative patterns and their spiritual roots from the business.

Which Format to Use?

There is a fundamental decision to be made about the plan for the Action Meeting(s). You will want to decide whether to conduct the ministry to the business one primary pattern/theme at a time or to apply God's solutions one at a time to all of the important primary patterns/themes. All things being equal, we suggest the "one primary pattern at a time" approach, the one we have been using in our example of "abandonment" throughout Part Three. Obviously you will need to decide based on your particular situation.

One Pattern/Theme Approach: "Ministry Target"
This approach organizes the ministry by the "primary pattern/theme." The plan is to take one primary pattern/theme and completely remove it and everything associated with it before moving on to the next primary pattern/theme (most likely at another Action Meeting). That is, first apply God's Solution to the Sins of the Founding and Resident Fathers with resultant Curses. Then minister to the Organizational Culture items associated with the same pattern/theme. Next pray for Gods healing of the hurts and losses associated with the same pattern/theme. Lastly, cast out the demons and demonic strongholds, then push back and displace the principalities associated with the same pattern/theme. Thus all five of God's Solutions to the five negative spiritual roots creating/underlying the one primary negative pattern/theme have been applied.

Since the Development Team will have found and organized the ministry for a number of negative patterns/themes, a "shorthand" way is needed to refer to the particularly pattern/theme selected for attacked during one of the Action Meetings. We have chosen the phrase "Ministry Target" for this purpose.

Let's use "Ministry Target."

The entire first Action Meeting will likely be taken to completely minister to one primary pattern/theme (especially being the first time this is done). Additional meetings can be scheduled with the plan to minister to one or two primary patterns/themes each meeting, until all of the 3-6 original primary negative patterns/themes are removed from the business.

Thorough Approach

This approach organizes the ministry according to the five negative spiritual roots. That is, God's solution for each type of negative spiritual root is applied to all of the 3-6 negative primary patterns/themes before moving on to the next type of negative spiritual root. For example, the first area of ministry would be to apply God's Solution to all of the Sins of the Founding/Resident Fathers and resulting Curses primary patterns/themes. After completing this, apply God's Solution to all of the Ungodly Beliefs and Organizational Culture items. Then the Lord's healing for all of the Organizational Hurts/Losses would be received. Finally, cast out the demons and demonic strongholds, and displace and remove all of the Organizational Oppression/Principalities.

Expect to need several Action Meetings to apply the Thorough Approach to the business. It will likely take the entire first Action Meeting to get started and maybe complete the Sins of the Founding/Resident Fathers and resulting Curses roots. Therefore, successive Action Meetings are needed to apply God's Solution to the other spiritual negative roots.

While this approach will work, it seems cumbersome compared to working with one Ministry Target at a time. We will not discuss it further in this book.

Planning the Meeting

With the format decided, the following needs to be planned.

Who, Where, and When?
Generally speaking we will want the same people to attend this meeting as the Preparation Meeting. If the time and location "worked" for the Preparation Meeting, it would be easy to use the same location and time of day.

Handouts and Overheads
HO

OH

You can help the employees invited to the Action Meeting make the transition from the current to the new Organizational Culture by giving them a handout listing the new beliefs/attitudes. Likewise, as you did for the Preparation Meeting, you can "copy and paste" the prayers, significant information, ministry steps, primary patterns/themes groups, and new Organizational Culture statements into a power point type presentation.[1]

Ministry Helpers
Depending on the number of people attending the meeting, it may be appropriate (and wise) to have some Ministry Helpers available. These people should be trained and able to minister to any individuals asking for or needing special assistance during the group ministry times. This could occur during the praying for healing of Organizational Hurts/Loses and during the deliverance/freedom ministry. The Leaders and Intercessors of the company are the most appropriate ones to bring this ministry to the attendees, if they are willing to be trained in basic Restoring the Foundations ministry.[2] Also, church teams and/or Healing

---

[1]   Trained TYB/HHN consultants have these power point presentations as part of their "equipping."

[2]   If the topics and approaches for healing of inner hurts, hurts from losses, and deliverance are new to the Leaders and Intercessors, it may be beneficial for the business to host at least the first and perhaps even the second Restoring the Foundations seminars to train the Leaders and Intercessors in the basics. Please refer back to page 118.

House Network teams trained in Restoring the Foundation ministry could be invited to attend the Action Meeting(s) to assist. Of course, if a TYB/HHN consultant is involved, he can assist as well.

Agenda for the Action Meeting(s)

The agenda for the Action Meeting, like the Preparation Meeting, is also fairly standard. The same type of ministry will be done for each meeting, and for every business. Only the details will be different based on the 3-6 primary negative patterns/themes active in each business. The agenda and its contents are in the Implementation section, starting on page 164. The Development Team will plan the details of the agenda for each Action Meeting.

13. Planning for Ongoing Transformation

After the first Action Meeting, the Leadership and Intercessors involved in the ongoing transformation of the business will begin to function.

Filling the Intercessor Positions

The task of finding, training, and releasing the Intercessors into the business may be easy or difficult, depending on the current spiritual maturity of the company and the Christians already present. Part Five discusses these topics (starting on page 238). The Development Team can plan how to transition the business from where it is to having a suitable staff of Intercessors. It can determine which positions within the company are to be staffed with Intercessors, perhaps those with Watchmen or Gate-Keeper callings.

Ongoing Vigilance

The Intercessor meetings discussed in Part Five (page 244) will be a normal part of implementing the Action Plan. These meetings should continue as the company transitions into the Ongoing Transformation phase.

Ongoing Celebration

Planning from the beginning just how the business and employees will honor and glorify the Lord is relevant. If the company is already doing this, then it is a matter of building on this. It is very important to begin implementing times of thanksgiving, worship, prayer, etc. A position of "Celebration Oversight" could be created for ongoing planning and coordination so such events. Other possibilities are to have a chaplain available for the employees, private chapel space, even a ministry department, etc. We know of one business, Maximum Significance International, supplying these services, as well as Intercessors, to businesses.[1]

14. Final Comments and Summary

You can include here any other facts, history, insights, prophetic words, etc., that have not been noted elsewhere that may be relevant as the Development Team prepares to implement the Action Plan.

---

[1] Maximum Significance, Inc. is listed on the Ministry Resources page in the back of this book.

III. Implementing the Action Plan

When the Development Team has finished their work and the Action Plan is completed, the Leaders of the Implementation Team swing into action. Besides the "startup" activities, their first main task will be to lead the Preparation Meeting. They will share with the employees the decision to bring change to the business, to align with the principles of God's Word as discussed in *Transforming Your Business*, and that this will be accomplished through an Action Plan that provides a step by step transition.

A. Select and Release Development Team

The Development Team will be selected and immediately released by the Leadership Team once the decision has been made to proceed with the Transforming Your Business process. Please refer back to page 119 for the discussion of their selection.

B. Select and Release Intercessors

The next step is to mobilize the company Intercessors. This is an important part of starting the Transforming Your Business process. This will be the first priority of the Development Team as they begin to meet. They can use the questions listed in the Planning section (page 133) and incorporate the information in Part Five (page 219) as they plan.

We would like the business to immediately begin to benefit from the Intercession of the Intercessors. However, they should not be released before they are ready. As in our teenage years, there may be an "awkward" time between identifying and beginning to train the Intercessors and their reaching sufficient maturity. Acquiring temporary outside help, or hiring employees that are already experienced Intercessors, may be appropriate.

The enemy's plans need to be exposed. The enemy's attacks need to be defused. Both the Leaders and Intercessors should be involved in this. This requires God's revelations to guide and direct as the Action Plan is put together. The bottom line is that the Leaders will want to hear from the Lord as to how to solve the immediate need for Intercessors. He will provide the best solution for you. He will insure that you have what you need as you need it.

C. Select and Release Implementation Team

The Development Team will specify the skill sets/giftings of the Implementation Team incorporating the suggestions starting on page 134. This team will "wait in the wings," staying informed of the developing plan, until it is time for them to lead the business through the transition. Their first "public" appearance will be as they lead the Preparation Meeting. If the most responsible Leader of the business (i.e., Owner, President, CEO, Chairman of the Board, etc.) is not the Leader of the Implementation Team, it would be good for this person to delegate authority and responsibility to the Implementation Team by the "laying on hands"[1] and praying for the team.

D. Provide Healing Ministry for Appropriate Leadership and Intercessor Families

Begin to schedule Leaders and Intercessors for personal Restoring the Foundations ministry with Healing House Network teams, as planned on page 135.

---

[1] We are following the principle expressed in Hebrews 6:2.

E. First Meeting: Preparation Meeting

Prepare Employees for the Transforming Your Business Process

It is time to have a meeting of everyone involved in the Transforming Your Business healing and freedom process. The necessary decisions will have been made and everything is ready to go.

1. Pre-Meeting Work

HO

OH

The Implementation Team has been working behind the scenes preparing the implementation of the Action Plan. They have been building on the work of the Development Team. They have copies of handouts with the agenda for the Preparation Meeting and the location, date, and time information about the Action Meeting. The "power point" presentation is ready. All those selected to attend the meeting will have been invited and a list of those expected to attend is ready to verify that only invited people are present. (Planning is on pages 149 and 297 with Implementation on page 305.)

The Intercessors have also been praying, binding, and loosing. They have been guided by the Holy Spirit as He has been showing them what to do.

2. Lead Preparation Meeting

Attendance and Handouts

HO

It would be good to use an attendance roster so that you can verify who attends the Action Meeting. It is important to have the right people present and equally important that no one be there who doesn't want to be or who would be put at risk by attending. As the people arrive and "sign in," you can also give them the handout.

Welcome and Introductions
The Leader of the Implementation Team introduces himself and states that he is presiding over the meeting. He welcomes everyone and expresses the truth that this meeting is the start of a historic transition in the life of the business. (This might also be a good time to introduce the other members of the team, the ones that will be "public.")

Opening Prayer
It is important to place the meeting under the covering of the Holy Spirit and His control as soon as practical. The Leader can do this by inviting everyone to join him in an Opening Prayer. We suggest using the following sample prayer, or use one created by the Development Team. It can be projected for everyone to read and pray together.

OH

Dear Lord. We come before you both individually and as a group of people engaged in a common purpose, the operation of (business name) to glorify You and to accomplish Your purposes.

We ask You to forgive us for our failings and disobedience. We are ready to hear Your voice and move forward in step with You. Thank You for forgiving us according to Your Word.

We choose to submit to You, Lord. Have Your way in the life of the business and in each one of our lives.

We apply the Blood of Jesus Christ to everyone here and also those not here; we apply the Blood to their homes and families, and all that concerns them. We apply the Blood to every aspect of the business and all that it is involved in.

We resist the enemy, and command him to flee. We bind all evil spirits arrayed against us, including all principalities and powers and wickedness in high places. We forbid you to have any influence in this meeting, any influence with the people associated with this business, or any influence in the days to come.

160

Come, Holy Spirit. Be in charge of this business and this meeting. We turn the meeting over to You and thank You for guiding every part of it.

In the name of Jesus Christ we pray, Amen.

Discuss the Purpose of the Meeting (and Ongoing Warfare)
While it is likely that everyone present already knows the purpose of the meeting, it is a good idea for the Leader to state it clearly and succinctly. He might say something like this.

We have come together to prepare for a very significant event in the life of our business. We expect this event to be a major milestone for us and that it will result in significant changes in how we do business.

We have been learning about the sources of problems within our company; how they are caused by negative spiritual forces. These are forces that we have brought into the company ourselves as well as ones that have been a part of the land and structures that we occupy. We will refer to these forces as "roots," since they are the basis, the cause, of many if not all of the problems we have been facing.

The purpose of this meeting is to prepare us to proceed with the removal of these negative spiritual roots from our company.

You have been asked to be a part of this event because you are a believer in the Lord Jesus Christ. Your participation will make this transition easier and quicker. As we join together in agreement, exercise our combined authority that has been delegated to us by the Lord Jesus Christ, and apply the solution of the Cross to these negative spiritual roots, we can all move forward individually and corporately into our Destiny.

Discuss and Impart Leaders' Vision and Heart

OH

The Leader then begins to discuss and impart the vision/destiny that the Lord has laid before the company.[1] He can express his heart to see the business succeed in fulfilling the vision and accomplishing all that God has put before them.

The Leader shares how putting into practice the Action Plan as presented in *Transforming Your Business* can accelerate and increase the fulfillment of the call. He states that the Action Plan lays out a path to transition the business from where it is now to where God wants it to be.

Explain TYB Principles and Action Plan

OH

It is time to explain the basic principles of *Transforming Your Business*. The Leader can present appropriate topics from Parts One and Two, as planned by the Development Team. The right topics can be chosen based on the general level of understanding of spiritual warfare and organizational dynamics. This choosing requires a careful balancing "act" between complexity and available time. Again, we must be guided by the Holy Spirit.

OH

The Leader discusses the elements of the Action Plan. He lets the people know that he will be leading the group through these elements during the Action Meeting. Projecting the elements of the Action Plan will help everyone see the big picture.

Provide a Time for Questions and Answers

As the Leader prepares to conclude the meeting, he provides a time for those present to ask questions and clear up any confusions or misunderstandings.

---

[1] The Development Team will have included an updated statement of the vision on page 1 of the Action Plan.

3. Bring the Meeting to a Close

The Leader insures that everyone knows the date, time, and location of the first Action Meeting.

Express Caution

If the business has employees that have not been selected to attend the Preparation and Action Meetings, the Leader lets those present know why they were selected to be a part of the ministry to the business. He asks them to not talk about the meetings or the purposes of the meetings to others. He explains it is not an issue of elitism or wanting to create suspicion but it is an issue of protection: protection of the company and protection of all the employees. He can ask the attendees to help by not providing any opportunity for the enemy to bring problems into the company that would divert energy and time from the main purpose of the Transforming Your Business process.

Closing Prayer

The Leader prays a suitable Closing Prayer to end the meeting. He can use the following sample prayer as he leads the group.

OH

Dear Father, we are so appreciative that You extended salvation to us and brought us into a position of Sonship with You. You have and are healing us, equipping us, and enabling us to partner with You.

We thank You for your hedge of protection about each one here, their families, and their place of belonging. We also ask You to place a hedge of protection around all the employees of our business, as well as the business itself. We receive your hedge of fire round about us, just as you put it about Jerusalem.

Lord, we look forward to the Action Meeting where we can begin to cooperate with You to remove all of the Baggage that has held us back. We are ready to accelerate and move forward in You.

In the Name of Jesus we pray. Amen.

It is time to dismiss the people and breathe a "thank you" prayer to the Father for bringing the business this far and launching the Transforming Your Business ministry.

F. Second Meeting: Action Meeting(s)

Apply God's Solution to Free the Business/Organization

Generally speaking, businesses do not know they are at war with negative spiritual forces. Thus they don't fight in this realm. Likely it has been a one-sided war up to this point, with the business on the losing side. They don't understand the spiritual roots of problems and thus they can't address these issues.

This is about the change for your company. The time has come for your business to engage the war and to begin to win. It is time to have a legal and formal Action Meeting to begin the process of freedom and healing. It is time to officially confess, do Identification Repentance, install a new Organizational Culture, seek God's healing of hurts and losses, and re- move/displace principalities. It is time to remove the spiritual roots of problems from your affairs.

1. Pre-Meeting Work

By this time, the Action Plan will be completed. The 3-6 most important primary negative patterns/themes and their roots will have been discovered, analyzed, and prepared for ministry. The planning for the Action Meeting(s) will be completed, as dis- cussed on pages 151 and 299, with the implementation informa- tion on page 306.

The Preparation Meeting has been held and all the selected peo- ple are primed and ready to participate in the Action Meeting. The Intercessors have also been praying: binding, loosening, seeking God's wisdom.

OH The Implementation Team is ready to go with the selected pri- mary negative pattern/theme, i.e., the Ministry Target (see page 152) for this particular Action Meeting. They have the prayers and the lists of sins and curses, Ungodly Beliefs/Organizational Culture, Organizational Hurts and losses, and principalities at hand and on "power point."

HO
Handouts have been prepared that have the Action Meeting's Ministry Target on it as well as the related ungodly aspects of the Organizational Culture (lie/truth pairs) listed. The Leader is ready to explain each ministry area and to lead the attendees through the ministry steps.

Any planned training or preparation of the Leaders and Intercessors to be helpers during the healing of inner wounds and during the deliverance/freedom ministry will have been completed. TYB/HHN consultants will be on hand to assist if desired.

2. Start Action Meeting

Attendance and Handouts

HO
We would suggest the use of an attendance roster so that you can verify who attends the Action Meeting. It is important to have the right people present and equally important that no one be there who doesn't want to be or who would be put at risk by attending. As the people arrive and "sign in," you can also give them the handout.

Welcome and Introductions
As in the Preparation Meeting, the Leader of the Implementation Team welcomes the attendees and introduces those that will be "public" during the ministry time. He welcomes them to the continuation of the historic transition of the business into a fuller dimension of God's purpose and destiny.

Opening Prayer
The purpose of the Opening Prayer is to not only set the spiritual context of the meeting and turn control over to the Holy Spirit, but to also begin the ministry at a general level. Thus this prayer is more lengthy and detailed than usual. Just as for the Prepara-

OH
tion Meeting, we suggest the words of the prayer be projected onto a screen so the Leader can lead everyone as they pray in agreement.

Here is a sample prayer that can be used or the Development Team can customize it for your business.

Father God, Lord Jesus, and Holy Spirit.

We come before You today as Your children. We come individually and corporately. We come seeking Your help and guidance as we and our business go through this ministry process. We ask You to release fresh faith and expectation. We know that You are a good God, desiring the best for Your children. We thank you for loving and accepting us just as we are, yet loving us too much to let us stay as we are.

Lord, help us take responsibility for our sins and short-comings, both individually and corporately. Open our eyes to every way we have been blind to our transgressions and the transgressions of those who have gone before us.

We now confess our sins before You. We confess the sins of our ancestors. We confess the sins of the former Leaders. We confess the sins of those living on the land before us. We choose not to hold any of these people accountable for the effects of their sins on our lives. We release all these ancestors: our biological ancestors, our Leaders as our spiritual ancestors, and the former inhabitants of the land as our resident ancestors. We release them from each and every way we have blamed them for our problems. And now, based on the finished work of Christ on the Cross, we renounce these ancestors' sins and release ourselves from their effects.

On the same basis we break the power of every curse coming against us or our descendants because of the sins of these ancestors. We cancel all legal rights of demons to oppress us, our descendants, and our business because of these ancestors' sins and curses. We cancel all dedications made by these ancestors of their descendants and those coming after them on the land. We are not "owned" by any demons, demonic strongholds, or principalities. We declare ourselves to be completely and eternally given to and owned by the Lord Jesus Christ.

Lord, we thank You for helping us recognize the lies that we have believed. We are ready to have our minds renewed. We are ready to identify and remove every ungodly aspect of our Organizational Culture. Father God, we want to think like You think; we want to do business according to Your nature, Your Character, and Your principles. We want to represent the Kingdom of God according to Your will. Thank You for Your enabling Grace to help us identify every ungodly aspect of our Organizational Culture. Thank You for carrying us through the process of changing these ungodly aspects into a Godly Organizational Culture.

Lord, we need You to help us discover our personal hurts and losses, as well as the Organizational Hurts and losses. Help us identify with the Organizational Hurts and losses and realize that they are also our own hurts and losses. We trust You to expose the lies helping to hold these hurts and losses in place. We ask You to clarify our perceptions that we may see these hurts and losses in the light of Your truth. We ask you to bring Your healing to all pain, hurts, and losses held by us individually and corporately.

Lord, if we have been upset, disappointed, or separated from You in any way; if we have blamed You for any of these problems, please help us see where the blame should be placed, whether on ourselves or on Satan. We want to clear out all hindrances in our relationship with You. We ask You to forgive us. We receive Your forgiveness.

Lord, You are our Deliverer. We ask You to set us free from every demon that has influenced or tormented us. Set us free from every demonic stronghold. Set us free from all influences of principalities affecting us and our business. We choose to use the authority You have given us over all the power of the enemy. We choose to no longer cooperate with the enemy but to cast out, remove and displace him. We choose to be totally set free and to continue to walk in that freedom.

Holy Spirit, thank You for revealing the truth we need to know and bringing healing and deliverance to every negative spiritual root. In the Precious Name of Jesus Christ we pray, Amen!

Purpose of Meeting (and Ongoing Warfare)

The purpose of the Action Meeting should be well known and understood by now. After all, the business has been working toward this moment for some time. However, people and memories are sometimes not perfect so stating the purpose of the meeting one more time will help everyone be "on the same page." So after the Opening Prayer, it would be good to again state the purpose. Here is a possible expression of the purpose that you may use.

At the Preparation Meeting we discussed and laid out a course of action to transform our business. The purpose of this meeting is to actually commence the application of the Action Plan to remove negative patterns/themes from our company by extracting the significant negative spiritual roots behind these patterns and themes.

We have been working toward this event for some time, so it is with high expectations that we begin this process. We expect that all of us, all of our lives, and all of the aspects of our business to be quite different once we complete the implementation phase of this process. We expect no less than radical transformation of our business, no less than radical fulfillment of the call of God on our lives and this business.

Primary Pattern/Theme: Ministry Target

The Leader transitions the meeting and prepares the attendees for ministry to the Ministry Target (primary negative pattern/theme) that will be addressed in this Action Meeting. We recommend that you projected the words describing the target onto a screen. The Leader might say:

OH

*One of the primary negative patterns/themes we see op-
erating in our business is _____. In this
meeting we are going to focus on the negative spiritual
roots of this pattern, the ones holding it in place and
empowering it. We are going to remove these roots
and their influence. This is our **Ministry Target** for this
meeting. So let's join together and unity in agreement
as we go for more freedom. As Paul wrote: "It is for
freedom that Christ has set us free."[1]*

The Leader can now prepare and lead the attendees through the
ministry steps to remove the influence of the chosen Ministry
Target. He will lead them through the ministry steps for each of
the five negative spiritual roots related to the Ministry Target
(assuming the Issue-Focused Format is being used).

3. Leader Leads in Sins of the
Founding and Resident Fathers
Confession and Repentance
(Identification Repentance)

For the current Ministry Target, the Development Team has the
patterns, groupings, and sub-groupings ready for ministry to
Sins of the Founding Fathers and the Sins of the Resident Fathers, and resulting Curses. They are diagramed and listed in
the Action Plan on page 292.

The Leader will lead the people through the ministry steps for
each group or sub-group. In other words, referring back to the
primary pattern of "abandonment" example on page 137, there
are four groups/sub-groups, 1A through 1D. So the ministry
steps would be repeated four times. The "control" example
would require five times through the ministry steps, for
groups/sub-groups 2A through 2E.

As the Leader is going through the ministry steps, he will come
to the "blank" lines in step 1 and step 5. The first time, he will
name the Ministry Target (i.e., "abandonment"), and then the

---

[1]   This truth is in Galatians 5:1.

associated sins of "denial," "enabling," and "manipulation." After completing all six steps for the "abandonment" pattern/group, the Leader will lead the people through all six steps again, this time for the "rejection" sub-group including its associated sins of "expected rejection," fear of rejection," and "perceived rejection." "Rebellion" would be the subject for the third time through the ministry steps, and "passivity" would complete the fourth time through the process.

Of course, for your Ministry Target, you will have your own set of group and sub-groups customized for your company. At this Action Meeting, you will be bringing their operation to a halt!

Ministry Steps for SOFFCs and SORFCs

OH

The following ministry steps are based on the discussion of God's Solution as discussed in Part Two (page 77). These steps can be projected so that all the attendees can repeat the words along with the Leader as he leads them.

> *(Leader states the name of the Ministry Target, i.e., "abandonment," then leads ...)*

1. *We confess the sins of our biological ancestors, the sins of our current and previous spiritual leaders, the sins of the previous inhabitants of the land and structures, and our own sins of _____, including the associated sins of _____, _____, _____, ...*

2. *We choose to forgive and release all of these people. We release them from every way their sins and the resulting curses have impacted our individual lives, our family lives, and our corporate life.*

3. *We ask You to forgive us, Lord, for each and every way we and our families have entered into these same sins and allowed them and the curses to influence us. We receive Your forgiveness.*

> *(Leader pauses to allow everyone to "receive" forgiveness from the Lord.)*

4. *Lord, on the basis of Your forgiveness, we choose to forgive ourselves for giving place to these sins and the consequences in our lives.*

5. *We now renounce all the sins and curses of _____, including the associated sins and curses of ____, _____, ___, ... We break the power of these sins and curses from our individual lives, from our family lives, and from our corporate life. We do all of this based on the redemptive work of Christ on the Cross.*

6. *We receive God's freedom from these sins and curses. We receive good gifts from the Father of Light. Thank You Lord for showing us a picture of Your good gifts.*

   (Leader waits while each person listens/watches for the Holy Spirit to bring revelation from the Father into their awareness. Leader suggests that each one records what he hears/sees.)

When you finish the steps for one group/sub-group, cycle back to step 1 for the next sub-group until the entire set of group/sub-groups is completed, i.e., until you have completed the ministry to Sins of the Founding/Resident Fathers and resulting Curses for the Ministry Target.

Be alert to the attendee's desire to express their joy and excitement about their new freedom. The Leader can give permission to "let it out" either at the end of each cycle through the ministry steps or at the conclusion of this part.

4. Leadership Commits to take (OPTIONAL STEP)
   Responsibility for the Land
   to Care for the Land and Bless It

(**PLEASE NOTE:** If at all possible, it is important to do this ceremony. However, it only needs to be done one time. Normally it will be done as part of the first Action Meeting; however, it may be done anytime thereafter, even during the very last Action Meeting. So skip over this section once it has been done.)

OH

We have discussed the importance of "possessing" and Marrying the Land on pages 44 and 82. The planning step is discussed on page 140. This point in the ministry is a good place to accomplish this, right after ministering to the SOFFCs and SORFCs. The following declaration/commitment is suggested. Project the words so everyone can repeat them and make a commitment to the land.

1. *Father God, we thank You that you are the maker of heaven and earth. We thank You that You have given us responsibility for a portion of Your earth.*

2. *We ask You to forgive us for every way we have not been a husband to the land; for everyway we have ignored, neglected, used, or abused the land and structures. We are sorry. We will no longer use or abuse the land and buildings. We receive Your forgiveness.*

3. *We affirm Isaiah 62 verses four and five regarding our land and structures.*

   "No longer will they call you Deserted, or name your land Desolate. But you will be called Hephzibah, and your land Beulah; for the LORD will take delight in you, and your land will be married. As a young man marries a maiden, so will your sons marry you; as a bridegroom rejoices over his bride, so will your God rejoice over you."

3. *We receive Your assignment to us of this land. We choose to be good stewards of the land and buildings. We each one choose to covenant with the land, as if in marriage, for as long as the Lord directs. We will do our part to redeem the land from all sins, curses, and principalities. We will protect and care for it so that it is blessed and fruitful. We bless the land in the Name of Jesus Christ.*

You might consider having a celebration at the end of the meeting to commemorate this "marriage ceremony." It could be very meaningful!

5. Leader Leads for Ungodly Organizational Culture

HO

Next is to legally cancel all agreements with the lies of the enemy that are related to the current Ministry Target (primary pattern/theme). The Development Team will have provided a list of 5-10 ungodly aspects of the Organizational Culture beliefs/attitudes that are a part of the Ministry Target. The attendees will receive a printed handout of these 5-10 for their ongoing prayer and meditation. As the Leader discusses and deals with each lie/truth pair, we suggest that they be projected.

OH

OH

As the Leader starts leading the people through the following ministry steps, they can be projected on the screen. When the people come to the "blanks," the Leader will have them read. First the ungodly statement from their handout will be read, and then later the Godly replacement truth.

Ministry Steps for Organizational Culture

These steps are based on the discussion of God's Solution in Part Two (page 83). The Development Team will have prepared 5-10 Ungodly and Godly Belief pairs for the Leader to use based on the Ministry Target.

(Leader reads the next lie from the handout, then leads the group as they say together ...)

1. *We confess the sins of our biological ancestors, the sins of our previous and current spiritual leaders, the sins of the previous inhabitants of the land and structures, and our own sins of believing this lie and allowing it to be a part of our Organizational Culture. The lie is:*

   _____.

2. *We forgive all those who have brought this lie into our Organizational Culture. We forgive them for setting us up to accept this lie such that we have lived our lives and conducted our business based on it.*

   (If there are any specific individuals or organizations that have had major influence in the organization receiving this lie, Leader leads the group in forgiving the individuals or organizations.)

173

3. *We ask You, Lord, to forgive us for receiving this lie, for incorporating it into our lives, and for doing business based on it. We receive Your forgiveness.*

   (Leader pauses to allow everyone to "receive" forgiveness from the Lord.)

4. *Lord, on the basis of Your forgiveness, we choose to forgive ourselves for giving place to this lie and allowing it to influence and control our lives and our business.*

5. *We renounce and break our agreement with this lie. We refuse to give it place any longer in our personal lives and in our corporate life.*

   - We cancel all of our agreements that this lie has provided for the kingdom of darkness.

   - We cancel these agreements with demons, strongholds, and principalities afflicting us.

   - We cancel these agreements locally, with us and with the land.

   - We cancel these agreements remotely wherever in the world they have given place to the kingdom of darkness.

6. *(Leader reads the truth to replace the lie from the handout, then leads the group as they say together ...)*

   Lord, we thank You that You are a standard of truth and righteousness that provides us a path to follow. We commit to follow your path of righteousness in our personal lives and as a business. We choose to accept, believe, and receive Your truth that: _____
   _____.

7. *Lord, I ask You to show me how to walk out/manifest this truth in my life, so that I contribute my part to our increasingly Godly Organizational Culture.*

The Leader will lead the group through the above steps one time for each ungodly/Godly pair of statements of the Organizational Culture. So this will be done 5-10 times.

If the attendees want to clap, cheer, shout, dance, or express their joy about their new freedom, by all means let them celebrate.

6. Leader Prays for
Organizational and Individuals Hurts/Losses

Some significant freedom will have been achieved from the above ministry to the Ministry Target. The level of influence and oppression over the individuals and the business will have been decreased. This will allow the Holy Spirit greater entry to bring healing of the Organizational Hurts and Losses.

Standby Help
Even though the main focus is on healing the business, praying for healing in a group setting will likely result in the Holy Spirit also touching some or maybe all of the attendees regarding their personal hurts. Sometimes significant hurts and losses will be triggered. As discussed in the Planning section, it is prudent to have the Leaders and Intercessors trained to help any individuals desiring or needing help during this part of the ministry. If a TYB/HHN consultant or Intercessor is also present, they can be available if a more severe situation occurs. If desired, Restoring the Foundations church teams could also be used.

Preparation of the Attendees
It is likely that many of the attendees will have never experienced God's healing of their wounds "on the inside." They have not known He wants to, or if they did know, they did not know how to receive healing from the Lord. Depending on the spiritual maturity of the people, the Leader may want to present some key scriptures on the overhead as part of transitioning into this portion of the Action Meeting. The goal is to stir faith in the attendees so that they will open their hearts to receive healing of their inner hurts from the Lord.

OH

175

Ministry

OH

With the list of hurts associated with the Ministry Target in hand, the Leader is ready to lead the people through the following ministry steps. As usual, it would be good to project first the list, then the ministry steps.

Ministry Steps for Organizational Hurts and Losses

OH

On page 93 we shared a procedure for receiving healing of our inner wounds from the Lord, including the wounds from hurts and losses of the organization. Here are the ministry steps for this approach. As usual, the Leader can prepare the people and then, with the steps on the overhead, lead them through the process one time for each hurt

(Leader shares the hurt or loss that is next on the list for God's healing, then lead with ...)

1. *We confess the sins of our biological ancestors, the sins of our previous and current spiritual leaders, the sins of the previous inhabitants of the land and structures, and our own sins that have been a part of this hurt/loss to our business and to ourselves. The hurt/loss is:*

   _____.

2. *We forgive all those who have brought this hurt/loss to our business and to ourselves. We forgive them for their sins again us and our business.*

   (If there are any specific individuals or organizations that have had major influence in the organization receiving this hurt/loss, Leader leads the group in forgiving the individuals or organizations.)

3. *We ask You, Lord, to forgive us for our sinful responses coming out of this hurt/loss, for burying our hurt (or loss) and not bringing it to you, and for letting it influence how we do our jobs and conduct our business. We receive Your forgiveness.*

   (Leader pauses to allow everyone to "receive" forgiveness from the Lord.)

4. *Lord, on the basis of Your forgiveness, we choose to forgive ourselves for carrying this hurt/loss and allowing it to influence and control our lives and our business.*

5. *Lord, we choose individually to share our wounded feelings with You. We want to share with You the pain, hurt, disappointments, loss, abandonment, etc., that we have carried. We give You all of these feelings. You did not design us to carry negative emotions. I gladly give all my negative feelings to You now.*

   (Leader says, "Go ahead and gather up all of your hurt and pain, whether disappointment, anger, bitterness, trauma, etc., to the Lord now." He pauses and allows time for the individuals to do this.)

6. *Lord, come now and heal our hurts/losses. We give You permission to go deep into our hearts. Come into my heart. I ask you to remove all of the affects of the wounding. I wait on You now to come and heal me.*

   (The Leader can be quiet for a minute or two to give each person time to interact with the Holy Spirit. When the Leader senses the go-ahead from the Holy Spirit, he can continue with the next step.)

7. *Lord, now we ask You to heal our business from all affects of this hurt/loss. Heal us collectively as well as individually.*

   (Again the Leader should be quiet for a minute while everyone listens for the Lord's healing.)

8. *Thank You Lord for healing me and for healing our business of this hurt/loss. We receive Your healing and we commit to walk in it.*

The Leader will repeat the above steps for each of the hurts and/or losses on the list for the Ministry Target. Once he comes to the end of the list, it is time to move on to the next and last area of spiritual roots.

If the Leader senses that a change of pace is needed, he can ask for one or two testimonies of what was experienced. It is always good to hear what the Lord has done in someone's life.

7. Leader Leads in Removing
Organizational Oppression/Principalities

It is time to war against the fifth and last spiritual root, the Organizational Oppression/Principalities. The Ministry Target provides the focus on which demons, strongholds, and principalities to deal with. The recovery of legal ground has been completed, so it is just a matter of a "mop-up" operation at this point.

The war will be waged using God's Solution as discussed in Part Two starting on page 94. We encourage you to re-read that section if it has been a while since you last read it. It will encourage you and build your faith as you get ready to engage the powers of darkness.

Standby Help
Again, it would be wise to have some people experienced in deliverance available in case any of the attendees need help. The trained Leaders and/or Intercessors can be part of the "standby" team, as well as a TYB/HHN consultant and/or other trained Restoring the Foundations teams.

Preparation of the Attendees
As with ministry to hurts/losses, it is possible that many of the attendees will have no experience with deliverance or displacing principalities. Again, depending on the spiritual maturity of the people, the Leader may want to present some key scriptures on the overhead as part of transitioning into this portion of the Action Meeting. The goal is to stir faith in the attendees so that they will "stand up" with their spirit man, step into the authority the Lord has delegated to them, and join in warfare with the Leader.

OH

Ministry

The ministry procedure is essentially the same as for the SOFFCs and SORFCs. The Action Plan list used for the SOFFCs and SORFCs ministry (page 292), plus the additions on page 296 form the basis for this ministry.

Ministry Steps for Organizational Oppression/Principalities

OH

These ministry steps come from Part Two, starting on page 96, where we discussed God's Solution for this negative spiritual root. These steps can be projected so that all the attendees can repeat the words along with the Leader as he leads them. It is particularly good to be in agreement and unity as the demonic hosts and principalities are being addressed.

> *(Leader states the name of the Ministry Target, i.e., "abandonment," then leads with ...)*
>
> *1. In the Name of Jesus Christ, we renounce the demons and strongholds of _____, including the associated demons of _____, _____, _____, ...,*
> ....
>
> *- We command the strongholds to be disassembled, torn down, uprooted, and overthrown.*
>
> *- We command the demons to come out of the strongholds.*
>
> *- We command all of the demons afflicted us and our business, to leave us individually and corporately. Leave this place and leave this planet.*
>
> *(Leader then leads the attendees in naming one demon at a time, commanding it to leave. Everyone continues commanding until the Leader discerns by the Holy Spirit that the demon is gone. Then he names the next demon and leads the people in removing it. This continues until the entire group/sub-group with all of its demons is removed. Then the Leader moves on to the principalities.)*

2. In the Name of Jesus Christ, we address the
  principalities and powers of _____, including the
  associated principalities of _____, _____,
  _____, ..., ...

  - We command you to loose your grip from us, our
  buildings, and our land.

  - We command you to remove yourselves from all legal
  ground you have claimed.

  - We command you to disconnect from every access
  opening you have had.

  - We command you to withdraw from us individually,
  corporately, and from our land and buildings.

  - We dismiss you from your assignments against us and
  our business.

  - We displace you and push you back from over our
  land, buildings, and business.

  - We command you to remove yourselves, draw back,
  and no longer attempt to hinder or block God's open
  heaven over us.

When the Leader discerns that these two steps are completed for one group/sub-group, it is time to cycle back to step 1 for the next sub-group of the Ministry Target. This continues until all of the group/sub-groups have been ministered to.

The Leader should continue to be alert to see if anyone is struggling as the deliverance and cleansing proceeds. He can direct one of the helpers to the person if needed.

8. Leadership Transfers Ownership
of the Business to God   (OPTIONAL STEP)

(**PLEASE NOTE:** This is an OPTIONAL step that the Leadership Team must decide whether to include or not. Please see discussions on pages 47 and 117, and the planning step on page 148.

Just as the step to Marry the Land is done just one time, the same is true for this step. It will normally be done as part of the first Action Meeting; however, it may be done anytime thereafter, even during the very last Action Meeting. Skip over this step once it has been done.)

OH

If the decision has been made to put God in charge of the business, the following declaration/commitment/transfer of ownership example may be used. Project the words so everyone can repeat them and be in Unity and Agreement as the business "title" is transferred to God.

1. *We come to You, Abba Father, as Your sons and daughters.[1] We come knowing that You are a good God, having our best interests on Your heart. We delight in being children of the Most High God.[2]*

2. *We acknowledge that You are Lord over heaven and earth and that everything belongs to You, including our business and its land and structures. We declare First Corinthians 10:26, "For the earth [is] the Lord's, and the fulness thereof."*

3. *We confess that we no longer desire to attempt to manager and operate our business using only our reason, logic, and desires. We confess that we are not able to consider all of the factors and make good system-wide decisions. We ask You to forgive us for our arrogance in thinking we could make better decision than You and for excluding You from the decision-making process and Your rightful place as owner of this business. We receive Your forgiveness.*

3. *We now transfer all legal and spiritual ownership of this business, including the lands and structure, into Your capable hands. We will accomplish whatever paperwork You desire to satisfy man's legal system as will as Your system.*

---

[1] Please see Romans 8:14 and surrounding verses.
[2] Please see Galatians 3:26.

4. We receive our assignment as Stewards of Your business, including the land and structures. We choose to be Your sons and daughters. We welcome the leading of the Spirit of God in all decisions and actions. We submit to You and expect You to guide us as You speak Your Word to us. We declare that we are united together as "God and sons." We thank You that You will cause us to be "fit" instruments in the Master's hand. We bless You, Lord, and thank You for blessing us. In the precious Name of Jesus Christ we pray, Amen!

This step is another wonderful event to commemorate. It is fitting to celebrate the transfer of the title to the new Owner of the business. This can be done after you finish the Action Meeting.

9. Concluding the Action Meeting

You have come to the end of the ministry for the Ministry Target for this Action Meeting. You have applied the complete Restoring the Foundations Integrated Approach to Ministry to the negative spiritual roots behind one of the primary negative patterns/theme manifesting in the business. It is a job well done. Finish the official ministry with a closing prayer of rejoicing and then celebrate another step toward healing and freedom.

Closing Prayer

OH

The Leader leads the people in a closing prayer. Project it so all may read it together. Here is an example that may be used.

Lord, we thank You for being with us during this action time of removing negative spiritual roots from ourselves and our business. We thank You for providing the way out, the solution to the effects of all these roots and the solution for removing them. Thank You, Jesus, for going to the Cross and making the way for us to do what we have done in this meeting. We are so appreciative that You have brought the revelation and insights to us that we needed to do this.

Lord, we have asked for forgiveness many times throughout this meeting. We thank You that Your Word in 1 John 1:9 promises that when we confess our sins, that You are faithful and just to cleanse us from all unrighteousness and to forgive us our sins. We receive completely Your cleansing and Your forgiveness.

We submit to You, Lord, according to James 4:7. We declare You are Lord over us and over our business. We declare that You are in charge and that we are Your stewards; of the business, of the people, of the structures, and of the land.

Lord, we thank You for providing the abundant grace we need to be serious and diligent about renewing our minds and bringing righteousness into our Organizational Culture. As we pray and meditate on the new truths we have received, help them move from our heads to our hearts. We commit to develop an Organizational Culture that is in alignment with Your Word, nature and character.

Lord, we receive the authority You give when we submit to You and we choose to use it to bind all remaining demons and demonic strongholds affecting us individually and/or corporately. We announce to the demons that your time is short, but in the meanwhile you can not function in any way. We agree that you do not have any opportunity to bring oppression into our lives in the area of the primary negative pattern/theme with which we have just dealt.

Lord, we choose to use Your delegated authority to bind and restrict all of the principalities that still claim legal ground to access us and the business. We forbid the principalities to use whatever access they claim. We apply the Blood of Jesus to the legal ground and do not allow them to use it. We serve notice on the remaining principalities that they will be totally displaced and removed as any remaining legal ground is reclaimed in future Action Meetings.

Lord, we ask for a fresh infilling of Your Holy Spirit. Thank you for filling us and for filling the business. We pray for Your healing of our bodies, souls, and spirits wherever it is needed. We ask for the presence and peace of Your Holy Spirit throughout the land and structures of our business.

Lord, we stand in agreement with You and with each other that any counter-attack is disarmed before it even begins. We agree that we as a business and as individuals will stand against Satan's strategies, that they will be uncovered and nullified before they can be put into operation.

In the precious and powerful Name of Jesus Christ we pray, Amen!

Celebration

It is appropriate to have a time of celebration for the victory over one primary negative pattern/theme. One down, several to go! If the marriage to the land also occurred during this Action Meeting, this is certainly a reason to rejoice. And if you put the Lord in charge, this too is worthy of remembrance. It is always appropriate to celebrate the Lord and His goodness to us. Perhaps someone could lead worship and help everyone praise the Lord, for His mercies are new every morning and great is His faithfulness.[1]

A passage that helps us express our excitement and joy over another step of freedom is Psalm 144, where David declares that the LORD teaches his hand to war. Then David declares the many ways the LORD is important to him in the fight.

Psalm
144:1 Blessed [be] the LORD my strength, which **teacheth my hands to war, [and] my fingers to fight:**
144:2 My goodness, and my fortress; my high tower, and my deliverer; my shield, and [he] in whom I trust; who subdueth my people under me.

---

[1]   This praise is found in Lamentations 3:23.

We can say a hearty "Amen" with David and conclude a successful Action Meeting.

10. Post-Meeting Work

The Implementation Team continues the follow-up work after the Action Meeting(s). The most important things are to:

- have the Intercessors continue on "high alert," working with the Holy Spirit, to discern any attempts to form a counterattack after the victory of each Action Meeting. They can continue to speak confusion into the ranks of the enemy, forgetfulness about their purpose, and cancellation of their assignment.
- promote the new Organizational Culture beliefs throughout the business to help the employees continue to change their attitudes. (see page 145)

11. Completing all the Action Meetings

When the business has held several Action Meetings, enough to complete the ministry for each of the original 3-6 primary negative patterns/themes selected by the Development Team, it is time to stop for a while. We suggest the company "consolidate" its gains, perhaps for two to three months.

Consider this. In 3-6 key areas, the business has eliminated the pressure of the ancestor's sins and curses. It has begun to align some key attitudes with God's truth. It has received healing of wounds; and it has pushed back the oppression of a number of principalities. This is all very significant. It is time to take possession of these wonderful gains and truly integrate them into the fabric of the company. As God directed to Moses in Exodus:

> *Exodus 23:30*
> *Little by little I will drive them out before you, until you have increased enough to take possession of the land.*

We want the business and all of the people involved to "take possession" of their land. Then, after a time of consolidation, the Leaders and Intercessors will have a good understanding of how the business is doing with the changes. It may be that a primary negative pattern not previously discovered has "popped up." It may be than one of the original 3-6 patterns did not "take" as well it should have and that more work needs to be done with it. In any event, when the time is right, the Development and Implementation Teams can devise a new set of 3-6 negative patterns/themes and begin another round of Action Meetings that will lead to further Transforming Your Business.

G. Ongoing Transformation

Once the original Action Meetings have been held, the business enters the "Ongoing Transformation" phase. This can be considered a "maintenance" operation, with certain people in the company functioning as "watchmen" and "gate-keepers," along with the normal Intercessory functions. Needless to say, all of this must be done with the Holy Spirit and His gifts in full operation.

If you have put God in charge of the business, He will insure that His business remains secure and that it functions profitability. All it takes is for the Leaders and Intercessors to remain stewards, seek His direction for managing the business, and succumb to the sins of the flesh to use reason and logic in running the business. Attempting to "take control" and ownership back from God is not a good idea!

1. Ongoing Vigilance

Certain people in the business should have a stance of "watchfully alert." Intercessors with the appropriate calls and giftings should be in key positions. They are to provide ongoing vigilance as the business moves further into its destiny.

> *Stance: Watchfully Alert!*

186

We can not emphasis enough the importance of having mature, gifted Intercessors actively functioning within the business to successfully remove the influence of the enemy and to keep out the influence. In Part Five, we discuss in detail how Leadership can properly protect and work with Intercessors. We strongly encourage you to put the suggestions in Part Five into practice.

Two of the characteristics of Satan are to keep coming back to try again, and reusing the same old deceptive tactics. There is no point in letting him catch you unaware. Work with the Intercessors to insure that there is a guard over the previous weak areas, and that all are alert to signs that Satan's agents are at work. This can be done by being sensitive to outbreaks of negative behaviors and/or feelings within the company. Watch the customers and vendors and see how these relationships are progressing. Watch the business and remain sensitive to how it is doing.

It is equally important, and maybe more so, to keep a check on our own relationship with the Lord; how our Christian walk is going. All of the Leaders and Intercessors must remain very sensitive to signs of the enemy's attempts to infiltrate and subvert any Leader, Intercessor, or other employee of the company. Exercise ongoing vigilance in all these areas.

Hiring New Employees
The Intercessors should be involved in evaluating potential employees. This is a sensitive area, and requires mature Leaders and Intercessors who can function in the proper use of discernment without slipping into judgment. Along with the usual interview, evaluations, personality tests, etc., we suggest including a spiritual giftings test and perhaps even the Restoring the Foundations application for ministry form. Also, depending on the importance of the position, a more intensive interview approach might be helpful, such as the Topgrading interview.[1]

---

[1] This book is listed in the Biography.

Upgrading Current Employees

Besides helping the business become more healed and free, the individuals attending the Action Meetings will have benefited in their personal lives from the group ministry. These employees should begin to be more productive and more involved in the affairs of the company. This makes an opportune time for Leadership to help individual employees discover their real giftings, callings, and loves. It is likely many, perhaps most of them, do not know these things. They have just moved through life, somehow ending up in your business. You can help them discover who they are; and then assist them to move sideways, up, or even "out" of the business if necessary, bringing them into their place of destiny. Those that remained in your business have the potential to become top producers; benefiting the company and bringing fulfillment to themselves.

Periodic Repentance

As we discussed in Part Two (page 106), it would be a good idea for the company Leaders and Intercessors to meet periodically. They can present themselves before the Lord for a time of listening, repenting, and waging any needed spiritual warfare. All new information gathered since the last Action Meeting can be analyzed and organized for the meeting.

2. Ongoing Celebration

With Ongoing Transformation and vigilance, why not also have ongoing celebration. This could take many different forms, depending on the situation. Whatever constrains there may be, some form of expression of thanksgiving, worship, praise, prayer, Bible study, etc. should be possible. At the least, those among the Leadership, Intercessors and employees who desire to can come together and celebrate the Lord.

If it is possible in your business, a Celebration person can be designated to coordinate and oversee celebrations.

PART FOUR

Common Principalities

The military is fond of the saying, "Know your enemy." Without this knowledge it is difficult, if not impossible, to wage, much less, win a war. It is imperative to recognize the enemy, identify when and where he is operating, and discern what he is doing. We must know our enemy in order to develop an effective strategy and Action Plan and have success in removing his influence from our businesses and lives.

In this Part, we will to expose the more "common" principalities that occur and operate over and through businesses to hinder/block them from flourishing and fulfilling their purpose. In all probability, some are afflicting your business, so become attuned to "know your enemy." Beyond these common principalities, we want to encourage you to be informed and wise about other principalities that are likely "seated" and operating in your area and/or over your business. Vital and important information will come by talking to local Intercessors, by spiritual mapping, by observing the dynamics within your business (and church), and by revelation from the Holy Spirit and being sensitive to His Voice, as discussed in the Action Plan (Part Three, starting on page 127).

As a reminder, most of the common principalities we will discuss here also manifest as individual demons that oppress individual people. Thus we will frequently use the phrase "demonic/principality" to signify that what is being said applies to both "personal" demons and business/land principalities.

If you are already well familiar with the concept, reality, and different types of demonic principalities, you may skim or skip this part of the book. You can go on to Part Five on Intercession or go right to the implementation of the Action Plan Template in Appendix A.

Intercessors

It is extremely important that business Intercessors be prepared and ready to fulfill their key role as the company prepares to implement the Action Plan. They are needed to identify people in the company that are unknowingly being influenced by demonic principalities. They are needed to stop the ability of the principalities to interfere with God's purpose. Of course, Intercessors are the very people many of these principalities, particularly the occult/religious ones, would most desire to control. Thus it is most important that the key Intercessors for the organization know and understand the enemy, and that they also receive their own healing and freedom by going though a ministry such as Restoring the Foundations as provided by the Healing House Network. It is imperative that they desire their own personal freedom, that they are committed to pursuing and receiving as much healing as possible at any given time. Only in restoration will they be able to strongly submit to the business leadership, respond in maturing love to the revelation they see (versus a knee-jerk reaction concerning others, in agreement with the influencing principalities), insuring that they do not provide **any place** to the enemy. We will have more to share about Intercession and Intercessors in Part Five.

I. Garden Variety Principalities

These are the lowest in hierarchy, most common, obnoxious and discomforting level principalities of the kingdom of darkness. Like noxious weeds, they are everywhere, affecting/influencing everyone, both individuals and organizations. They can create an "atmosphere" of dysfunction. This includes the employees of your business and most likely, you.

The following titles are used because they describe the function, behavior, and/or manifestations of these types of demons/principalities.

A. Disobedience/Rebellion

The first sin (by man) mentioned in the Bible is the disobedience/rebellion by Adam and Eve as they fell to the deception of the serpent, questioned God's Word, believed the lie, and ate of the forbidden fruit (Gen 3:1-6). They turned from submission and fellowship with God to disobedience/rebellion and isolation from God. The tendency to sin in this way then passed down generation after generation to every human being. It is deeply embedded into each one of us to say "No!" and go our own way, separated from God and from each other.

This sin tendency manifests in business just as much as it does in home and families. Individuals within an organization may submit and serve their boss, or they may not. Most of the time, it is a mixture; sometimes "submit," sometimes "do your own thing." They may resist, subvert, go around, or do any number of things to benefit themselves rather than support their boss, their "team," and to work for the good of the organization. They may strive for their own career advancement and recognition versus embracing the team approach[1] of working together for the advancement of the organization and its God ordained purpose. This is such a common issue, it has become the theme of a number of books written with that sole purpose: to empower individuals to advance their own personal careers.[2]

Here is how principalities are given place and become entrenched. As the Founders form an organization and are joined by others, each person brings his "legal ground" for the personal demonic stronghold of Disobedience /Rebellion into the business. The personal strongholds merge with and strengthen the already existing regional/territorial principality of Disobedience/

---

[1] The book "Good to Great" shows how the team approach makes all the difference. We refer to this book on page 37. Please check out the Biography on page 331.

[2] Just doing a simple search (in February, 2006) on Amazon.com using the words "corporate ladder" yielded 77 books and articles, while "career/job" had 15,895 results.

Rebellion. This principality continually strengthens itself as it works in and through the people in the company, establishing itself as a territorial principality over the land and structures of the business itself, as well as gaining increased influence over the broader region.

People lose, organizations lose, communities lose–everyone loses in this case. The individuals making up the organization find it harder and harder to relate to, trust, and work with others. The unity factor decreases and the business finds itself less than successful in its purpose. The enemy is winning; the Kingdom of God is not. Now is the time to turn this trend around! Now is the time for the Kingdom of God to advance in every business.

Common Facets of Disobedience/Rebellion
The Disobedience/Rebellion principality, as with the personal demonic stronghold, may include a number of different facets. We want to deal with all of the different contributing parts that are important (i.e., operating) in our organization. Here are some of the more common facets. We suggest that you deal with all of these components as well as others operating in your business when implementing the Action Plan. You may check out the larger list in Appendix A.[1]

> _Disobedience/Rebellion_
> → _Disrespect_
> → _Independence_
> → _Resistance_
> → _Self-Sufficiency_
> → _Stubbornness_
> → _Undermining_

---

[1] The template Action Plan in Appendix A contains lists of potential ancestral sins as well as principalities. These lists start on page 266.

B. Abandonment/Isolation

Returning to Genesis again, the result of the first mentioned sin of Disobedience/Rebellion by Adam and Eve was their Abandonment of God.[1] Immediately, they discovered they were naked, i.e., that they had shame. So they attempted to cover themselves and hid from God. Because of the potential of their living forever with this defect, God then Abandoned Adam and Eve by withdrawing fellowship, driving them from His presence and their dwelling place in the Garden, leaving them to die. Everyone lost. Adam and Eve lost their home, fellowship with God, and their lives. God lost the fellowship of Adam and Eve, the primary reason He had created them. Adam and Eve immediately experienced spiritual death (separation from God) and eventually physical death.

We see this sin of Abandonment/Isolation continuing to manifest in the human race. For example, Cain is disobedient with his sacrifice. Out of his anger at God rejecting (abandoning) his sacrifice, he kills Abel. Again, death is the ultimate abandonment/separation, as it was for Adam and Eve. Today, it is common for us to abandon each other, as we withdraw and isolate ourselves, attempting to protect ourselves from further hurt.

When we bring this ancestral sin and demonic oppression into our business, we resist being part of a team. As we discussed earlier, "team" is all important if we are going to have agreement and unity. Without these, we will not fulfill purpose and destiny.

---

[1] Genesis 3:8 describes when Adam and Eve hid themselves. This sad story extends throughout the entire chapter.

Common Facets of Abandonment/Isolation
Here are the more common facets of this ancestral sin and principality. Again, please check out Appendix A for additional possibilities.

Abandonment/Isolation
→ *Abdication*
→ *Loneliness*
→ *Rejection*
→ *Separation*
→ *Self-Pity*
→ *Victimization*

C. Deception

A common thread running through the above two "Common Characters" is "Deception." Adam and Eve were deceived by the serpent, resulting in Disobedience/Rebellion and Abandonment/Isolation. Deception is *"to cause to believe what is not true; to mislead."* In other words, when we believe a lie, we have been deceived. The serpent, i.e., the devil, specializes in Deception. After all, he is the father of lies.[1] This is one of his major tactics he uses to keep us trapped and depressed. Clearing Deception from the "air" over the business and its employees can be a tremendous benefit in improving communications, reducing isolation and Fear, and promoting teamwork.

Common Facets of Deception
Deception can come in many of forms. Here are several common aspects. As usual, Appendix A has a more detailed list.

> *Deception*
> → *Lying*
> → *Secretiveness*
> → *Betrayal*
> → *Confusion*
> → *Self-Deception*

---

[1] Jesus declares the devil's identity in John 8:44.

D. Shame

Shame is the conviction that "I am uniquely and fatally flawed."

This is an identity lie about "Who I am." There are a number of possible identity lies (or Ungodly Beliefs), but this one about Shame is one of the most entrapping identity lies that exists. It sucks the very life out of a person as it causes him to live continually on guard, always afraid that someone is about to discover and expose his "flaw." The lie is that, "I am different." Of course, this is being "different" in a "bad" way.

This identity theft is worse than losing one's social security number and credit cards. This theft is very hidden, and it stays that way throughout the person's entire life.

What makes this demonic stronghold even worst is that the Shame gives place to demons of **Fear**. Since the person is fearful of exposure, he gives place to a stronghold of Fear. This can become entrenched, perhaps even as another identity lie; "I am fearful."

And then there is the ultimate entrapment. Fear gives place to **Control**, as Control promises to protect the individual and keep others from discovering or exposing the "flaw" of "being different." This Control can manifest in a number of different ways in different people. Thus there is no one personality that we can point to and say, "That is a Shame, Fear, and Control based person." For example, usually we see the Control focused turning outward, attempting to Control others. However, sometimes it turns inward and controls the person himself (this usually appears as passivity).

These three principalities combine into one super-stronghold of Shame-Fear-Control. This super-stronghold is very subtle and deceptive for as it victimizes its captives, it keeps them self-

196

focused, continually protecting and shielding themselves from the world.[1]

Of course, Control is not able to deliver on its promise to prevent exposure of the "flaw," (to prevent further hurt and pain), and so the person is continually experiencing new shaming events. However, since he doesn't know anything else to do, he just keeps building higher walls and retreating from others even more.

When this person comes to work, he may do a good job, he may even be brilliant, but it is hard for him to become a team player. He is too self-focused to develop a team/company point of view.

For individuals, getting free of this demon/stronghold usually requires personal ministry. Ministry by a team trained to discern, expose and remove such strongholds is the best way to really insure freedom. However, sometimes much freedom/healing can be obtained in a group ministry setting. How much will depend of how passive/active the person is and how much he wants to break free of this oppression. We have seen great victories after teaching and then ministering to this super-stronghold of Shame-Fear-Control.

Of course, once the individuals of the organization are free, it becomes possible to remove the influence of Shame principalities from the company. We feel this is a key aspect of setting the business free for fulfillment of destiny. Shame is so crippling of individuals, and thus the company, that not dealing with this stronghold is akin to surrendering to the will of the enemy.

---

[1] You may learn more about the Shame-Fear-Control Stronghold, including its fruits and roots, from our two-tape resource. There is also a short chapter in "Restoring the Foundation." Please check the Resource page at the end of this book.

Common Facets of Shame

Shame has many different sources and personalities. They are all "cover-ups!" These components are quite common. Appendix A has a more detailed list.

<u>Shame</u>
→ Anger
→ Condemnation
→ Deception
→ Failure/Defeat
→ Guilt
→ Hatred
→ Passivity
→ Self-Hatred
→ Victimization
→ Unworthiness

E. Fear

It is amazing how many different fears we humans have. Besides the Fear of exposure and of rejection mentioned above as we discussed Shame, there seem to be almost as many different ways to be fearful as there are people. Of course, we have the God-designed fears/cautions to help us survive potentially harmful situations. However, we seem to have many more fears, excessive, irrational fears, than what is needed for survival. Maybe this is why God has so many "Fear nots" in the Bible.

Fear is an emotion (for some, a lifestyle) that comes from the expectation of imminent danger. It has to do with expectation of death or harm of some type; physical or emotional. Even if the Fear is about an unlikely-to-occur situation, the body and emotions stay continually alert, ready to flee if necessary. What comes to mind is an image of a rabbit eating grass. He is always watching, muscles tense, and ready to spring away at the slightest hint of danger.

Fear can also be an identity lie, particularly when it is based on Shame, as discussed in the previous section. In this case, a deceptive stronghold of fear will be at the core of the person. It will be intertwined with the God-created personality, such that the person has no idea that he has a counterfeit personality. As far as he is concerned, "This is just the way I am!" As with Shame, it usually requires ministry by a team trained to discern and remove such strongholds to really be effective.

How will this person perform at work? Most likely, he will "play it safe." This is not the person to have in your sales or marketing department, not if you want him risking rejection and failure in order to make a sale or win a contract. As a manager, this person likely will be passive and permissive with those under him. He will not confront nor correct when it is needed. This is too risky; he might get someone upset with him. In other words, you will have a department that is not really managed. Each person will be doing his own thing.

Common Facets of Fear
There are probably as many kinds of Fears as there are people.
Here is a list of very common ones. As usual, Appendix A has a
more detailed list.

Fear
→ *Anxiety*
→ *Dread*
→ *Intimidation*
→ *Paranoia*
→ *Worry*
→ *of Authorities*
→ *of being Wrong*
→ *of being a Victim*
→ *of Death*
→ *of Poverty*
→ *of Punishment*
→ *of Rejection*

F. Control

This one is interesting. Now we enter the realm of applied Deception. In our experience, no one views him/herself as a controller, and yet every one of us is to various degrees. We all are busy insuring that we are safe and that we "get our way," which is, of course, the right thing. Frequently, our very value, self-esteem, and yes, even our identity, are wrapped up in whether what we "do" is accepted by others. If there is a threat of not being accepted, either us or our work (i.e., what we "do."), we press and argue, and even fight and abuse to have our way. Sometimes it is not safe to "fight" out in the open, and so the "in-fighting" goes on behind the scenes, underground. All of this is Control in different forms.

Part of the healing process for the organization is for the individuals and the company as a whole to shift their need for **significance** and **security** from being based on "what they do," to "who they are." We are again back to the need for an Integrated Approach to Ministry, to deal with the complex interactions between Sins of the Fathers and Resulting Curses, Ungodly Beliefs, Soul/Spirit Hurts, and Demonic Oppression. Both

> *Who He has created us to be is what gives us value, who He is is what gives us safety.*

the individuals and the organization need healing and freedom from the many ways the group and territorial principalities have access to them. The identity of each individual, and certainly that of the business, needs to be based on our value as one of God's creations. Who He has created us to be is what gives us true value, who **He is** is what gives us safety.

In our book, *Restoring the Foundations*, we discuss four levels or degrees of Control. These four are: Direct Control (out in the open), Overt Control (not necessarily obvious), Indirect Control (manipulation), and Hidden Control (occult/witchcraft). We give a number of examples of how these different levels manifest. Is it safe to say that the best team building and fulfillment of destiny will occur when none of these four levels are operating? God has provided healing and freedom from any underlying Shame and/or Fear, or from any other legal ground allowing the principality of Control to have place over and throughout your business. Tension, separation, rejection, being-on-guard, strife, taking over, competition, usurping authority, jealousy, etc., are all better removed from your company. Let's get rid of Control.

Common Facets of Control
The list for Control is shorter than for Fear, but there are still plenty of ways one may Control. These are the more common ones. Check out Appendix A for more possibilities.

Control
→ *Appeasement*
→ *Denial*
→ *Defending*
→ *Enabling*
→ *False Responsibility*
→ *Jealousy*
→ *Manipulation*
→ *Passivity*
→ *Possessiveness*
→ *Pride*
→ *Witchcraft*

G. Anger

People tend to be of two types when it comes to Anger. The explosive type erupts all over everyone close at hand, then it is over. That person has blown his anger out by spewing it all over everyone else. He is now at peace, but everyone else is fuming. What a way to build a team!

Or they might be the "bury-it-down-deep" type. On the surface, things look calm. However, the stuffed anger festers and smolders. Who knows when, if ever, it will come out? Brooded upon anger eventually becomes bitterness. Both the Anger and the Bitterness provide legal ground for demons of destruction. These negative emotions, plus the demons, frequently result in a crippling disease such as arthritis and/or other auto-immune dysfunction.

Neither type of person is good for your company. Both have deep wounds needing cleansing and healing. Both will alienate their co-workers and make your company an unpleasant place to work. Sooner or later, their fellow employees will decide, "I don't need this; I don't have to put up with this." And so they leave for another job, taking your investment in them elsewhere.

And what about when your Angry employee blows up with your best customer? The chances are you will lose them both. This is a place where an ounce of cure is worth a pound of regret. Helping your Angry employees become healed, with the Anger given over to the Lord, will pay good dividends.

This demonic stronghold and principality can be cleared from your organization and cleared from the land. You don't have to put up with its destruction of God's plan for you and your business.

Common Facets of Anger
Here is the list for Anger. As usual, these are the more common ones. Appendix A has more possibilities.

Anger
→ *Bitterness*
→ *Frustration*
→ *Hatred*
→ *Punishment*
→ *Rage*
→ *Resentment*
→ *Retaliation*
→ *Violence*

H. Mammon/Finances

One of the reasons a business exists is to make money. So what is the problem? The problem is that there is a difference between "making money" and "loving money." It is not good if we are "possessed" by money, by possessions, or materialism. This is the realm of the god of Mammon, an idol/demonic principality. God makes it very clear in the second commandment that He hates idols, and that we are not to worship them.[1]

While there is argument about whether the word "Mammon" as used in the Bible[2] (and other literature) is referring to a spirit/demon or not, it is clear that sin surrounding money issues is rampant in the world today. Thus, for convenience sake, we will use this term to represent demons and principalities involved with the love of money and/or possessions, greed and fear of loss. Most businesses, unless they have dealt with these sins, will be oppressed by the spirit of Mammon. At the very least, many of the employees, customers, and vendors will be influenced by Mammon. Does it seem like a good idea to do what we can to minimize the ability of Mammon to impact our companies?

In 1 Timothy, Paul writes:

> *1 Timothy 6:9-10 (NIV)*
> *6:9 People who want to get rich fall into temptation and a trap and into many foolish and harmful desires that plunge men into ruin and destruction.*
> *6:10 For **the love of money is a root of all kinds of evil**. Some people, eager for money, have wandered from the faith and pierced themselves with many griefs.*

---

[1] The second commandment is first given in Exodus 20:4-6. You may check out the discussion of this commandment on page 19.

[2] Jesus uses the word "Mammon" in Matthew 6:24 and Luke 16:9, 11, and 13, as He contrasts serving God or Mammon. Thus He uses the word as a personification of wealth and riches.

Notice that it is **not money** that is the root of all evil, but the **love of money**. Jesus, in Luke 16, makes it clear that we are to use unrighteous Mammon to win favor for Christianity, but that we are not to **serve** it. If we "serve" Mammon, we are putting our trust in an idol. This activates/releases the ancestral curse contained within the second commandment.[1]

Common Facets of Mammon
A much more extensive list is in Appendix A,[2] but this list is a good starting point for the more vicious aspects of Mammon.

Mammon/Finances
→ *Failure/Bankruptcy*
→ *Cheating God*
→ *Fear of Loss*
→ *Greed*
→ *Love/Idolatry of Money*
→ *Poverty*
→ *Stealing*

---

[1] The second commandment is discussed on page 19.
[2] These lists start on page 266.

II. Occult Variety Principalities

Let's move on from the Garden Variety to the more sinister and deceptive principalities. These are higher level entities in the kingdom of darkness, the Occult/Religious demons and principalities.

The definition of "Occult" is:

1. Of, relating to, or dealing with supernatural influences, agencies, or phenomena.
2. Beyond the realm of human comprehension; inscrutable.
3. Available only to the initiate; secret: occult lore.
4. Hidden from view; concealed.

For our purposes, a "working" definition is *the seeking of hidden knowledge or power*." When people strive for supernatural power and influence without the true and living God, they are moving into the realm of the occult. God hates our seeking hidden knowledge or power from any substitute or counterfeit source. This is the sin of idolatry, as expressed in the second commandment.[1] When we become involved "in the occult," we give place to individual occult demons as well as to occultic principalities. These entities seem to be at a higher level of empowerment, as they traffic in human deception and rebellion.

When you look at the ancestral sins and principalities groups in Appendix A, you will find the Occult list is the largest (on page 275). There are so many ways to seek hidden knowledge and power. It is as if Satan will provide us with whatever will draw us away from the true and living God. And so over the years many different practices and secret organizations have developed to ensnare us humans.

As we minister to individuals as well as to organizations, we want to perform careful and detailed spiritual mapping to insure

---

[1] The second commandment is discussed on page 19.

all of the significant occult forces are discovered so that we can include them as we recover the legal ground of oppression.

The principalities we are about to discuss are included because of the major impact they can have on an organization. Essentially, these principalities are variations of strong occult, religious evil forces or powers. It seems likely that they travel together, *since each one seems to be present whenever any one of them is present.* However, they may not all be present in any one business at any one time, but it is important to know about them so that their manifestations can be recognized when they do appear. The Leaders and Intercessors want to be prepared to recover the legal ground and to displace these especially destructive principalities.

A. Queen of Heaven

This name occurs in the Bible in the book of Jeremiah,[1] where God expresses His anger about the Israelites worshiping this idol/demonic power. It seems appropriate to apply the title "Queen of Heaven" to the main/principal occult/religious spiritual entity that is over all occult, religious principalities and powers.[2] Other names also given to the Queen of Heaven are: Isis, Ashtoreth, Ishtar, and Astarte, all idols worshipped in different nations and cultures.

The origins of the title "Queen of Heaven" are, of course, lost in antiquity. However, legend has the title beginning with the death of Nimrod.[3] His mother retained her place of power by creating a woodcut portrait of herself and the baby son for the masses to worship. It seems reasonable that all mother-son religions have this as their basis.[4] It might interest you to know

---

[1]   Please note Jeremiah 7:18 and 44:17-19. ,

[2]   One authority on Babylon is Alexander Hislop. Please see his book, "The Two Babylons," 1917.

[3]   Nimrod is first mentioned in Genesis 10:8-9.

[4]   If you check this out, you will find that most false religions have a mother-son basis.

that the Catholic Church has given Mary, the mother of Jesus, the title "Queen of Heaven."[1]

We suspect that the occult/religious territorial principalities around the world are directly under the Queen of Heaven in Satan's chain of command. One clear example would be Diana of Ephesus.[2] Others may be Athor of Egypt, Virgo Deipara of Tibet and China, Hestia of Greece, and Juno of Rome.

For the purposes of Transforming Your Business, the demonic realm hiding behind this title is what we are interested in. It is likely that we will not be dealing with the Queen of Heaven[3] directly as we bring cleansing to our organizations, but rather, we will be dealing with demonic powers/principalities directed and controlled by the Queen of Heaven. These next several principalities are of this category.

B. Jezebel

The name "Jezebel" strikes terror into the hearts of many. The current activity and reputation of this demonic spirit has increased so strongly, that many Christians fear this spirit hoping it will never come their way. In fact, many have made a covenant with this demon/principality, reasoning that if they ignore it, it will ignore them.[4] While this tactic may seem reasonable, it does not work. All that results is that Jezebel is *unhindered* in her destructive works.

---

[1] Mary has been referred to as the "Queen of Heaven" by Catholicism since ancient times. One famous painting by Filippo Lippi, the "Coronation of the Virgin," shows Mary being crowned as the Queen of Heaven. It was painted around 1444. In 1954, Pope Pius XII officially declared Mary, the mother of Jesus, the "Queen of Heaven."

[2] The "great goddess" Diana is mentioned in Acts 19:24-28 and 19:34-35.

[3] If we do need to deal with the Queen of Heaven directly, the Holy Spirit will let us know we are to bind her influence from our businesses.

[4] The covenant with Jezebel may have been made without really thinking about it, but it is present and real nevertheless.

209

Many books and messages have been written and spoken in recent years regarding Jezebel. It is as if the Lord declared that it is time for this vicious demon/principality to be exposed, identified and removed from the church.[1] Based on the number of people we have ministered to, who were either the victim of attacks by this spirit, or who were being used by the spirit to attack others, we agree it is time for all Christians to know about and understand the purposes of this Enemy of the Church.

There are two key things to know about Jezebel. The first is that while this spirit has a feminine name (based on the Jezebel of the Bible), it is just as eager to influence/control a man as a woman. Any warm "body" will do where she can rule to accomplish hell's purpose. Thus we have no reason or right to reserve the word "Jezebel" for women. Any of us are susceptible to giving place to this demon/principality. However, the spirit is a deceptive, seductive spirit. It tends to feminize whoever it is influencing; men become weak and woman become seductive.

The second thing to know is that the primary purpose of Jezebel is to stop the Word of God. She does this by "killing" the true Word of the Lord.[2] She then does her best to become the "messenger," bringing her version of the "Word of the Lord." Of course, this word will be a mixture of truth and error, counterfeiting the true word of God. It is usually a controlling word, designed to stifle Christian growth, promote passivity, stop the anointing, and promote the messenger.

---

[1] We have taught and ministered for a number of years about how individuals may become an "Unwitting Instrument" of this occult religious demonic stronghold. We give a number of scriptural characteristics of the manifestations of Jezebel so that each of us may do self-examination. You may obtain a copy of this tape through our resource department (contact information on page 345).

[2] Please note 1 Kings 18:13, 19:2, where Jezebel kills the prophets of the Lord and then threatens the life of Elijah after his great victory on Mount Carmel.

The devil wants death and destruction. We have observed a number of marriages being destroyed by Jezebel spirits. We have also watched (from afar) several churches being destroyed by Jezebel demons and principalities. We have also been privileged to be a part of several marriages being restored as the people humbled themselves and came for Restoring the Foundations ministry. Contrary to how some feel, it is possible to defeat the Jezebel spirit. All it takes is for the people to become aware that they are being used as "Unwitting Instruments" and decide to stop cooperating with this spirit that is destroying them and through them others.

Here is a table summarizing Jezebel's characteristics.

Jezebel's Characteristics

Strong Occult Force/Power	Will Inhabit Any Body
Motive: Kill Word of God	Motive: Bring Correction to Leaders
Tactic: Replace True Word of God with Her Version	Methods: Spreads Rumors, Forms Cliques, Creates Divisions/Strife/Organizational Splits.
Manner: Sweet Until Resisted, Then Becomes Ruthless.	Easily Offended when Confronted. Can't Work Things Out.
Personality: Negative, Bitter	Forgets Agreements.
Unteachable	Never Repents
Accuses Others of Being a Jezebel	Practices Mind Control

As we consider the action of this spirit in the marketplace, it is not a pretty picture.

Let's say we have one or more people in the company who have woundings such that they are afflicted with Abandonment and Rebellion issues. (Thus giving place to these demons and principalities.) There will likely be father and/or mother issues of

Abandonment, which is likely to be projected onto any authority, i.e., company leaders. In order to cover the Shame (as discussed above) and Fear (discussed above) coming from the Abandonment and Rebellion, the person usually will give place to Control. In severe cases, this can be Jezebel level Control. Without even realizing what he/she is doing, the person becomes an impediment to the company moving ahead in God's purposes. He/she is negative about proposals and suggestions that are from the Lord and positive about their own agenda. They strive to manipulate their way into leadership, moving from position to position. *He/she will then begin to set up his own little kingdom.* The demon attempts to destroy those who stand in its way, yet is crafty in its ability to look innocent to leadership. It "knows" leadership's weaknesses and needs, and will exploit that information to gain and secure its position. It particularly likes to emasculate strong men, turning them into slaves and servants. He/she most likely won't be able to coordinate/cooperate well with other departments, unless he has Control over the other leader(s).

Since the main target is leadership, it is imperative that the leaders of the business set up a system of protection for one another. To not do this is to surrender before the war begins. Her deception is supernatural, the craftiness is wicked, and the scruples non-existent. It is naive for a leader to think that he is immune to all of this. All one has to do is read the newspapers to see the destruction Jezebel is bringing to the church world.

If the person is confronted by Leadership, it is likely that he will go into attack mode, accusing and blame shifting. It takes a leader who understands how the spirit operates through the person and its manifestations to handle the situation well. Binding the Jezebel spirit is recommended, of course, as well as commanding the other principalities over the company to remain disengaged. The goal is to help the person realize that he is being an Unwitting Instrument and that he is helping bring about his own destruction. If the leader can accomplish this, he will be able to both protect the company and offer redemption (healing and freedom) to the person.

C. Ahab

With every Jezebel there is an Ahab. In the Bible, Ahab was one of the kings of Israel. He took as wife Jezebel, the daughter of the king of Sidon, a Baal priest.[1] She brought a strong occult ingredient into an already corrupted line of Israel's kings.

Ahab represents weakness, passivity, wickedness. As a demon or as a principality, it influences people into situations where they can be easily controlled by occult, religious spirits, such as Jezebel. It causes people to give up without trying, to admit defeat before the battle even begins, and to run from inferior forces.

In a church situation, it causes the pastor to allow others to run the church. He becomes their puppet.

In business, associates control the company rather than the owner/CEO. They use their "usurped" authority to keep people trapped and "down," continually turning plans and directives coming from their oversight to their own purposes.

Wherever you find a Jezebel, you will find an Ahab, whether ministering to an individual or an organization. It is important to look for both of them. Together, they seek to Control and take over the rightful and productive operations of others. Ahab will be the figurehead, with Jezebel behind the scenes running the show. The company will not be allowed to fulfill God's destiny.

D. Leviathan

Leviathan is known as the King of Pride and as the "twister" of communications. He is described in the book of Job, with the entire 41st chapter devoted to him. The last verse declares him the "king over all that are proud." Ugh! Who would want Leviathan over him as king? He feeds from the fleshly human nature and does his best to get us into pride and keep us there.

---

[1] We have this story in 1 Kings 16:29-33.

Pride is strengthen by Control (perhaps from Jezebel?) and covered by Deception so that we don't even realize we have slipped into Pride. We become self-sufficient and think that we don't need God in our lives. In fact, the tendency is to become our own "god." In fact, it is unlikely we will even think about God. We just keep moving ahead, secure in our own strength and abilities.

Leviathan is a serpent. Isaiah 27:1 declares him to be a piercing and a crooked serpent. He is known to so twist communications that confusion and frustration become the norm. He can change what both the sender and the receiver hear. The receiver will hear something different than what the sender said. Then, when the receiver summarized what he heard back to the sender, the sender hears the communications further twisted. We have found it necessary to write notes to each other when under the influence of a strong Leviathan principality, including repeating back to each other what we thought the other person said. It is hard to believe this can happen until one experiences it. Let us assure you, this is a real phenomenon. We should be prepared to deal with twisted communications when Leviathan is exerting its influence.

Leviathan seems to always be present with Jezebel, so the leaders will have the fun of dealing with several occult religious demons/principalities at the same time.

E. Python

Python is a constrictor, a serpent that kills by squeezing the life out of its victim. It is known for its ability to move stealthily and with great secrecy until it is in position to strike. Once it strikes, it twists and turns, wrapping itself about its victim with great distortions of itself and the victim. When this name is used to describe a demon or principality, it is referring to the life being squeezed out of a person, a ministry, a business, a vision, etc. It does this through underhanded and deceptive ways.

It works with Leviathan to bring confusion, distortion, and twisting into an individual or organization. Anything that God has called to purpose and destiny, Python, along with Jezebel and Leviathan, will be there to attempt to stop and subvert God's Will. We bind this spiritual power and stop its function so that we can go about the business of clearing the legal ground of all of the demons and principalities. Then we cast it out, displace it, and remove it along with the others.

F. Absalom

Absalom was one of King David's sons. He decided to subvert his father's authority and kingship and take over the kingdom for himself. His tactic was to stand by the side of the road leading to the city gate and win the people's favor. The Bible states that "he stole the hearts of the men of Israel."[1] The spirit of Absalom is still doing this today, as he works with Jezebel to bring insubordination, disruption, strife and confusion into the organization. They work together to spread rumors about the leaders, win the hearts of the people, and cause factions and cliques to form. In churches, splits are the result. In businesses, it is more common to have an uncooperative department or division. However, occasionally a group of people will leave and form another company, taking trade secrets and proprietary procedures that are hard to replicate.

While God wants us to raise up spiritual sons and daughters, particularly those that will assume the leadership of the business, it is here that Absalom attempts to find a place. Thus it is important that the prospective leader respect and submit to the current leader. It is very important that he understand the tactics of the religious occult demons and principalities so that he can *choose into* personal ministry and *choose out* of cooperating with the enemy.

---

[1]   We can read about Absalom's strategy in 2 Samuel 15:1-6.

III. Occult Secret Organizations

We want to complete Part Four with a discussion of occult organizations and their effect on the employees of the business as well as the entire business.

This is an area of great Deception. There are many church and business leaders who are members of occult/secret organizations and lodges who do not seem to see the dichotomy of both claiming to be a Christian and belonging to one of these organizations. This really fits the admonishment of Paul in 2 Corinthians 6:14-17, where he declares, "Come out from them and be separate," as he contrasts righteousness and wickedness. The likelihood is high that at least some of your employees belong to an occult organization.

Occultic/secret societies, lodges, and organizations are characterized by, well, their "*secretiveness.*" Their members are not allowed to share with outsiders the rules, procedures, and purpose of the organization. While in many cases this may be "harmless fun," what distinguishes an occult/secret organization from the others is the use of "bloody" oaths. That is, the rites used for initiation and for advancing through the organization's various levels include the member making vows to not divulge the secrets of the organization upon penalty of death via some horrible occurrence. For example, the Freemason initiate will be instructed to declare:

> *Binding myself under no less a penalty than having my throat cut across, my tongue torn out by its roots, and buried in the rough sands of the sea...*

At the next degree level, the oath includes the following words:

> *Binding myself under no less a penalty than that of having my left breast torn open, my heart plucked out and given as prey to the wild beasts of the fields and the fowls of the air...*

216

At the third or Master Mason's Degree every Mason must swear an oath including the following:

Binding myself under no less a penalty than that of having my body severed in twain, my bowels taken from thence, and burned in ashes...

While the people may think this is harmless fun and has no real meaning, the kingdom of darkness is delighted with the Open Doors these oaths provide them into the lives of the people. And of course, the people bring their "secret society" demons with them when they come to work.

Typical fruit from these bloody oaths and curses for the Freemason and his descendants is physical diseases, particularly associated with the parts of the body mentioned in the bloody oaths. The fruit also includes spiritual oppression and torment such as being fearful, sexual perversion, failure, shame, and other defeat and "loser" attitudes. It is hard to understand why anyone would want to pass these types of curses on to their descendants. It shows the level of Deception associated with occult activities.

In our books[1] we discuss how God taught us about the effects of Masonry by bringing to us several granddaughters of Masons for Restoring the Foundations ministry. In each case, they were suffering from many different physical afflictions, sexual sins, fears, and control issues. As we applied God's principles of healing and freedom, breaking the power of the grandfather's bloody oaths, each one came out from under the cloud of oppression. Particularly beneficial for them was the "casting out" of the demons that had legal ground because of the oaths, and that were doing their best to carry out the curses of the oath. As frequently happens when dealing with occult demons, the manifestations of their leaving was very evident. Each woman knew that something significant had happened and that Demonic Oppression was very real. We enjoyed being a part of their newfound freedom!

---

[1] These books are listed in the footnote on page 13.

Occult Organizations
In Appendix A on page 276 we have included a list of many occult organizations. You will find they range from overtly witchcraft to psychic to secrecy lodges. As mentioned above, Satan will design and create as many different types of organizations as necessary to insure that every man and woman is tempted to seek gratification, i.e., security and significance, from a source other than the true and living God.

If you or any of your ancestors was/is involved in a secret society, we recommend that you find out what type of secret society it is. Most likely, you will want to apply the ministry steps discussed in Part Two to gain freedom from the ancestor sin and Demonic Oppression.[1]

---

[1] A prayer to free oneself from the curses of Freemasonry can be downloaded from the **www.HealingHouse.org** website. Click on the "Ministry Downloads" link on the left.

PART FIVE

Intercession—Spiritual Warfare

Have you noticed that the words "Intercessors" and "Intercession" are mentioned more than once in this book? That is because this is an important subject. From its introduction in Part One (page 40), we have discussed the different aspects of being an Intercessor and Intercession at significant points along the way.[1] We now want to go more in depth about Intercession and its importance. We will emphasize how it relates to the warfare of freeing the business and then maintaining that freedom. And then, we will follow up with how to take care of those called as Intercessors. These are all significant areas of support to the success of the Action Plan.

We mentioned often the importance of business Leaders interceding for the business, interceding for each other and employees, and for God's calling in the business. However, it is also important that those within the company with the spiritual call and gifting as Intercessors be identified, properly recognized, and placed. These people are the "watchmen on the wall," and the "keepers of the gates." We believe that God provides Intercessors within every group of people. Whether they are properly utilized or not is the responsibility of the leaders and managers. When properly positioned, Intercessors will do their protective and offensive functions easily and naturally. After all, they are just being who they are.

The spiritual entities over the land, buildings, and people making up the business will continue to bring destruction onto the land and all that is on it for as long as we allow. Whether we like warfare or not, whether we prefer to think all is peaceful or not,

---

[1]   Please check the Index for pages numbers where significant comments about Intercession and Intercessors are located.

we are at war. We enlisted in the army of the Lord when we experienced the new birth. Now that we are ready to implement the Action Plan, we are going on the offence against the principalities arrayed against us. We are escalating the spiritual warfare with the intent of totally removing and displacing the principalities. God planned for the Intercessors to be a part of this. They act as eyes and ears to hear from the Lord what the enemy is planning, what legal ground he still has, and what strategy the Lord is giving us to continue to remove him from our affairs. Then they go into action following the Lord's strategy to defeat the enemy.

Not an Intercessor?
We should comment for just a moment that not everyone is called as an Intercessor. Is this obvious? As important as Intercession is, it is just another "job description" in the Body of Christ. If we are called to it, we should respond and do it. If we are not, then we need to find where we do fit. There is no place for envy, jealousy, or superiority/inferiority attitudes. As Paul writes in 1 Corinthians 12, each cell, joint, eye, etc., has its place and its function. As Leaders in our businesses, we are responsible for helping each person be in his place of calling and gifting, including the Intercessors. It is in "being in our place" that each one finds fulfillment, joy, significance, security, anointing, blessing, and destiny.

I. Importance of Intercessors

We want to again emphasize the Intercessors' vital role as a business becomes awakened, aware, and enters a new level of comprehension about negative spiritual roots and their impact. In this book, we have written more than 16 significant paragraphs about Intercessors and their different functions during this transition. We summarized the more significant roles in the box.[1] It is not too strong a statement to say this; that without

---

[1]   If you would like to read these paragraphs again, please check in the Index under Intercession.

proper alignment of Intercessors and Leadership, and without the proper care and relationship established between them, the business will likely fail in making the jump from the uninformed and untaught captive to the aware and activated overcomer.

Major Functions of Intercessors

Seeking Knowledge and Wisdom
- to properly place employees, team members, intercessors
- to discern employees needing help in getting free of demons, demonic stronghold, and/or principalities
- to receive revelation about:
  - sins and curses baggage on the people and on the land
  - ungodly Organizational Culture
  - Organizational Hurts/Losses
  - primary principalities over business and in the region
  - planned attacks/counter-attacks by the enemy
  - business strategies: which markets, proposals, ventures
  - marketing strategies: how, when, and where

Spiritual Warfare
- cover Leadership, other Intercessors, and business
- cover meetings and interactions with rest of world
- discern intentions/purpose of each visitor. Apply appropriate countermeasures as necessary.
- bind enemy over employees and business
- exercise authority to cleanse people and land
- apply *Transforming Your Business* freedom process
- remove/displace principalities from land and structures
- ongoing vigilance, protection, and covering

This is an impressive list. While other people, including the Leaders, can also do some of these functions, this list serves to highlight our contention that every business needs to know, "Who are our Intercessors?" The business must find the Intercessors and insure and secure these persons as properly healed, protected, prepared, placed, and released to function on behalf of the business and God's destiny for the business.

221

II. Importance of Leaders and Intercessors Working Together

Leaders and Intercessors are different. While there are all types of people that are Leaders and all types of people that are Intercessors, in general they have a different "drive" or focus in life. This can make it "interesting" as they attempt to relate to each other. Yet one without the other will not make it in today's spiritual climate. The warfare is heating up and God's call to destiny has never been more widespread and significant. The Bible calls us to "run the race" to win.[1] If you do not want to settle for "also ran" in the race of life, you will want to partner with the "other" part of God's team. You will want to have a significant, trusting, mutually respectful, and team relationship with either a Leader or an Intercessor. Leader or Intercessor, God will have you work together in unity, unless you want to allow the devil to have his way!

You see, God has arranged and purposed it so that each one needs the others. In a properly functioning business, each one protects the other.

> *Leaders pray for and cover Intercessors. Intercessors intercede for and protect the Leaders. They share the revelation knowledge they are receiving from the Holy Spirit. Together, they can obtain all the pieces of God' plan for every aspect of a transformed business.*

Not Able to Relate to Leadership?

If you are an Intercessor and you do not have a trusting and mutually respectful relationship with the Leaders of the business of which you are a part, if you feel that you can not develop such a relationship, then it is important to check with the Holy Spirit to see where the problem lies and what He would have you do. For example, it might be that you just need some significant healing and freedom from father and/or mother issues, that you can not

---

[1]   Our "race" is discussed in 1 Corinthians 9:24-26, Galatians 2:2, and Hebrews 12:1.

and do not trust anyone. We would suggest the thorough format Restoring the Foundations ministry to help you break free from the old patterns. On the other hand, it may be your Leader needs the healing and freedom because he has wounds that cause him to just not be trustworthy. Either way, for whatever reason, you need the Holy Spirit to speak to you and your family to know which path He would have you take. God wants you in a place where your gifts are appreciated and useful, where you are covered and protected, and where you are fulfilled and satisfied.

A. Leaders Cover Intercessors

Whether in businesses, or in churches, or civic clubs and government, or home, these organizations work best when Leaders cover and protect the Intercessors. Intercessors are on the "front line" and deserve the best Leadership can bring to them.

Let us repeat; the Leaders are responsible to pray for and cover the company's Intercessors, other Leaders, and the rest of the employees. Leaders can pray together and/or individually. Ideally, this is done daily (but not as rote), as prompted, and often. Leaders do best in this role if they will accept that they are the pastors of the employees. God has entrusted the people of the company into their care, and business leaders/owners are stewards of the people as much as every other company resource.

Let's peek in on an Intercessor's meeting at two different companies. One is covered by the Leadership and the other one is not. Do you think it will make a difference?

Covered Meeting
When Intercessors meet for a time of Intercession, at least one top-level Leader should also be present. The Leader, in general, will not be in charge of the meeting (the designated Intercessor is), but he is there to pray for and protect the Intercessors as they seek the Lord for revelation knowledge and for spiritual warfare.

As the meeting is started, the Leader prays: for the Intercessory team, to bind any attempted demonic interference that might try to come against any of the Intercessors; to delegate authority to the Intercessors to represent the business before God; to ask for a release of discernment; and to declare an "open heaven" over the Intercessors.

When this type of covering is provided by a Leader, and the Intercessors can intercede with great freedom and anointing, it sets the stage for the Holy Spirit to do awesome things. There is no way to know ahead of time what might come out of the meeting, except with God, it is always a blessing.

The Intercessors take notes of what they are hearing from the Lord. They pass all revelation from the Lord on to the Leadership, including comments regarding any out-of-the-ordinary happenings during the meeting. The attending Leader submits his comments to the other Leaders as well. This can be done in writing or perhaps more efficiently, by voice recording the highlights.

Uncovered Meeting
When Intercessors meet by themselves without any Leadership covering, it is a whole different situation. While they might have great intentions and Godly motives, they are in a dangerous position. They are like sheep without a shepherd, or an army recruit on the battle field without a general. Sooner or later, something bad is going to happen. Somebody is going to get hurt.

An uncovered Intercessory group is a prime target for takeover by Jezebel. In Part Four we discussed Jezebel and its characteristics in some detail (see page 209). It is not a pretty picture. With great cunning and deceptiveness, the spirit will use a host (a person who becomes an Unwitting Instrument) to work its way into leadership of the Intercessory group. It soon will have all of the people (that continue to come) under its influence.

An automatic selection process will take place, as the Intercessors that are not susceptible to the control and deception of the spirit will feel "uncomfortable" with the up and coming new leader. They will "vote" with their feet and stop coming to the meetings. This leaves Jezebel with a covey of idolizing, desiring-to-be-controlled people who will support the group leader and stick with him even if eventually confronted by the Leadership. The prayers that are prayed, the revelation about leadership that comes forth, the plans made about what to do if the group is "persecuted," are generally not from the Holy Spirit, but move into the realm of witchcraft and idolatry.

The Unwitting Instrument of Jezebel seems a nice enough person. Unfortunately, usually through the wounding of abandonment, he/she has become shame-based and is "just" trying to survive in this "cruel" world. So fear and control are given "place," leading to the Shame-Fear-Control Stronghold becoming firmly entrenched in the person's life. With occult ancestral sins and curses, the control can escalate to the Jezebel level. This person, not realizing he/she is yielding to a spirit that is out to "kill" him/her and others, goes through life manipulating and positioning (controlling) to keep the shame hidden from view at all costs. As we said, it is not a pretty picture.

We have not seen much good come out of an uncovered Intercessory group. Please do not do this to yourself or to the company, but especially not to your Intercessors. Leaders, you must care for and protect your Intercessors. They are there for you; God has provided them for you. They want to do their job. Provide what they need to function with safety and effectiveness.

B. Intercessors Cover Leaders

The relationship between the Leaders and Intercessors is truly symbiotic. Each needs the other to be maximally effective and efficient. In a like matter to the Leaders covering, protecting, encouraging, respecting and properly placing the Intercessors, the Intercessors cover, protect, and shield the Leaders from the onslaughts of the enemy. They "cover the backs" of the Leaders. Their work allows the Leaders to "lead" and remain focused on all of the aspects of running a successful and rapidly growing company. The Leaders do not have to worry about enemy attacks or inroads into the finances, mutiny or sabotage from the employees, wholesale departure of customers, etc. The

Leaders can lead to their maximum potential. They can do this in a state of peace, knowing that the entire company "team" is functioning under the control of the Holy Spirit with each person in his place, doing his job, all under an Intercessory prayer shield. This is as good as it gets in a business environment here on this earth.

III. The Hazards of being an Intercessor

Prime Target
It would be unfair to stress the importance, necessity, and honor of being an Intercessor without also disclosing the hazards that go with the job. This front-line position means that each Inter- cessor is also a front-line target. It is as if each Intercessor has a big "bull's eye" painted on his back. We want to insure that each Intercessor is aware of and watchful of the many ways the devil will try to deceive them and maneuver them so that they can be "taken out," rendered ineffective in the army of the Lord.

If every Intercessor is aware of the different schemes of the devil, he at least has the choice of saying "No!" when the Tempter comes around. By the way, the more healed and free he/she is, the easier it is to say "No!" Let us look at some of the "wiles" of the devil with which he will try Intercessors.

A. Warning Scriptures

We want to highlight five scriptures that warn us about how the enemy will try to entrap us. Knowing this gives us an opportu- nity to not succumb to his schemes.

Unforgiveness

> *2 Corinthians 2:10-11 (NIV)*
> *2:10 If you forgive anyone, I also forgive him. And what I have forgiven--if there was anything to forgive--I have forgiven in the sight of Christ for your sake,*
> *2:11 In order that Satan might not outwit us. **For we are not unaware of his schemes.***

The context is forgiveness. Paul is being careful to forgive everyone completely. He doesn't want to be outwitted by Satan. This is one of his schemes to ensnare and entrap people.

Intercessors, you can not afford to hold unforgiveness. If this is a family characteristic, be thorough in dealing with ancestral sins and curses and changing all mind sets and attitudes.

Giving Place

> *Ephesians 4:26-27*
> *4:26 Be ye angry, and sin not: let not the sun go down upon your wrath:*
> *4:27 Neither give **place** to the devil.*

We discussed this scripture in Part One on page 18. We want to mention it again because it is so important that Intercessors not sin out of anger, or for any other reason for that matter. We can't afford to give "place" to the devil, opening a door through which he can access us.

Now being human, it is likely that we will sin, sooner or later. However, as soon as we realize what we have done, we can quickly forgive others, repent, and slam shut the door we just opened, reclaiming the "place" given.

Ungodly Attitudes and Mental Strongholds

> *Ephesians*
> *6:11 Put on the whole armour of God, that ye may be able to stand against the wiles of the devil.*

In this scripture we have the word "wiles." The Greek word translated "wiles" has to do with strategies, battle plans, and activity in the mind; i.e., the intellectual area. We want to stand firm against the battle plans of the enemy, against his logical constructs. We could easily extend this into the area of Ungodly Beliefs and ungodly Organizational Culture. Satan tries to constructed attitudes of thought and patterns in our minds that give him place, which cooperates with his schemes. And Paul writes to not allow Satan to do this.

A parallel verse is:

> *2 Corinthians*
> *10:5* **Casting down imaginations,** *and* **every high thing** *that exalteth itself against the knowledge of God, and* **bringing into captivity every thought** *to the obedience of Christ;*

Clearly Paul expects us to be vigilant about what goes on in our mind. Removing strongholds of the enemy is important; otherwise he has an Open Door through which he can control us.

Opposing the Truth, Being held Captive

> *2 Timothy 2:25-26*
> *2:25 Those who oppose him he must gently instruct, in the hope that God will grant them repentance leading them to a knowledge of the truth,*
> *2:26 And that they will* **come to their senses** *and escape from the trap of the devil, who has taken them* **captive to do his will.** *(NIV)*

This passage has also been discussed before, in Part 1 on page 39. The context is unfruitful arguments and discussion, even strife, even being in opposition to the "truth." Intercessors must stay alert against foolish discussions and beliefs leading to captivity. Is it obvious that we can do better in this life and our Christian walk if we stay "sane?"

If your family line had people that were involved in the occult, such as in witchcraft, spiritualism, Satanism, or freemasonry, then it is likely that mind binding, mind blocking spirits were waiting for your arrival on the earth scene. When one lives his entire life with this type of oppression, it is accepted as "normal" and so no attempt will be made to receive freedom. Receiving some Restoring the Foundations ministry can be a big help in obtaining a sane and clear mind!

Summary

So we want to be wise as serpents and harmless as doves when it comes to unforgiveness, giving place, ungodly mindsets, and foolish quarrels. We certainly don't want to do anything to be held captive to do the devil's will!

B. Going Outside Your Boundaries

It is important that Intercessors know their boundaries. Why you ask? Because going outside of your boundaries is hazardous to your health! Boundaries are demarcations of authority and safety. They are set by human authorities and by God.

What is our Sphere of Operation?

In Exodus 23, where God gives the strategy for conquering Canaan land, He also sets the limits of the territory He is giving to the Israelites. This is so important that He reiterates the placement of the boundaries many times throughout the Old Testament. Exodus 23 contains important understanding for everyone, but particularly for Intercessors.

> *Exodus 23:31*
> *I will fix your boundaries; from the Red Sea to the Sea of the Philistines. From the wilderness to the Euphrates, ...*

God fixed the boundaries of the Israelites. He set the East and the West, the South and the North boundaries. While Israel possessed the entire area only once, during King David's reign, the entire area continues to belong to them even today. For their part, they never attempted to possess land that was outside the boundaries set by God.

Know Your Boundaries

First of all, we should mention that there are several types of boundaries. There are our family and household boundaries, our place of business boundaries, our church boundaries, and our spiritual warfare boundaries.

We have personal boundaries (i.e., our family), and household boundaries, which come from God's initial delegation to Adam and Eve stewardship of the earth. God established the family, parental, and household authority and responsibility. We have always had every right to wage spiritual warfare over our households.

We have boundaries at work. These are established by our employer as he delegates responsibility and thus authority to accomplish our job description. We can conduct spiritual warfare at work within our area of operation.

Owners and company officials have boundaries according to the vision of the company and their job descriptions. Companies have delegated authority and responsibility from the "state," which gets its authority from God's establishing of the nations.

Boundaries come from Leaders

We believe spiritual leaders, particularly church five-fold ministers, have authority they can delegate to other ministers within their organization. Likewise, business Leaders have authority that they can delegate to others, including Intercessors, within the business. They can release the Intercessors to function within the boundaries of the company, i.e., within all that concerns the company and its operations. Thus they can go outside the "walls" of the company, outside the property line, to wherever Intercession is needed on the company's behalf. Now, what the Intercessors will encounter "out there," and whether they will be successful or not, depends on many factors, many of which we are discussing in this book. One important factor is God's commissioning, which we discuss in the next section.

Boundaries come from God

What we are really interested in is this: *what are the boundaries within which we are authorized and commissioned by God to conduct spiritual warfare?* As Leaders and Intercessors, we want and need to know the scope of God's call. It might be within the bounds of our company or church, it might be within our neighborhood, or it might be our entire city. When it comes to spiritual warfare, God calls and commissions each one of us individually. He set the boundaries of our operation. Within these boundaries, we have delegated authority to represent God and His Kingdom over all the power of the enemy. Within these boundaries, God will anoint us and provide everything we need to be successful.

He will even provide a copy of this book so that you and others can deal with "place," "legal ground," and "Open Doors." He will help you understand the negative spiritual roots of problems you have been struggling with. And as you deal with and clear out the personal and corporate Baggage, it is likely that God will expand your scope of operation. It may move from the city to the state, to the nation, to the world. It all depends on God's call and on your ability to mature into it. As you grow and mature, you should become a more able warrior. You should also be becoming more healed and free, reducing the size of the bull's eyes on your back!

As the Leaders select and commission Intercessors for the business, they need to seek the Lord to discover the delegated scope of operation for each Intercessor and assign them accordingly to the various tasks laid out in the Action Plan.

What Happens Outside Our Boundaries?
When we go too far in our spiritual warfare and move beyond what God has set as our boundaries, we become vulnerable. We are no longer covered by the organization's legitimate sphere of operations nor by God's commissioning and anointing. We are "on our own." This is like a rabbit in the center of a pack of wolves or a seal surrounded by killer whales–not a safe place to be–not a place we are likely to escape from unscathed.

This reminds us of an old pilot's saying; "There are old pilots and there are bold pilots, but there are no old, bold pilots." Being submitted and obedient to God and the company Leaders might be the key to a long and satisfying life as we respect the boundaries established by God, however narrow or broad they may be.

C. Sins of the Flesh

The third area of hazards we want to mention are the ordinary, garden variety sins of the flesh. While these sins are not unique to Intercessors, the ones we want to mention are of special importance to them. As a front-line ministry, Intercessors can not afford to indulge these sins. Yet, because of their gifting and call, Intercessors can easily succumb to these sins, and thus give "place" to the enemy. They must commit to guard these areas. Submitting to company Leaders, who are charged with oversight and protecting, is one way to stay humble and safe.

Most of the following sins were discussed in Part Four from the point of view of Principalities. As you read the following sections, you might reflect back to those sections to check if you are unknowingly being influenced by demons/demonic strongholds, and/or principalities.

1. Control

We know this will be a surprise to you, but everyone controls, whether they are willing to admit it or not. We are talking about illegitimate control now, not God delegated legitimate control. We control to get our way, to cover shame, to avoid expected danger, and to have power. If we are afflicted by Jezebel (page 209) and/or other religious spirits, we might control for all four reasons. In fact, sometimes we think these demons control just for the fun of it, just to see what they can get away with!

As God reveals His secrets to Intercessors, particularly strategies for Leaders such as are needed to implement the Action Plan and for spiritual warfare, it is very tempting to an Intercessor to use this information to control the Leadership. He can do this by "shading" things just a little bit. He can change the words he uses when explaining the revelation, or he might adjust the implications of the information. He can manipulate Leadership's understanding to his advantage. He can magnify what the Holy Spirit has brought to him to enhance his status and gain more influence. There are a number of ways the Intercessor can control either directly or indirectly.[1] This might be to accomplish his agenda, or it may be to accomplish an agenda of which he is not even aware.

This sin is obviously a huge invitation to the powers of darkness to further invade and influence the person. In fact, it is tantamount to treason, since the Intercessor is yielding to the enemy and obeying him (*"being taken captive to do Satan's will"*) rather than supporting God's purpose for the business. This will eventually spell destruction for the Intercessor unless he realizes what he is doing, seeks help, and goes through a restoration process such as Restoring the Foundations ministry.

Of course, Intercessors are the very people the principalities, particularly the occult/religious ones, would most like to control. They are most fearful of an on-fire, sold-out, empowered, Holy Spirit led Intercessor. So guess why Intercessors are the prime target as the business embarks on the Transforming Your Business road to freedom.

We strongly encourage all Intercessors to maintain an attitude of submission and obedience to the Leadership of the business. In return, it is completely appropriate for the Intercessors to expect and insist on proper covering and protection from the Leaders. It takes this partnership to help the Intercessors avoid being drawn into the sin of illegitimate control.

2. Pride

Pride is another pervasive sin that easily goes unnoticed by the person committing it. This is because pride is "built in" as part of the human psyche. Adam and Eve gave place to pride when they chose to be "as God."[2] in Genesis three, releasing to the entire human race the knowledge of "good and evil."

---

[1]   We expose the Control-Rebellion-Rejection Stronghold and the different ways to control in a chapter in our book, *Restoring the Foundations*. Please check the Resource page at the back of this book for more information.

[2]   The serpent initiated this dreadful condition with his question in Genesis 3:4-5.

John has some choice words for pride:

> *1 John 2:15-17*
> *2:15 Love not the world, neither the things [that are] in the world. If any man love the world, the love of the Father is not in him.*
> *2:16* **For all that [is] in the world,** *the lust of the flesh, and the lust of the eyes, and the* **pride of life,** *is not of the Father, but is of the world.*
> *2:17 And the world passeth away, and the lust thereof: but he that doeth the will of God abideth for ever.*

It would appear that John sums up the world as having two primary characteristics: "lust" and "pride." If it were not for the mercy of the Father, we would all still be completely in the world. The point we are making is that pride is very prevalent. It takes work and commitment, and probably a lot of grace, to not give "place to" and walk in pride.

Here are two more well-known verses concerning pride. These should cause us to pause and consider, "Where am I, Lord, regarding this pride thing?"

> *Proverbs 16:18*
> **Pride** *[goeth] before* **destruction,** *and a haughty spirit before a* **fall.**

> *1 Timothy 3:6*
> *Not a* **novice,** *lest being* **lifted up with pride** *he fall into the condemnation of the devil.*

The verse in Proverbs is the source of the saying, "Pride goeth before a fall." While this saying is a mis-quote, it is accurate in its message. Allowing pride to get a grip puts us on the slippery path to destruction.

In First Timothy, Paul is presenting some character issues to consider in selecting leaders. He wants mature people selected as leaders. While this is not a guarantee, it does make it less likely the leader will "fall into the condemnation of the devil."

As usual, there is a major occult principality, Leviathan (page 213), ready and willing to take advantage of the fleshly sin of pride. As the King of Pride, he is always looking for subjects that will serve him.

Intercessors are "setup" for this sin: "After all, "I am one who receives revelation from God Himself. The success of the company depends on me."

The safeguard is for all Intercessors to keep in mind that every skill and talent they have is a gift from God. None of us can take pride in "our" gifts. Gifts are "given," not earned. We did not do anything to obtain the gift. While we do have a stewardship responsibility to develop and use the gift, we can not let the existence of the gift "puff us up."

Another temptation occurs when people appreciate and compliment Intercessors on their abilities. The Intercessor then has a choice to make. He can silently or "out loud" express his thanksgiving to God for "gifting" him to be a service and a blessing to others, to be a help in accomplishing His purposes within the company; or he can accept the appreciation as his own and give place to pride. Keeping the focus on God and His goodness rather than the gifting will help keep *Leviathan* at bay.

3. Elitism: Spiritual Pride

There is another possible "step up" when it comes to pride. When occult/religious spirits are present and have an influence, pride can escalate into "spiritual pride." We begin to believe that "we have the truth and 'exceptional' anointing." This is how Christian sects, or worst, false religions get started and continue.

Intercessors may not plan to start a "false religion," but they are at risk for this sin. "After all, if it wasn't for me, the Leadership wouldn't know what to do. I am the only one who can hear from God." And so they move into elitism. Then, the more God reveals things to them, the more at risk they become. It's so easy to say, "Wow, God's showing me all of these things. I must be really special."

Well, yes, Intercessors are special. But then, so are all of God's children. It is helpful to remember that we are "just" operating our God given gifts and talents in obedience to the call and destiny God has for us. None of us are more important than anyone else in the Body of Christ. It is with a humble heart that we can realize that the God of the universe has chosen us to represent Him here on the earth; expressing His character and bring His love and Word to others.

As usual, there is a safeguard. Intercessors, your safety depends on your humbling yourself and staying under the covering and protection of the business Leadership.

4. Isolation, Self-Sufficient: "a Lone Ranger"

"Just Jesus and me! That's all I need."

How many times have you heard someone make a statement of this type? We suspect that all of us feel this way at times, particularly right after experiencing another hurt from church leadership or a "supposed" close friend. We all have a tendency to withdraw and lick our wounds when offended and rejected. Those called as prophets may have the greatest tendency to become a "lone ranger" when hurt, but Intercessors are not far behind in wanting to escape and avoid relationships with leaders.

The common Ungodly Belief is, "Leaders will just hurt you and hold you back."

Leaders are "in process." Leaders do hurt people. They operate out of their wounding just as everyone else does. That is why it is so important that Leadership receive their healing and freedom since their influence and impact is multiplied throughout the organization (we are referring to Principles of Principalities #4). *We would submit that church leaders in particular are the most in need of ministry and the most fearful of asking for it.* Our plea to all leaders, especially church leaders, is to press past the enemies attempts to keep you trapped in shame, fear, pride, ego, and control; and seize the opportunity to become a healed leader that brings healing to all those God has placed in your care.

However, Intercessors, let us encourage you to not let wounded Leaders keep you from your calling and destiny. Being a "Lone Ranger" is not the answer. In fact, it is a good way to be "taken out" by the enemy. It is easier for him to pick you off and render you ineffective when you are all alone and unprotected, like a sheep without a shepherd. It reminds us of the old Lone Ranger joke:

> *A thousand Indian warriors are bearing down on the Lone Ranger and Tonto. The Lone Ranger turns to Tonto and asks him "What should we do, Tonto?" To which Tonto replies, "What do you mean, 'We,' White Man?"*

A "Lone Ranger" prophet or Intercessor is all alone without hope or help, with a thousand demons bearing down on him. When he most needs help is when "Tonto" betrays and deserts him. It seems the events of life (with a little help from the demons) set him up to become angry and bitter as he broods over his wounds and rehearses the past rejection and abuse. This is no way for a man or woman of God to live.

It is better to be under covering and protected. Best is for both the Leaders and the Intercessors to be healed and free and operating as a team. Again and again, we have watched church leadership come into unity and peace as they receive the Restoring the Foundations ministry. They receive healing for their wounds and they remove the devil from their lives and organization and become the unified army God has called them to be. No wonder the enemy deceives and lies to us to try to keep us isolated and alone. He knows the trouble he will have when we get out from under his bony finger and into unity under the direction of the Holy Spirit.

IV. Preparation and Release as an Intercessor

Now that we have reached this point, do you still want to be an Intercessor? Have we totally frightened you out of this calling?

We hope not. It is a noble calling and worthy of proper recognition and respect.

So let us look into several aspects of preparing and releasing business Intercessors. We want to do this so that they are protected and able to operate with the greatest effectiveness. We will conclude Part Five with a suggested procedure for conducting an Intercession meeting.

A. Finding the Intercessors

You may already know the people in your business who are called as Intercessors. Our prayer is that you have at least one seasoned, healed, and mature Intercessor who can step into the role of Prophetic Intercessor for the Implementation team as well as lead the company Intercessors. Ideally this person will already be knowledgeable in the topics we are discussing. He will meet or exceed all of the "specifications" for the Prophetic Intercessor as discussed in Part Three on page 121.

However, if you do not know who are the Intercessors, you might be asking, "How do I find the business Intercessors?" In this case, you will need to search out the Intercessors, help them receive their healing, train and equip them, and allow some time for them to mature as they "practice"[1] their calling. One way to speed the process is to bring in one or more recognized and able Intercessors as consultants to help raise up the business Intercessors. This could be a very worthwhile investment, particularly since an anointing would be deposited into the company Intercessors by the experienced Intercessor.[2]

---

[1]   Hebrews 5:14 expresses the concept of "practice" or "exercise" to improve one's discernment.

[2]   We have listed a number of equipping ministries on the Ministry Resources page 343.

Let us answer the question, "How do I find the Intercessors?" The short answer is "by prayer." As you ask the Lord to reveal His Intercessors, you may hear names or see faces. This is a wonderful starting point. However, we will not stop with this. We discuss, in a few pages (page 249), how God protects us by having us confirm every word by two or three witnesses.

If the business is publicly Christian, with most if not all of the employees Christians, it will be easy to find the Intercessors. Just ask around. Find out who likes to pray. Find out who prays "without ceasing," with periodic "burdens" the Lord asks the person to carry. When you find people who would rather pray than eat, it is likely you have found the Intercessors. The next step is to find out how they pray. Is it strong and forceful, full of declarations and decrees, even emotional? If so, it is almost 100% that you have the right ones. We will let time and fruit provide the rest of the confirmation.

If the business is not overtly "Christian," has people of different beliefs and religions (or anti-religion), it is more of a challenge to find the Intercessors. Yet even here, it seems God has His underground "grapevine." Ask some people whom you know are Christians. They probable know other Christians who know other Christians who …. Soon, every Christian in the company will know you want to meet those called as Intercessors. This will get you started even if there are more who do not yet know their calling. As the spiritual atmosphere over the company shifts, and Intercession becomes public, the others will also be identified. The sanctification of the many by the "tithe" will be "working."

Hiring an Intercessor

A suggestion or plan to speed things along is to hire one or more experienced Intercessors to intercede for the business. There appears to be two ways of doing this. One way is to hire a consulting Intercessor who contracts for a certain number of hours of prayer. This could be "on-site," or the person could pray from his/her home. The second way is to hire the Intercessor as an employee who spends some part of his/her day praying for the company. While in many ways obtaining an Intercessor should be no different than hiring any other staff or filling a Leadership position, in terms of spiritual covering and authority, there is a difference. So we prefer the "hiring" approach to obtain an Intercessor. On the other hand, if the consultant Intercessor is coming to also train and equip the company Intercessors, this could be a very beneficial temporary situation. As usual, the best solution will become clear when we pray and ask the Father to reveal His will.

Business "Watchmen" and "Gate Keepers"

As we consider hiring one or more Intercessors, a question that is often asked is, "How do we 'make it work' having Intercessors as employees for our company. We have to have them doing something useful besides 'praying' all day?" This raises another question, "What is 'useful'?" Some would contend that spiritual work is more useful than physical work in that it produces more long-lasting fruit. However, perhaps there is a combination that will satisfy everyone.

One suggestion is that you look for and hire Intercessors that have a special anointing as "Watchmen" and/or as "Gate Keepers."[1] They can be positioned to oversee all that enters and leaves the company. They have a special gifting to discern deception and evil plots. These people might answer the phone, be the receptionist, manage the receiving department, etc. Please let your Holy Spirit creative "juices" flow to discern where your business can use Watchmen and Gate Keepers.

The key to success with this arrangement is close communication between the Intercessor and his/her oversight Leader. There should be an agreed upon method of communication that insures the Intercessor is adequately protected from all eventualities and that all gleaned information is promptly gotten to the right Leadership. Remember, the company is now at war. We want to use Holy Spirit strategies to outwit and out-maneuver the enemy.

---

[1] There are a number of Biblical references for watchmen and gate keepers. A few are: 2 Kings 11:6, Psalm 127:1, Isaiah 21:6, 62:6, Jeremiah 31:6, **Ezekiel 33:2-7.**

B. Preparation for Intercession

At long last, we are finally going to get to pray! Well, almost. There are just a couple of other things we suggest you to attend to on the way to the prayer room. Let's look at them.

1. Receive Personal Healing and Freedom

We have stressed the importance of receiving one's own healing, particularly for Leaders and Intercessors (page 117). There is nothing else to compare with becoming healed and free. Our experience over many years of bringing Restoring the Foundations ministry to individuals and couples (not to mention our own 20+ years of healing) is that this is essential for effective and fruitful ministry. Other than being born again, there is no other event that changes lives for the good in such a radical way.

As Leaders and Intercessors prepare to develop and implement the Action Plan, the receiving of their own personal Restoring the Foundations ministry from a Healing House Network team is a vital part of the plan. We need to recover as much legal ground as possible before serious engagement with the enemy. We do not want to engage him in warfare with vulnerable openings. We want to remove all access points that exist because of Sins of the Fathers and Resulting Curses. We want to cancel all agreements with the demonic because of Ungodly Beliefs and renew our minds with Godly Beliefs. We want to receive healing to our heart for all wounds so the pain is gone and we no longer react sinfully when someone pokes in a (formerly) tender place. And then we want to have the fun of kicking out the demons that have taken advantage of all of these things through lies and oppression all along the way. We want complete healing and freedom, receiving all we can get.

We will then be ready for the next step as we prepare to conduct spiritual warfare.

2. Receive Equipping

We have not emphasized "equipping" in this book. Our purpose here is to acquaint you with the sources of problems, the negative spiritual roots behind them, God's solution for these problems, and the procedure to go through to remove the negative spiritual roots, thus eliminating the problems. There are many books available that will help someone become a better Intercessor, as well as proficient in other areas of ministry, i.e., the prophetic. There are anointed ministries that we can go to for training and practice. So we will not detail this aspect of preparation, even though we do want to encourage you to become a competent warrior, ready for battle.

On the other hand, it would be good if the person selected to be the Prophetic Intercessor member of the Implementation Team is already equipped and experienced. If not this person, then it would be good if at least one company Intercessor was already matured and seasoned in his/her gifting and call. We would caution, however, that even a mature Intercessor should desire to receive personal healing and freedom to insure minimum access for the enemy before assuming the role of primary Intercessor for the company. This is a high level position, a high profile target position, and the Leaders must insure that this person is free of the hazards we detailed earlier and is free from any infiltration or influence by the principalities over the company.

Books and Practice
You will also want to provide for the Intercessors some of the many good books available on Intercession, spiritual warfare, hearing the voice of the Lord, the prophetic, gifts of the Holy Spirit, and the demonic. We have included a number of the ones we feel are "on track" with God in the Bibliography.[1] Between what is presented in this book, in the *Restoring the Foundations* book, and in these other books, there are ample resources available. However, the most important thing that will blend all of

---

[1] We have also listed a number of ministries that are called to equip in these specialized areas in the Ministries Resource page at the end of this book.

the Intercessors into an effective team of Intercessors is "practice." After their basic training, having the Intercessors come together to "practice" their gifts and calling using the approach presented here will help them mature and season faster than any number of books. We would also suggest an ongoing training program be a part of the practice sessions.

As the Intercessors begin to practice, they can practice on the "real" issues of the business, the Development of the Action Plan and the needed revelation from the Lord. The only cautions are to not allow them to go beyond their boundaries for their level of healing and maturity and to evaluate all "words" carefully. It is the Leaders responsibility to cover and protect the Intercessors as they grow and mature.

The quality and quantity of Intercessors in your business will determine how rapidly you can implement an Action Plan. Attempting to implement it before suitable mature Intercessors are available is unwise. It is probably better to continue "as is" until the Holy Spirit gives the "go-ahead."

C. Commissioning of Intercessors

It is past time to change how Intercessors are recognized and treated. They are no longer the "little old ladies" meeting on Tuesday or Thursday morning. They may be "little old ladies," but they, and others, are being updated and anointed for today's battles. Praise the Lord for these serious prayer warriors.

It is time for formal and official commissioning and release of Intercessors as respected and trusted partners of God's team. It is time for public recognition for all to see and know who the Intercessors are. It is time for public declaration that the organization's Leaders and Intercessors are joint partners in carrying forward the Kingdom vision of the Lord.

The benefit of the public commissioning and release of the Intercessors is the official declaration of covering, protection, responsibility, respect, authority, and anointing to them. It is the public display of righteous Leadership coming together with righteous Intercessors, in unity and agreement, for purpose and destiny. This can be powerful. It is two sides of a spearhead being readied for thrusting into the enemy's camp.

For a business or a church, we recommend that during a public meeting the organization's Intercessors be introduced to the group. They can be prayed for, prophesied over, commissioned, anointed, and released into their ministry. If they have the more specialized calling of Watchmen or Gatekeeper, this calling can be recognized and released as well.

For the business preparing to implement the *Transforming Your Business* Action Plan, the Preparation Meeting is a good time to publicly introduce, commission, and release the Intercessors.

IMPORTANT
The only exception to having a public meeting is if the Intercessors need to be protected from people that might attend a general meeting, including possible "plants," i.e., witches or other enemy agents in the organization. If they need to be kept hidden from public view for a season until the Holy Spirit has begun to cleanse the company, a meeting with just the Leaders and Intercessors is the more prudent thing to do. The public meeting can come later, when the enemy is no longer active within the individuals of the business.

D. Procedure for Spiritual Warfare

Now we can pray. Let's go to the prayer room and begin!

1. Leader's Prayer

We discussed the importance of at least one of the Leaders being present to cover and protect the Intercessors and the meeting. We will refer you back to page 223 for these details. In essence, the Leader is present to represent the entire company: all of the other Leaders, all of the Intercessors, and all of the other employees. His responsibility is to start the meeting with an Opening Prayer. We suggest that the prayer include ingredients such as:

- thanksgiving to God for the privilege of knowing and serving Him
- thanksgiving for the vision and God's purpose for the business
- thanksgiving for God's ordained success as the business pursues God's plans and purposes
- submission to the authority and sovereignty of God
- affirming the ownership of the business by God (if transfer of the business to God can be done and has been done)
- declaring the expectation that God will provide everything needed for successful management and operation of the business.
- declaring that the business is to display the Lord's glory to the world and advance the Kingdom of God further into the marketplace and society.
- forgiveness of all who have sinned against the company and its personnel
- confession of any and all sins not already repented of and covered by the blood of Jesus Christ (pause for a minute to allow each Intercessor to confess their personal Baggage)
- binding all demons/demonic strongholds/principalities that would try to interfere in or disrupt the meeting
- delegating to the Intercessors authority to represent the business and the Leaders before the throne of God
- inviting the Holy Spirit to come and control the meeting
- asking the Holy Spirit to release and impart His gifts, with special mention of the gifts of Word of Knowledge, Word of Wisdom, faith, prophecy, discerning of spirits, and healings
- asking the Holy Spirit to release discernment and revelation of negative spiritual roots, strategies of the enemy, planned counter attacks, people that need help, and any other hidden thing that the Leaders need to know.

The Leader need not pray every one of these items every time the Intercessors meet. The point is to be sensitive to the Holy

Spirit and pray prophetically, being aware that these are important ingredients to consider with Him whether to include or not.

The Leader continues to pray for and cover the lead Intercessor and the group as they intercede for the business.

2. What's on God's Heart?

As the Leader releases the Intercessors into prayer, we would suggest a period when everyone prays at the same time. The purpose is to align our spirits with the Spirit of God, to become more sensitive, to "tune in" to the Voice of the Lord. Those who have their prayer language can pray using it, so that the Holy Spirit is controlling what they pray.[1]

After a short time, the Intercessors can begin to inquire of the Lord, "What is on Your heart at this time? What do You want us to pray so that Your Will, will be accomplish here at this time?" As each one listens to the still small voice[2] of the Holy Spirit, he can begin to write or type on a notebook computer the impressions he is sensing to share later for group prayer.

3. Spiritual Warfare Prayers

The meeting can flow in several different directions as the Intercessors move into the next phase of the meeting. Since the control of the meeting has been turned over to the Holy Spirit, He will orchestrate it according to His purposes.

Protocol
In order to follow the Holy Spirit, we recommend that there be an agreed upon protocol that only one person, the lead Intercessor in charge of the meeting, be responsible for "steering" the

---

[1]　Roman 8:26-27 lets us know that the Spirit of God prays God's will on our behalf even when we do not know what or how to pray.

[2]　God's "still small voice" is identified in I Kings 19:2 and Psalm 40:10.

flow of the meeting. He is responsible for synthesizing the various sensing from the different Intercessors, and what he himself is discerning of the ebb and flow of the Spirit. His job is to stay in alignment with the Spirit, and the other Intercessors are to follow his lead. If he misses it and the Holy Spirit turns "right" while he continues straight ahead, or turns "left," the others are to still follow his lead. We trust that God is bigger than our mistakes and maturing struggles and that the Holy Spirit will get the Intercessors back on track if necessary. Usually a "flurry" of sensings will occur and a stream of notes will be passed to the lead Intercessor helping him/her realign with the Holy Spirit.

Normally, the group will begin to pray what they hear from the Holy Spirit as He answers their question, "What is on Your heart, God?" With the lead Intercessor and others agreeing, one person at a time can pray "into" what he sensed from God. At least one person should record what is being expressed. We do not want to lose what God is saying. It is likely that much of it will pertain to issues the Leaders are facing.

The group might ask other questions of the Lord (one at a time, of course) as the meeting progresses. They might ask questions such as:

- "Lord, what preventative/defensive measures do we need to do today, to stop the enemy before he can get started?"
- "Lord, what do we need to do to advance our business and thus the Kingdom of God today?"
- "Lord, what new Open Doors do we need to pray about?"
- "Lord, what is on Your heart and mind that You want us to agree with You about today?"

As the Intercessors hear the answer to the question, they can either pray out God's will or submit their sensing to the lead Intercessor for his discernment as to what to do. He can then lead the group in appropriate declarations, prophetic acts, intense praying in the Spirit, etc.

As the business is developing and then implementing the Action Plan, we would expect much of the dialog with God to bring forth knowledge and wisdom needed to effectively execute the Action Plan. We emphasized a number of times in Parts Two and Three that we would want to inquire of the Lord to obtain the details needed.

We also expect, that at times, the Holy Spirit desires Intercession for the employees of the company. He will have us bind the prince of the power of the air and his ability to confuse and blind the minds of the people. There might be intercession to free them from hooks and traps and other things keeping them from whole-heartedly participating in the Action Plan and even their destiny. Sometimes there might be intercession regarding legal ground to be taken back. Other times the Holy Spirit will have us interceding that Satan's strategies fail, that confusion, turmoil, and forgetfulness be released into the enemy's camp, that groups assigned to attack the business be disbanded and their assignments canceled. All sorts of amazing things can happen in the "heavenlies" when we come together in unity and agreement that God's will be done here on earth as it is in heaven! An Intercession meeting should be the high point of the day!

4. Meeting Wrap-up

When it is time to bring the Intercession to a stop, the Leader again assumes responsibility for the meeting. He has two important tasks to accomplish.

Covering and Release

The Leader prays to close the meeting. As he does this, he prays for the Intercessors: that *the blood of the Lamb cover and protect* them as they separate and go their own ways; and that they be enabled *to release all false responsibility* for the revelations that have come forth.

We would encourage the Intercessors to make deliberate declarations of release, and that they turn all responsibility for the interpretation and understanding of the revelations over to the Leaders.

Their job was to do the spiritual warfare so as to enable the receiving of the revelations. It is the Leaders' job: *to seek* the Lord; *to verify* what is from God and what (if any) is not; and *to incorporate* the results into the operation of the business and the Action Plan.

5. Confirming His Word

One of the major safeguards the Lord has given to us as we seek to hear His voice is the confirmation of His Word. God, knowing that we can miss His voice in and amongst the clatter and confusions of many demonic voices and our own human spirit voice, established a principle for verification. Jesus declares in Matthew 18:16 *"that in the mouth of two or three witnesses every word may be established."* Jesus based this on Deuteronomy 17:6 and 19:15, where God established the principle of multiple witnesses. This is, by the way, still in use in our court rooms today.

IMPORTANT
As the Leaders ponder the reports from the Intercessors meeting: They can pray and hear God's voice for themselves as to the validity (or not) of the different revelations; If they are not sure what God is saying, or they are not in agreement, they can "table" that part and come back to it another time. Or they can "send it back" to the Intercessors, requesting that they ask God for more clarity. **God really wants us to have success. He will work with us to insure we get it right if our heart attitudes are right**; i.e., humble and submitted.

E. Counterattacks and Strategy

In the introduction to Part Three, we discussed Preemptive Strikes by the Intercessors to shut down the enemy even as the business was preparing an Action Plan (page 111). We also have mentioned possible counterattacks by the enemy as the battle is engaged and advances are made. Generally speaking, the enemy will attempt to stop and reverse the gains *as they are made*. We don't have to be naive and allow him to do this. As

249

we quoted in the introduction to Part Four, the *"best defense is an offense."* The Bible gives many examples of counterattacks by the enemies of Israel after great victories. However, when they sought God, He always gave them creative alternative strategies to thwart the enemy and bring another victory.

The focus of the counterattacks will be the Intercessors, Leaders, their families, customers, employees, and vendors, as well as the equipment, facilities, and internal functioning of the business. The demonic principalities will check every potential "Open Door," looking for an avenue that will allow them to bring maximum havoc to the company.

This situation can be handled in a 1-2-3-4 approach. First, the Intercessors are given the assignment to apply the Blood of Jesus to each potential "Open Door" and seal it so that the demonic/principalities can not use it. This is particularly important before the "Initiate Action" meeting. Second, as the Leaders and Intercessors go through their personal Restoring the Foundations ministry, they will "close" many of their own Open Doors, reducing their vulnerability. Third, at the Initiate Action Meeting and thereafter, the company itself will have fewer Open Doors available for counterattacks. Fourth, the Intercessors will continue to function as Watchmen on the wall to discern planned attacks, so that the Leaders and Intercessors together can speak confusion into the ranks of the enemy and dismiss each demon and principality before the battle can be launched.

This approach will greatly, if not completely, help the company proceed rapidly through the elements of the Action Plan and onward.

Ending

Hasta La Vista

We have come to the end of the main portion of the book. We pray that this journey we have taken together has helped you become more spiritually aware than when you started, and that you are ready to take spiritual charge of your life. You now have the basics and the

> *You are ready to take spiritual charge of your life!*

procedures to remove the negative spiritual roots from your business, church, civic club, governmental unit, and any other organization of which you are a part. Write and let us know how it goes.

God Bless You,
Chester Kylstra

PS: Look for the second edition of *Transforming Your Business* with the included case studies. Perhaps a part of your story can be included in it. We are planning for a mid-year, 2008, release.

PPS: Also look for the companion first edition of *Leading a Transformed Business* early in 2007.

Appendices

Appendix A

Action Plan Template
Information Gathering

Appendix A contains an Action Plan Template that can be filled in and completed for your business. It is ordered the same as the components of the Action Plan: Information Gathering, Planning, and then Implementing (pages 125, 132, and 157). You may copy these pages and customize them for your business or organization. Even better, you may download a Word Document version of this Appendix A from the web site at www.TransformingYourBusiness.org. Using the Word Document will allow you to easily expand the form and to "fill in the blanks."

Contact Information

Name of Person(s) filling out this form: _____

Date: _____

Mobile Phone & Email Address: _____

_____

I. Organization Information

Name: _____

Address: _____

_____

_____

Phone: _____ Web Site: _____

Email: _____

Vision and Mission Statement: _____

_____

_____

_____

_____

_____

_____

_____

_____

_____

Product(s) and/or Service(s): _____

_____

_____

_____

_____

_____

_____

_____

_____

_____

_____

_____

_____

II. Current Leaders/Principals

1) Name: _____

Position: _____

Contact Information: _____

How Long with Organization?: _____

Decision Influence (1-10): _____

Willing to "Stand In" for current and former Leaders? _____

Willing to examine his contribution to existing problems?: ____

2) Name: _____

Position: _____

Contact Information: _____

How Long with Organization?: _____

Decision Influence (1-10): _____

Willing to "Stand In" for current and former Leaders? _____

Willing to examine his contribution to existing problems?: ____

3) Name: _____

Position: _____

Contact Information: _____

How Long with Organization?: _____

Decision Influence (1-10): _____

Willing to "Stand In" for current and former Leaders? _____

Willing to examine his contribution to existing problems?: ____

III. Historical Baseline Data

It is important to have good baseline data before starting the ministry for Transforming Your Business. Otherwise, how will we know if any benefit has come from the ministry? How will we know if there are certain areas within the business that do not seem to be responding to the ministry and thus may need additional focused ministry? The following is the type of data we suggest you "extract" from your historical records.

A. Overall Business

Gross income (Sales by products, by services, by departments, by time, by price), expenses (officer salaries, management salaries, employee salaries and wages, inventory valuation, inventory Cost of Goods Sold (COGS), expense breakdowns by activity/budget including taxes by jurisdiction/type, etc.).

_____

_____

_____

_____

_____

B. Marketing

Budgets, channels, percent of sales, percent of expenses, estimated effectiveness, etc.

_____

_____

_____

_____

_____

_____

C. Production

Product/Service lines. For each line or department: its budget, value added, income producing rank, percentage of employees, estimated effectiveness, etc.

_____

_____

_____

_____

_____

_____

_____

D. Employees

Number of employees, by department or production/service line, growth rate, turnover rate; employees' satisfaction level with their job, employers' satisfaction level with employees' performance, gifts and personalities matched with jobs (using spiritual gifts and personality determination questionnaires or the equivalent); salaries and bonuses, percent of total expenses, growth rate (anything else of significance).

_____

_____

_____

_____

_____

_____

_____

E. Customers

Number of customers, growth rate, their satisfaction level, spending levels and amounts, frequency of purchasing, personalities and attitudes survey, loyalty, etc.

_____

_____

_____

_____

_____

_____

_____

_____

F. Vendors

Number of venders, growth rate, satisfaction level, cost levels and amounts, frequency of orders, personalities and attitudes survey, loyalty, etc.

_____

_____

_____

_____

_____

_____

_____

_____

IV. "Beginnings" Information

Date Organized/Started: _____

Where Organized: _____

Purpose Organized: _____

Original Location Land/Structures: _____

_____

_____

Significant Information about Location: _____

_____

_____

2) Intermediary Location Land/Structures: _____

_____

_____

Significant Information about Location: _____

_____

_____

3) Intermediary Location Land/Structures: _____

_____

_____

Significant Information about Location: _____

_____

_____

_____

V. Previous Leaders/Principals

1) Name: _____

    Position: _____

Contact Information: _____

How Long with Organization?: _____

Decision Influence (1-10): _____

Contribution(s) to existing problem(s): _____

_____

_____

_____

_____

_____

2) Name: _____

    Position: _____

Contact Information: _____

How Long with Organization?: _____

Decision Influence (1-10): _____

Contribution(s) to existing problem(s): _____

_____

_____

_____

_____

_____

VI. Organizational Patterns: Fruit

Please list and explain the dominant characteristics of your business/organization. In other words, what do people (customers, vendors, employees) say about you? What is your reputation? For what are you known? What do other people/companies expect you to do? How do you respond to requests from the outside? How widely spread is your influence? In other words, what do people "see" and expect when they think about your business?

_____

_____

_____

_____

_____

_____

_____

_____

_____

_____

_____

_____

_____

_____

_____

VII. Historical Spiritual Mapping

Sins of the Founding Fathers and resulting Curses
Sins of the Resident Fathers and resulting Curses

We want to begin to find out about past sins and curses for both the founders and previous leaders, as well as for those living on the land and occupying structures. We want to list all occurrences of significant sinful events, sinful patterns, or other important influences that have happened on the land and/or within the structures, or that the founders have experienced. Consider including books and citing historical references that add to the understanding of what has happened in years past. Long-time residents of the area may also be a significant source. Please be as thorough as possible to insure that all significant negative influences given place in the past can be removed.

_____

_____

_____

_____

_____

_____

_____

_____

_____

_____

_____

_____

_____

_____

VIII. Revelation Spiritual Mapping

Sins of the Founding Fathers and resulting Curses
Sins of the Resident Fathers and resulting Curses

On the previous page we listed natural knowledge, i.e., information available to us through natural means. We are still looking for sources/roots, but now we will list what the Holy Spirit shows regarding past occurrences of significant sinful events, sinful patterns, or other important influences that have happened on the land and/or within the structures, or with the founders and previous leaders.

_____

_____

_____

_____

_____

_____

_____

_____

_____

_____

_____

_____

_____

_____

IX. Organizational Sins and Curses Groups: Open Doors/Roots

Contributed by:
F -- Founding/Previous Fathers
R -- Previous Resident Fathers
C -- Current Leadership

OPEN DOORS (Gen 4:7)

Please consider the following groups of Sins of the Fathers and Resulting Curses for the two set of Fathers: the Founding and previous Fathers of the business/organization (SOFFCs) and the previous Resident Fathers (SORFCs) that occupied the land and structures. We are looking for known character and personality traits that are **negative, undesirable, undermining, and most likely, sinful**. As you review the following tables check the items that apply. Check the first column "**F**" for the **F**ounders and previous Leaders of the organization. Check the second column "**R**" for the previous **R**esident Fathers (the ones occupying the land and the structures). Please check the third column "**C**" for those characteristics and personality traits that you observe in the **C**urrent Leadership, including yourself if you are one of the leaders. Please pray and ask the Holy Spirit to highlight each item that should be checked, whether or not you have natural knowledge concerning the item.

F R C   **F R C**

__ __ __ **ABANDONMENT**	__ __ __ **RELIGION**
__ __ __ Abdication	__ __ __ Antichrist
__ __ __ Blocked Intimacy	__ __ __ Betrayal
__ __ __ Desertion	__ __ __ Denominationalism
__ __ __ Divorce	__ __ __ Division
__ __ __ Isolation	__ __ __ Hypocrisy
__ __ __ Loneliness	__ __ __ Injustice
__ __ __ Neglect	__ __ __ Legalism
__ __ __ Rejection	__ __ __ Liberalism
__ __ __ Separation	__ __ __ New Age Practices
__ __ __ Self-Pity	__ __ __ Religiosity
__ __ __ Victimization	__ __ __ Rules, Excessive
__ __ __ _____	__ __ __ Spiritual Pride
__ __ __ _____	__ __ __ Traditionalism
	__ __ __ Unforgiveness
__ __ __ **REJECTION**	__ __ __ _____
__ __ __ Expected Rejection	__ __ __ _____
__ __ __ Perceived Rejection	
__ __ __ Self-Rejection	__ __ __ **PERFORMANCE**
__ __ __ _____	__ __ __ Competition
__ __ __ _____	__ __ __ Driving
	__ __ __ Envy
__ __ __ **REBELLION**	__ __ __ Jealousy
__ __ __ Contempt	__ __ __ People Pleasing
__ __ __ Deception	__ __ __ Perfectionism
__ __ __ Defiance	__ __ __ Possessiveness
__ __ __ Disobedience	__ __ __ Rivalry
__ __ __ Disrespect	__ __ __ Striving
__ __ __ Independence	__ __ __ Workaholism
__ __ __ Insubordination	__ __ __ _____
__ __ __ Resistance	__ __ __ _____
__ __ __ Self-Sufficiency	
__ __ __ Self-Will	
__ __ __ Stubbornness	
__ __ __ Undermining	
__ __ __ Usurping Authority	
__ __ __ _____	

267

F R C   **F R C**

MAMMON/FINANCES	**DECEPTION**
Bankruptcy	Cheating
Cheating	Confusion
Covetousness	Denial
Debt	Fraudulence
Deception	Infidelity
Delinquency	Lying
Dishonesty	Secretiveness
Failure	Self-Deception
Fear of Loss	Treachery
Greed	Treason
Idolatry of Possessions	Trickery
Irresponsible Spending	Untrustworthiness
Job Failures	_____
Job Losses	_____
Lack	
Lawsuits	**MENTAL PROBLEMS**
Love of Money	Craziness
Poverty	Compulsions
Not Tithing (Robbing)	Confusion
Stealing	Distraction
Stinginess	Forgetfulness
_____	Hallucinations
_____	Hysteria
	Insanity
ANXIETY	Mind Binding
Burden	Mind Blocking
False Responsibility	Paranoia
Fatigue	Mind Racing
Heaviness	Schizophrenia
Nervousness	Senility
Restlessness	_____
Weariness	_____
Worry	
_____	
_____	

F R C   **F R C**

_ _ _ **ADDICTIONS/**	_ _ _ **ESCAPE**
DEPENDENCIES/	_ _ _ Daydreaming
ESCAPE	_ _ _ Fantasy
_ _ _ Cocaine	_ _ _ Forgetfulness
_ _ _ Downers/Uppers	_ _ _ Hopelessness
_ _ _ Marijuana	_ _ _ Isolation
_ _ _ Non-Prescription Drugs	_ _ _ Laziness
_ _ _ Prescription Drugs	_ _ _ Passivity
_ _ _ Street Drugs	_ _ _ Procrastination
_ _ _ Tranquilizers	_ _ _ Sleep/Slumber/
_ _ _ _____	Oversleeping
_ _ _ _____	_ _ _ Trance
	_ _ _ Withdrawal
_ _ _ Alcohol	_ _ _ _____
_ _ _ Caffeine	_ _ _ _____
_ _ _ Cigarettes	
_ _ _ Computers	_ _ _ **UNMOTIVATED**
_ _ _ Food	_ _ _ Irresponsibility
_ _ _ Gambling	_ _ _ Laziness
_ _ _ Internet	_ _ _ Procrastination
_ _ _ Pornography	_ _ _ Undisciplined
_ _ _ Overspending	_ _ _ _____
_ _ _ Sex	_ _ _ _____
_ _ _ Sports	
_ _ _ Television	
_ _ _ Video Games	
_ _ _ _____	
_ _ _ _____	

F R C

F R C

_____ **UNBELIEF**	_____ **MOCKING**
_____ Apprehension	_____ Blaspheming
_____ Double Mindedness	_____ Cursing
_____ Doubt	_____ Laughing
_____ Fear of being Wrong	_____ Profanity
_____ Mind Blocking	_____ Ridicule
_____ Mistrust	_____ Sarcasm
_____ Rationalism	_____ Scorn
_____ Skepticism	_____ _____
_____ Suspicion	_____ _____
_____ Uncertainty	
_____ _____	_____ **ANGER**
_____ _____	_____ Abandonment
	_____ Feuding
_____ **PRIDE**	_____ Frustration
_____ Arrogance	_____ Hatred
_____ Conceit	_____ Hostility
_____ Controlling	_____ Murder
_____ Egotistical	_____ Punishment
_____ Haughtiness	_____ Rage
_____ Leviathan	_____ Resentment
_____ Prejudice	_____ Retaliation
_____ Self-Centeredness	_____ Revenge
_____ Self-Importance	_____ Spoiled Little Boy/Girl
_____ Vanity	_____ Temper Tantrums
_____ _____	_____ Violence
_____ _____	_____ _____
	_____ _____

F R C **F R C**

_ _ _ _ **BITTERNESS**	_ _ _ _ **DEPRESSION**
_ _ _ _ Accusation	_ _ _ _ Dejection
_ _ _ _ Blaming	_ _ _ _ Discouragement
_ _ _ _ Complaining	_ _ _ _ Despair
_ _ _ _ Condemnation	_ _ _ _ Despondency
_ _ _ _ Criticalness	_ _ _ _ Gloominess
_ _ _ _ Gossip	_ _ _ _ Hopelessness
_ _ _ _ Judging	_ _ _ _ Insomnia
_ _ _ _ Murmuring	_ _ _ _ Misery
_ _ _ _ Ridicule	_ _ _ _ Oversleeping
_ _ _ _ Slander	_ _ _ _ Sadness
_ _ _ _ Unforgiveness	_ _ _ _ Self-Pity
_ _ _ _____	_ _ _ _ Suicide Attempt
_ _ _ _____	_ _ _ _ Suicide Fantasies
	_ _ _ _ Withdrawal
_ _ _ _ **VIOLENCE**	_ _ _ _____
_ _ _ _ Abuse	_ _ _ _____
_ _ _ _ Arguing	
_ _ _ _ Bickering	_ _ _ _ **TRAUMA**
_ _ _ _ Cruelty	_ _ _ _ Abuse, Emotional
_ _ _ _ Cursing	_ _ _ _ Abuse, Physical
_ _ _ _ Death	_ _ _ _ Abuse, Mental
_ _ _ _ Destruction	_ _ _ _ Abuse, Sexual
_ _ _ _ Feuding	_ _ _ _ Abuse, Spiritual
_ _ _ _ Hate	_ _ _ _ Abuse, Verbal
_ _ _ _ Mocking	_ _ _ _ Accident
_ _ _ _ Murder/Abortion	_ _ _ _ Loss
_ _ _ _ Retaliation	_ _ _ _ Imprisoned
_ _ _ _ Strife	_ _ _ _ Rape
_ _ _ _ Torture/Mutilation	_ _ _ _ Torture
_ _ _ _____	_ _ _ _ Violence
_ _ _ _____	_ _ _ _____
	_ _ _ _____

271

F R C   **F R C**

_____ **GRIEF**	_____ **UNWORTHINESS**
_____ Agony	_____ Inadequacy
_____ Anguish	_____ Inferiority
_____ Crying	_____ Insecurity
_____ Despair	_____ Self-Accusation
_____ Heartbreak	_____ Self-Condemnation
_____ Loss	_____ Self-Hate
_____ Pain	_____ Self-Punishment
_____ Sadness	_____ _____
_____ Sorrow	_____ _____
_____ Torment	
_____ Weeping	_____ **VICTIM**
_____ _____	_____ Appeasement
_____ _____	_____ Betrayal
	_____ Deportation
_____ **SHAME**	_____ Entrapped
_____ Anger	_____ Helplessness
_____ Bad Boy/Girl	_____ Hopelessness
_____ Condemnation	_____ Mistrust
_____ Disgrace	_____ Passivity
_____ Embarrassment	_____ Self-Pity
_____ Guilt	_____ Suspicion
_____ Hatred	_____ Trauma
_____ Inferiority	_____ Unfaithfulness
_____ Self-Accusation	_____ _____
_____ Self-Hate	_____ _____
_____ Self-Pity	
_____ _____	_____ **FAILURE**
_____ _____	_____ Boom/Bust Cycle
	_____ Defeat
	_____ Loss
	_____ Performance
	_____ Pressure to Succeed
	_____ Striving
	_____ _____
	_____ _____

272

F R C

F R C

				INFIRMITIES/
				DISEASE
				Accidents (falls, cars)
				Anorexia/Bulimia
				Arthritis
				Asthma
				Barrenness/Miscarriage
				Bone/Joint Problems
				Cancer
				Congestion/in lungs
				Diabetes
				Fatigue
				Female Problems
				Heart/Circulatory
				Problems
				Lung Problems
				Mental Illness
				MS
				Migraines/Mind Binding
				Physical Abnormalities
				Premature Death

_____ _____ _____ _____

_____ _____ _____ _____

_____ _____ _____ _____

_____ _____ _____ _____

_____ _____ _____ _____

_____ _____ _____ _____

_____ _____ _____ _____

CONTROL

_____ _____ _____ Appeasement

_____ _____ _____ Denial

_____ _____ _____ Enabling

_____ _____ _____ False Responsibility

_____ _____ _____ Female Control

_____ _____ _____ Jealousy

_____ _____ _____ Male Control

_____ _____ _____ Occult Control/Jezebel

_____ _____ _____ Passive Aggression

_____ _____ _____ Passivity/Ahab

_____ _____ _____ Possessiveness

_____ _____ _____ Pride (I know best)

_____ _____ _____ Witchcraft

_____ _____ _____ _____

_____ _____ _____ _____

_____ _____ _____ _____

_____ _____ _____ _____

_____ _____ _____ _____

_____ _____ _____ **Leadership Style**

_____ _____ _____ Authoritarian

_____ _____ _____ Abusive

_____ _____ _____ Coercion

_____ _____ _____ Domineering

_____ _____ _____ Double Binding

_____ _____ _____ Manipulation

_____ _____ _____ Micro-Managing

_____ _____ _____ _____

_____ _____ _____ _____

_____ _____ _____ _____

_____ _____ _____ _____

F R C **F R C**

	FEARS		Fear of Public Singing
___ ___ ___	Anxiety	___ ___ ___	Fear of Success
___ ___ ___	Bewilderment	___ ___ ___	Fear of Violence
___ ___ ___	Burden	___ ___ ___	_____
___ ___ ___	Dread	___ ___ ___	_____
___ ___ ___	Harassment	___ ___ ___	_____
___ ___ ___	Heaviness	___ ___ ___	_____
___ ___ ___	Horror Movies	___ ___ ___	_____
___ ___ ___	Intimidation		
___ ___ ___	Mental Torment	___ ___ ___	**SEXUAL SINS**
___ ___ ___	Over-Sensitivity	___ ___ ___	Abortion
___ ___ ___	Paranoia	___ ___ ___	Adultery
___ ___ ___	Phobia	___ ___ ___	Bestiality
___ ___ ___	Superstition	___ ___ ___	Demonic Sex
___ ___ ___	Worry	___ ___ ___	Defilement/Uncleanness
___ ___ ___	Fear of Authorities	___ ___ ___	Exposure
___ ___ ___	Fear of being Abused	___ ___ ___	Fantasy Lust
___ ___ ___	Fear of being Attacked	___ ___ ___	Fornication
___ ___ ___	Fear of being Wrong	___ ___ ___	Frigidity
___ ___ ___	Fear of being a Victim	___ ___ ___	Homosexuality
___ ___ ___	Fear of Cancer	___ ___ ___	Illegitimacy
___ ___ ___	Fear of Death	___ ___ ___	Incest
___ ___ ___	Fear of Diabetes	___ ___ ___	Incubus
___ ___ ___	Fear of Exposure	___ ___ ___	Lesbianism
___ ___ ___	Fear of Failure	___ ___ ___	Lust/Fantasy Lust
___ ___ ___	Fear of Heart Attack	___ ___ ___	Masturbation
___ ___ ___	Fear of Infirmities	___ ___ ___	Pornography
___ ___ ___	Fear of Loss	___ ___ ___	Premarital Sex
___ ___ ___	Fear of Man	___ ___ ___	Prostitution/Harlotry
___ ___ ___	Fear of Performing	___ ___ ___	Rape
___ ___ ___	Fear of Poverty	___ ___ ___	Seduction/Alluring
___ ___ ___	Fear of Punishment	___ ___ ___	Sexual Abuse
___ ___ ___	Fear of Rejection	___ ___ ___	Succubus
___ ___ ___	Fear of Sexual	___ ___ ___	_____
	Inadequacy	___ ___ ___	_____
___ ___ ___	Fear of Sexual		
	Perversion		

274

F R C   **F R C**

____ **OCCULT**	____ Mediumship
____ Abortion (Molech)	____ Mental Telepathy
____ Accident Proneness	____ Necromancy
____ Ahab	____ Non-Christian Exorcism
____ Animal Spirits	____ Ouija Board
____ Antichrist	____ Palm Reading
____ Astral Projection	____ Past Life Readings
____ Astrology	____ Pendulum Readings
____ Automatic Writing	____ Psychic Readings
____ Behemoth	____ Psychic Healing
____ Black Magic	____ Python
____ Books, Occult/Witchcraft	____ Reincarnation
____ Clairvoyance	____ Satanic Worship
____ Conjuration	____ Séances
____ Control, Occult/Witchcraft	____ Slavery, Occult
____ Crystal Ball	____ Sorcery
____ Death, Suicide	____ Spells
____ Demons, Dispatching	____ Spirit Guide(s)
____ Demon Worship	____ Spiritism
____ Divination	____ Superstition
____ Eastern Meditation	____ Table Tipping
____ Eight Ball	____ Tarot Cards
____ Evil Eye	____ Tea Leaves, Reading
____ ESP	____ Third Eye, Using
____ False Gifts (Occult)	____ Trance
____ Fortune Telling	____ Transcend. Meditation
____ Handwriting Analysis	____ Vampire
____ Hexing	____ Victim, Occult
____ Horoscopes	____ Voodoo
____ Hypnosis	____ Water Witching
____ I Ching	____ Werewolf
____ Idolatry (of ____)	____ White Magic
____ Incantations	____ Wicca
____ Jezebel	____ Witchcraft
____ Levitation	____ _____
____ Leviathan	____ _____

OPEN DOORS (Gen 4:7)

INVOLVEMENT IN SECRET SOCIETIES, LODGES, CULTS, FALSE RELIGIONS, OCCULT AND MIND CONTROL ORGANIZATIONS

Please check all organizations that the Leaders are joined with or to which they belong., even if they were members for just a short time.

(The following are examples of groups which omit the foundations of the Christian Faith, such as the Trinity, the Atonement, the Blood of Jesus, or the Divinity of Jesus. Many are also "secret" societies that require the initiates to take a bloody oath not to divulge the secrets of the organization.)

F R C

F R C

____ Armstrong/Radio Church of God	____ Mormonism
____ Bahai	____ New Age Movement
____ Buddhism	____ Odd Fellows Lodge
____ Buffaloes	____ Orange Lodge
____ Christadelphians	____ Rainbow Girls Lodge
____ Christian Science	____ Rebekahs Lodge
____ College Fraternities	____ Religious Science
____ College Sororities	____ Rosacrucianism
____ Daughter's of the Nile	____ Santeria
____ De Molay Lodge	____ Satanism
____ Druids Lodge	____ Scientology
____ Eastern Religions	____ Shamanism
____ Eastern Star Lodge	____ Shintoism
____ Edgar Cayce	____ Shriners
____ Elks Lodge	____ Silva Mind Control
____ Freemasonry	____ Spiritualism
____ Hari Khrisna	____ Swedenborgianism
____ Hinduism	____ Knights Templars
____ Indian Occult Rituals	____ The Way International
____ Inner Peace Movement	____ The Christian Educational Society
____ Islam	____ Theosophy
____ Jehovah's Witnesses	____ Unitarian Church
____ Job's Daughters Lodge	____ Voodoo
____ Kabbala	____ Wicca
____ KKK	____ White Shrine
____ Knights of Columbus Lodge	____ Witchcraft
____ Knights of Templar	____ _____
____ Masonic	____ _____
____ Moonies	
____ Moose Lodge	
____ _____	
____ _____	

X. Ungodly Organizational Culture: Attitudes and Beliefs

Beliefs, Expectations, Ethics, Procedures, Practices

These lists of possible ungodly attitudes, beliefs, expectations, practices, etc., are here to provide you a starting point as you discover and define the Organizational Culture.

A. General

☐ (Deception) The end justifies the means.

_____

_____

☐ (Deception, Dishonesty) A little cheating here and there is OK as long as it is not obvious.

_____

_____

☐ (Fear Based Decisions) We must insure that the board is not able to talk to the employees.

_____

_____

☐ (Deception, Fear, Expected Rejection) I have to be guarded at all times. Anything I say will likely be misunderstood or used against me.

_____

_____

_____

_____

B. Founders/Owners/Managers/Leaders

☐ (Rejection, Self-Pity) No one appreciates all of the hard work I do, or the leadership I provide.

_____

_____

☐ (Loneliness, Deception, Fear) People in this organization do their job, but they never really catch the vision of the company.

_____

_____

☐ (Deception, Fear, Hopelessness) Our company will never get ahead. We just go from one crisis to the next.

_____

_____

☐ (Distrust, Fear of being Cheated) We have to insure our employees "toe the line" and work a full eight hours each day.

_____

_____

_____

_____

_____

_____

_____

_____

_____

C. Employees/Members/Helpers/ Contractors/Consultants/Volunteers

☐ (Favoritism, Dishonesty) Promotion by favoritism (not achievement) is fine.

_____

_____

☐ (Favoritism, Strife, Resentment, Jealousy) Family members related to the Leader(s) are always "right" and should be respected above others.

_____

_____

☐ (Favoritism) The opinions of family members (related to the Leader(s)) should not be challenged.

_____

_____

☐ (Control, Anger) The only way to get somebody to do something is to appear angry and yell at them.

_____

_____

☐ (Competition, Killing, Fear, Rejection) Character assassination through gossip is fine – everybody does it.

_____

_____

_____

_____

☐ (Strife, Division, Hopelessness) Strife and division are normal. It is just the way it is.

_____

_____

☐ (Competition, Strife) It is OK to pit one department against another (or one group of workers against another).

_____

_____

☐ (Mistrust, Insecurity) I can't depend on the company "rules" staying the same. The company leaders change them whenever they want.

_____

_____

☐ (Hopelessness, Helplessness) Creativity will always be stifled. There is no place to share new ideas where they will be heard and appreciated.

_____

_____

☐ (Hopelessness, Helplessness, Depersonalizing) People don't matter. All that matters is just meeting the production quotas.

_____

_____

☐ (Victimization, Resentment) Even when the company does well, only the leaders will benefit.

_____

_____

☐ (Distrust, Resentment) The Leadership will say one thing but do something else. There is no consistency.

_____

_____

☐ (Discouragement, Victimization, Hopelessness) We have to keep sacrificing to try to get ahead but we never will.

_____

_____

☐ (Fear, Rejection) If anyone challenges the Leader(s), he will pay for it!

_____

_____

☐ (Victimization, Unfair) Leaders can be angry at employees, but there is no place for the employees to be angry or upset, or express what they feel.

_____

_____

☐ (Victimization, Unworthy) No one every listens or hears me.

_____

_____

_____

_____

_____

_____

_____

_____

D. Customers/Clients

☐ (Deception, Dishonesty) It's okay if we short-change our customers. They won't notice.

_____

_____

☐ (Deception, Dishonesty) Customers are so naive. I can tell them anything about our products and they'll believe me.

_____

_____

_____

_____

_____

_____

_____

_____

_____

_____

_____

_____

_____

_____

_____

_____

E. Vendors/Suppliers

☐ (Deception, Dishonesty, Fear) Our vendors will cheat us if we don't watch them and their paper work closely.

_____

_____

☐ (Deception, Dishonesty, Fear) While our customers should pay us within 30 days, it is OK to delay payment to our vendors in order to maximize our cash flow.

_____

_____

_____

_____

_____

_____

_____

_____

_____

_____

_____

_____

_____

_____

_____

XI. Organizational Hurts/Losses
Fractures, Divisions, Rebellion, Anger, etc.

In filling out this section, you might consider significant losses, such as loss of important contracts and proposals, personnel, leaders, etc. Also consider inter-departmental strife, gossip, rumors, attempted or successful management/leadership takeovers, rebellion, etc.

_____

_____

_____

_____

_____

_____

_____

_____

_____

_____

_____

_____

_____

_____

_____

_____

_____

XII. Organizational Oppression/Principalities

As you examine the historical record of the land and structures, the inheritance from the Founding Fathers, and the revelation from the Holy Spirit, you will become aware of which principalities are likely exerting influences on your organization. There is no need to list again the ones which are identical to the Sins of the Founding/Resident Fathers and resulting Curses listed in section IX. If you find additional ones, you can list them here. Attempt to classify them as either major or minor influences. You can combine principalities of similar natures into groups similarly to what we did in section IX.

_____

_____

_____

_____

_____

_____

_____

_____

_____

_____

_____

_____

_____

_____

_____

XIII. Final Comments

_____

_____

_____

_____

_____

_____

_____

_____

_____

_____

_____

_____

_____

_____

_____

_____

_____

_____

_____

_____

_____

_____

_____

Appendix A

Action Plan Template
Ministry Planning

Discussion for this part of the Action Plan starts on page 132.

I. Planning to Select and
Release the Development Team

This step will be done immediately by the Leadership Team once they begin the process of Transforming Your Business.

_____

Leader/Oversight: _____

_____

Prophetic Intercessor: _____

_____

Researcher(s): _____

_____

_____

_____

Strategist: _____

_____

Implementer: _____

_____

II. Planning to Select and Release the Intercessors

The plan for the Intercessors can vary widely depending on the answers to the questions on page 133. The plan can range from obtaining the services of outside consultants to hiring Intercessors to raising up current employees to already having mature Intercessors on staff. Whatever your situation, the Leadership Team can pray for the Lord to direct the business as the Action Plan is developed to select and release quality Intercessors to function within the business.

_____

_____

Plan to find business Intercessors: _____

_____

_____

Plan to find well-known Intercessor to hire as a consultant for training, for oversight: _____

_____

_____

Plan to equip/train/season Intercessors: _____

_____

_____

_____

Plan to oversee/cover Intercessors as they meet for prayer: _____

_____

_____

_____

III. Planning to Select and Release the Implementation Team

Select the several key individuals who will implement the Action Plan. To have some carryover, include at least one person from the Development Team. The Implementer or the Prophetic Intercessor are two possibilities of a person to serve on both teams but do what is best for your situation. You might review the skill set/gift mix suggested on page 134.

The release of the Implementation Team will officially start with the Preparation Meeting. However, this team should be well acquainted with the work of the Development Team and involved with the planning for implementation.

_____

_____

Public Leader:

_____

_____

_____

Prophetic Intercessor:

_____

_____

_____

Implementer:

_____

_____

_____

_____

IV. Planning Healing Ministry
for Appropriate Leadership and Intercessors

Select key Leaders and Intercessors (and their spouses) who are to receive personal Restoring the Foundations ministry (15 hours each, Thorough Format, plus combined sessions for married couples). Obtain their available dates. Possibilities include founders/owners, officers, major decision makers, top managers, marketing, and others whose freedom and healing is important to the company and the Action Plan. Planning comments are on page 135.

Organize RTF ministry through
Healing House Network office

Call office: 800-291-4706.

Begin the process of scheduling Leadership/Intercessor couples with HHN Teams.

Leader: _____

Ministry Date: _____

HHN Team: _____

Location: _____

Intercessor: _____

Ministry Date: _____

HHN Team: _____

Location: _____

V. Planning to "Marry" the Land

The Leadership Team, along with others, should decide with the
Holy Spirit whether to "Marry" the Land or not. If so, develop
the plan (page 140) for the commitment/dedication ceremony as
part of the Action Meeting.

VI. Planning for Ministry to Sins of the Founding/Resident Fathers and resulting Curses – "Open Doors"

Develop the plan for ministering to the Sins of the Fathers and
resulting Curses, both from the founding leaders and from the
residents on the land. You can use a clean copy of the "Organizational Sins and Curses Groups: Open Doors" (starting on
page 266) as work sheets for the ministry.

Select which form to use. Either the primary pattern/theme
group and sub-groups as shown on page 137 or the outline form
shown on page 139.   Here is a skeleton outline form you may
fill out. (You can "copy and paste" the lines so that you have as
many as you need for the sub-groups and Open Door lines.)

❑ ___ Ministry Target _____

  ❑ 1A Primary _____

    ❑ ___ Open Door _____

    ❑ ___ Open Door _____

    ❑ ___ Open Door _____

    ❑ ___ Open Door _____

  ❑ 1B Sub-Group _____

    ❑ ___ Open Door _____

    ❑ ___ Open Door _____

    ❑ ___ Open Door _____

    ❑ ___ Open Door _____

VII. Planning for Ministry to Ungodly Organizational Culture
– Attitudes and Beliefs

This area has a number of parts, as detailed starting on page 141. First is the identification of the ungodly Organizational Culture items by the Development Team. They will work with a clean printout of the Ungodly Organizational Culture list starting on page 278. They will use natural knowledge and also listen to the Holy Spirit for supernatural knowledge as to the applicable ones.

As the ungodly aspects of the Organizational Culture are identified, the Leaders and Intercessors can begin to seek the Lord for revelation about His truth, about what He wants in the company in exchange for the ungodly beliefs and attitudes. Prepare for the Preparation Meeting and the Action Meeting. Ask the Lord for the strategy for introducing the new Organizational Culture to the entire company. Discuss the strategy to use at the Preparation Meeting, as well as for the Action Meeting. Finally, plan the strategy to continually "hold" the new Organizational Culture in front of the entire company. Ask the Holy Spirit for creative ways to do this.

_____

_____

Identify Ungodly Culture: _____

_____

_____

_____

Determine Primary Patterns/Themes: _____

_____

_____

_____

Discover God's Truth:

_____

_____

_____

_____

Consequences of introducing God's Truth:

_____

_____

_____

Preparation Meeting: Defining Organizational Culture

_____

_____

_____

_____

Action Meeting(s): Presenting God's Truth

_____

_____

_____

_____

VIII. Planning for Ministry to Organizational and Individuals Hurts/Losses

The Development Team will complete the list of Organizational Hurts and losses on page 285. They are to pray and ask the Lord which hurts and losses, and in which order, He wants to heal at the Action Meeting. There is no real need to rewrite that information here. The Implementation Team will follow the procedure discussed in Part Two starting on page 93.

_____

_____

_____

_____

_____

_____

_____

_____

_____

_____

_____

_____

_____

_____

_____

_____

IX. Planning for Ministry to Organizational Oppression/Principalities

The Groups/Sub-Groups Sins of the Founding/Resident Fathers and resulting Curses list from page 266 is the basic list for ministry to principalities. The list is expanded by additional principalities listed on page 286. The procedure for ministry starts on page 94. The ministry for principalities is a part of the Action Meeting(s).

_____

_____

_____

_____

_____

_____

_____

_____

X. Planning to Transfer Ownership of the Business to God

As with the decision to "Marry" the Land, the Leadership Team and others should consult with the Holy Spirit whether put God in charge of the business. If so, the Team will need to decide "how far to go," as we discussed on page 148, how to do the transfer, and at which Action Meeting it should be done..

_____

_____

_____

_____

XI. Planning for First Meeting: Preparation Meeting

This is the meeting we have been building toward, to publicly announce our intentions to declare our engagement of the enemy in the already ongoing war. As usual, it is important to have the Intercessors preparing the way. The planning information is on page 149, while the implementation activities are on page 159. The Action Plan Implementation is on page 305.

1. Assign Intercessors
Assign Intercessors to keep business covered and principalities over it "shut down" in the weeks leading up to Preparation Meeting. Also bind all demons attempting to influence the employees.

_____

_____

2. Select Public Leader(s)
Decide which Leaders are to publicly support the Leader of the meeting and presentation of the Action Plan.

_____

_____

3. Decide on Public versus Private Activities
Decide what activities, such as Intercession and Spiritual Warfare, can be done publicly versus privately.

_____

_____

4. Select Invitees/Attendees

_____

_____

_____

5. Date and Location of Meeting

_____

6. Pre-Meeting Activities

Person preparing Invitation list and Sign In Sheets:

_____

Prepare roster and have at meeting.

Person preparing Handouts:

_____

Prepare handout with purpose of the Preparation Meeting, and the agenda and time of the Action Meeting.

Person preparing Power Point:

_____

Prepare power point with prayers, purpose, vision, selected teachings from _Transforming Your Business_, and location and time of the Action Meeting.

Person inviting (and reminding) employees to meeting:

_____

Decide date, time, and place.

Person in charge of insuring Agenda prepared for Preparation Meeting:

_____

7. Agenda for Preparation Meeting

Plan the Agenda for the Preparation Meeting based on the outline contained in the Implementation section (starting on page 305).

_____

XII. Planning for Second Meeting: Action Meeting(s)

In this meeting we will officially declare war and engage the enemy. We want the Intercessors continuing to pray. The planning information is on page 151, while the implementation activities are on page 164. The Action Plan Implementation is on page 306.

1. Choose Format
Decide on either the **One Pattern/Theme** approach or the **Thorough** approach for the Action Meeting(s).

_____

2. Assign Intercessors
Insure the Intercessors are assigned to keep business covered and principalities over it "shut down" after the Preparation Meeting and while preparing for the Action Meeting. Continue to bind all demons attempting to influence the employees.

_____

_____

_____

3. Select Public Leader(s)
Decide which Leaders are to be public, either leading the meeting or supporting the Leader of the meeting.

_____

_____

4. Select Invitees/Attendees
These probably are the same people who were invited to the Preparation Meeting.

_____

_____

_____

5. Date and Location
Select the date and location for the Action Meeting.

_____

6. Selection of Primary Pattern/Theme: Ministry Target
Select the Ministry Target for this meeting. This will set the associated groups/sub-groups as well.

_____

_____

7. Choose Meeting for Ceremony to "Marry" the Land
(This is an Optional but Recommended Step)
If the Leadership and Intercessors sense the Lord is asking them to do this step, then select the Action Meeting (generally either the initial or final meeting of the first set of primary negative patterns.) at which the ceremony to commit to receive responsibility for the land will be done.

_____

8. Choose Meeting for Leadership to Transfer
Ownership of the Business to God
(This is an Optional but Recommended Step)
This is another decision for the Leadership and the Intercessors based on what the Lord is asking. Select the Action Meeting (generally either the initial or final meeting of the first set of primary negative patterns.) at which the ceremony to put God in charge and transfer ownership of the business to Him will be done.

_____

9. Planning the Meeting Details

Person preparing Invitation list and Sign In Sheets:

_____

Prepare roster and have at meeting.

Person preparing Handouts:

_____

Prepare handout with purpose, agenda, and ungodly/Godly Organizational Culture statements. Insure availability at meeting.

Person preparing Power Point:

_____

Prepare power point with prayers, vision statement, ministry steps, primary patterns/theme/groupings, new Organizational Culture statements, and location and time of the (next) Action Meeting.

Person inviting (and reminding) company employees about the meeting:

_____

Decide date, time, and place.

_____

If using Ministry Helpers, person responsible for arrangements.

_____

Decisions about what type(s) of Restoring the Foundations ministers to invite, their training level, where from, costs, etc:

_____

_____

_____

Person in charge of insuring Agenda ready for the Action Meeting(s): _____

_____

XIII. Planning for Ongoing Transformation

Planning for Ongoing Transformation is "just another mainte-nance" function.

Select Positions to be filled with Intercessors:

_____

_____

_____

_____

Choose Intercessors:

_____

_____

_____

_____

Plan Meetings:

_____

_____

_____

_____

_____

Frequency: _____

Location: _____

Choose Celebration Person:

_____

XIV. Final Comments

_____

_____

_____

_____

_____

_____

_____

_____

_____

_____

_____

_____

_____

_____

_____

_____

_____

_____

_____

_____

_____

_____

Appendix A

Action Plan Template Implementation

I. Select and Release Development Team

The Leadership Team is to immediately select and release the Action Plan Development Team once the decision is made to go ahead with Transforming Your Business. After each member of the team accepts their position and responsibility, we recommend the Leadership Team meet with the Development Team and pray for them, commission them, and release them to the task of developing the Action Plan.

II. Select and Release Intercessors

The selection and release of the Intercessors will depend greatly on the unique circumstances of the business. The plan is on page 289.

III. Select and Release Implementation Team

The selection and release of the Implementation Team is done by the Development Team after the above two items have been accomplished. Planning for implementation is on page 290.

IV. Provide Healing Ministry for Appropriate Leadership and Intercessor Families

The Development Team can oversee this function. It should commence as soon as possible, based on the Action Plan, page 291, with discussion on planning and implementation on pages 135 and 158.

V. First Meeting: Preparation of Organization

The planning information for this meeting is on page 149, while the implementation description is on page 159. The Action Plan planning is on page 297. You can "check off" the check boxes as you complete the individual items.

A. Pre-Meeting Work

The following tasks and preparation will have been completed.

- ☐ The Action Plan has been completed (or nearly so)
- ☐ The selected Attendees have been invited and primed for the meeting
- ☐ The Intercessors have been given their assignment and they are covering the meeting
- ☐ The Leader of the meeting has been prepared to lead the Preparation Meeting
- ☐ The handout for the meeting has been prepared
- ☐ The overheads (power point) are ready to go

B. Lead Preparation Meeting

- ☐ Have "Sign-In" list
- ☐ Give out Handouts
- ☐ Leader Welcome and Introductions
- ☐ Leader leads in Opening Prayer
- ☐ Discuss the Purpose of Meeting (and Ongoing Warfare)
- ☐ Discuss and Impart Leaders' Vision and Heart
- ☐ Explain TYB Principles and Action Plan
    - ☐ Share basic principles of *Transforming Your Business*
    - ☐ Explain the elements of the Action Plan. Provide a time for Questions and Answers
- ☐ Caution about talking to others about the transition of the business
- ☐ Leader leads in Closing Prayer

VI. Second Meeting: Action Meeting(s)

The planning information for this meeting is on page 151, while the implementation description is on page 164. The Action Plan Planning is on page 306. You can "check off" the check boxes as you complete the individual items.

A. Pre-Meeting Work

The following tasks and preparation will have been completed.

- ❏ The Action Plan has been completed (before the first Action Meeting).
- ❏ The selected Attendees have been invited and primed for the meeting.
- ❏ The Intercessors have been given their assignment and they are covering the meeting.
- ❏ The Leader of the meeting has been prepared to lead the Action Meeting.
- ❏ The Ministry Target for this Action Meeting has been selected.
- ❏ The primary group/sub-groups has been selected and lists prepared.
- ❏ The Organizational Culture ungodly/Godly statements matching the Ministry Target are prepared.
- ❏ The handout for the meeting have been prepared.
- ❏ The overheads (power point) are ready to go.
- ❏ The Ministry Helpers have been selected and trained as necessary.

B. Start Action Meeting

- ❏ Have "Sign-In" list
- ❏ Give out Handouts

❑ Leader Welcome and Introductions

❑ Leader leads in Opening Prayer

❑ Discuss the Purpose of Meeting (and Ongoing Warfare)

❑ Present the Ministry Target for the Meeting.

C. Leader Leads in
Sins of the Founding and Resident Fathers
Confession and Repentance
(Identification Repentance)

❑ The Leader leads the Attendees through the ministry steps for each Group/Sub-Group.

D. Leadership Commits to take (OPTIONAL STEP)
Responsibility for the Land
to Care for the Land and Bless It

❑ Leader leads the attendees through the declaration/commitment to "Marry" the Land.

E. Leader Leads for Ungodly Organizational Culture

❑ Leader leads the attendees through the ministry steps one time for each pair of ungodly/Godly Organizational Culture statements.

F. Leader Prays for Organizational and Individuals Hurts/Losses

❑ Leader prepares attendees for the ministry.

❑ Leader leads the attendees through the ministry steps one time for each hurt/loss.

❑ Leader release the ministry Helpers to assist individuals as needed or desired.

G. Leaders Leads in Removing Organizational Oppression/Principalities

☐ Leader prepares attendees for the ministry.

☐ Leader leads the attendees through the ministry steps one time for each Group/Sub-Group.

☐ Leader release the ministry Helpers to assist individuals as needed or desired.

H. Leadership Transfers Ownership of the Business to God (OPTIONAL STEP)

☐ Leader leads the other Leaders and attendees through a dedication and transfer of the business title to God.

I. Concluding the Action Meeting

☐ Leader leads in Closing Prayer.

☐ Everyone released into Celebration.

J. Post-Meeting Work

☐ Have Intercessors continue on high alert.

☐ Promote the new Organizational Culture.

VII. Ongoing Transformation

A. Ongoing Vigilance: Spiritual Warfare/Intercession

Information Gathering Person: _____

Designate who is to be responsible to continue to collect information as new sins, curses, etc., as revealed by the Holy Spirit, whether via continued historical research or revelation to the Intercessors and others.

Date for next Periodic Repentance Meeting: _____

Intercessors

Lead Intercessor: _____

Intercessor, Position: _____

Intercessor, Position: _____

Intercessor, Position: _____

Intercessor, Position: _____

Intercessor, Position: _____

Gate Keepers

Person, Position: _____

Person, Position: _____

Person, Position: _____

Person, Position: _____

Person, Position: _____

B. Ongoing Celebration

Person Responsible: _____

VIII. Final Comments and Summary

_____

_____

_____

_____

_____

_____

_____

_____

_____

_____

_____

_____

_____

_____

_____

_____

_____

_____

_____

_____

_____

_____

_____

Appendix B

Scriptures For Transforming Your Business

The following scripture references are presented here as additional supportive material. We encourage you to add to your understanding of God's provision for healing and freedom both at the individual and organizational levels. Please note that this is not an exhaustive list of scriptures pertaining to Transforming Your Business, but a representative list.

A. Hearing the Voice of the Lord

John 10:4
1 Corinthians 2:7-16

B. Confession and Forgiveness

Leviticus 26:40
1 Kings 8:47-50
Nehemiah 1, 9
Ezra 9
Daniel 9

C. Identification Repentance

II Chronicles 7:14
Jeremiah 30:13
Ezekiel 22:30

D. About the Founders and Leaders: SOFFCs

Joshua 6:26, I Kings 16:34
Matthew 26:31
Luke 11:46, 52
James 3:1

E. About the Land and Those Living on the Land: SORFCs

Leviticus 18:25-30
Deuteronomy 24:4, 28:18, 38-40, 42, 29:22-24, 27-28
Isaiah 24:1-6
Ezekiel 36:17
Jeremiah 16:18, 44:22

F. About the Ungodly/Godly Organizational Culture: Attitudes and Beliefs

Genesis 6:5
Exodus 32:9, 22
Psalms 83:4-5
Isaiah 55:7-9
Jeremiah 4:14
Matthew 18:19-20
Philippians 2:1-3

G. About the Wounds of the Organization: Organizational Hurts/Losses

Jeremiah 30:10-19
Luke 19:41-44

H. About the Influence of Principalities On/Over the Land

1. Entrapping Principalities

2 Corinthians 2:10-11
Ephesians 4:26-27, 6:12
2 Timothy 2:25-26

2. References to Principalities

Daniel 10:12-13
Romans 8:38-39
Galatians 3:1
Ephesians 1:21, 3:10, 6:12
Colossians 1:16, 2:15
Revelation 2:1-3:22 (seven churches)

3. How to deal with Demons and Principalities

Matthew 18:18
Luke 10:19
Mark 16:17

Appendix C

Restoring the Foundations Ministry for Individuals

As stated on page 13, the organizational ministry approach presented in this book builds on the Restoring the Foundation (RTF) ministry approach for individuals. Here is the story of how it came to be.

In the mid-1980s, as my wife Betsy and I were attending Bible College, the Lord give us several exciting revelations on how to bring healing to a person's life. It was an awesome time as we learned how to work with the Holy Spirit ministering to others. As we look back on that time, we feel He gave us these revelations for two primary reasons. First, we ourselves needed the healing. We were quite wounded from the events (or lack of them) in our early years and needed much healing.[1] Second, we were two very unlikely candidates to be carriers of His healing grace. That apparently qualified us according to First Corin-

---

[1] Betsy's autobiography, *Twice Chosen*, is the story of our pathway to healing. It starts with her difficult illegitimate beginning, then her adoption, then how these set her up to be controlled by fear and shame, i.e., her "dark side." She also includes the wounding of abandonment experienced by Chester at age two as his father dies and how this marked his life for many years. Like all good stories, this one has a happy ending. It is the healing and freedom the Lord began to bring into our lives while we were in Bible College and how it was formulated into the Integrated Approach to Biblical Healing and the birth of our ministry. This book is available from Proclaiming His Word Publishing as well as from your nearby Christian book store and online retailers such as Amazon.com, etc.

thians 1:26-31, where Paul writes about God choosing the weak, foolish, and unnoticed to confound the strong, wise, and influential. We both struggled with shame, fear, and the resulting control.[1] We both felt totally unworthy to serve God, yet we wanted to do this with all our hearts. At last, we gave up resisting His call and went to Bible College. That is when our personal healing began in earnest and the pieces of the revelation came together.

Integrated Approach to Biblical Healing Ministry

We call this ministry approach the Integrated Approach to Biblical Healing Ministry. It is integrated because we minister to four problem areas in an interdependent, harmonious way. In fact, to obtain deep and permanent healing and freedom, it is *necessary* that the relationship between each of the four areas be removed as well as the destructive effects of each area itself.

The first area is the ***Sins of the Fathers and Resulting Curses***. We all have to contend with this area because of the second commandment.[2] God expresses His hatred of idolatry in this passage. He expresses His jealousy when our love goes to anything or anyone other than Him. When this occurs, the curse described in this Bible passage is activated, causing the iniquity of the fathers (and mothers) to pass unto their children for the next three and four generations. Since essentially the entire human race has violated this commandment, this curse is continually propagated from one generation to the next.

---

[1] Our early healing resulted in another revelation about the dynamic interaction between shame, fear, and control strongholds and how they deceive their host into believing that they are part of his personality. Both of us needed freedom from this very destructive bondage. The details of this "super" stronghold are provided in a tape set. We also expect to have it in book form. This resource may be obtained from Proclaiming His Words Publishing. (Please see Author's page at end of this book.)

[2] The second commandment is written the first time in Exodus 20:5.

When we see a struggle area in a whole family line, we are seeing a curse in operation. When the different members of the family succumb to the curse and enter into the same sin, we are seeing another round of the curse pass onto an additional three and four generations. Common examples are alcoholism, criminal behavior, isolation and rejection within families, anger and feuding, criticalness and bitterness, etc. The list goes on and on.

Even though we all have to contend with these curses and sins, it is also true that blessings come down our family line as well. We hope you picked a family line with more blessings than curses!

God, knowing we would be trapped and helpless, provided a way to freedom from the generational sins and curses. The first mention of the principle of confession occurs in Leviticus 26:40. God wants us to acknowledge our sin and take responsibility for breaking His law (i.e., sin). Once we do this, then He is faithful and true to cleanse and forgive us.[1] He provided His Son, Jesus Christ, to carry our punishment and the consequences of our sin on the Cross.[2] Thus He has provided a way for us to get free of these ancestral sins and curses. We "just" have to believe and receive in order to obtain freedom from family curses.

We call the second problem area **Ungodly Beliefs**. It obviously has to do with the mind and what we believe. It works like this. We grow up in our family with the sins and curses of our ancestors and the blessings in operation. Since there is no perfect family, over time, everyone is hurt by someone, and maybe several "some ones." Based on these hurts, we begin to draw conclusions about life, about daddies, mommies, sisters and brothers. We decide what and who is safe and what and who is not. We make decisions about what we have to do in order to survive and be safe. As these numerous decisions accumulate, they

---

[1] This aspect of confess comes from First John 1:9.

[2] In Galatians 3:13, Paul writes that Jesus took upon Himself the penalties (curses) due us.

form the core of our belief system. So out of our experiences, many of them hurtful, we make decisions and form beliefs about ourselves, others, and God. These form our world view, our belief system. Unfortunately, many of these beliefs are lies. They do not agree with the truth of God's word. While they **are** based on our experience, they **are not** based on what God says about us, others, and the world.

As we get older and adventure out with people other than our families, we are exposed to another realm of potential hurts. Peers, authority figures (pastors, teachers, etc.), girl and boy friends all add to the load of hurt, and thus also to the distortions and lies of our belief system.

When we examine a person's belief system, we find that some of the beliefs may be based on truth (as expressed by God[1]), but usually many of them are not. This is why we need to have our minds renewed.[2] For example, out of my experience of my dad dying when I was two years old, I began to believe that "Important people will abandon me." As I dealt with this by withdrawing and isolating myself, my belief that "No one wants to be with me." was confirmed and strengthened. Of course, I never thought about the fact that because I isolated myself, no one could **find** me to be my friend. The point is that the hurts of our childhood lead to our forming Ungodly Beliefs. These need to be converted into the truth, i.e., into what God says about us and the situations of life. The Lord has given us an effective procedure for converting Ungodly Beliefs into Godly Beliefs as we work with the Holy Spirit to renew our minds.

The hurts we experience growing up in our families also lead to hurts on the inside of us that no one can see. This is the third problem area, *Soul/Spirit Hurts*. These hurts can be in the soul or in the spirit realm. Wherever they are, we ask the Lord to heal them. The Lord has given us a safe procedure in this

---

[1] Jesus states in John 14:6 that, "I am the way, the **truth**, and the life."

[2] Paul admonishes us to renew our minds in Romans 12:2.

Soul/Spirit Hurts area that leaves the Holy Spirit completely in charge of the healing and leaves the ministers in the position of facilitators. We just help the ministry happen. We ourselves do not, and can not, bring the healing.

It is no accident that Jesus, in Luke 4:18, quoted Isaiah 61:1-3. He read, "He (the Lord) has sent me to heal the broken-hearted, to preach deliverance to the captives, ... to set at liberty them that are bruised." As we bring Restoring the Foundations (RTF) ministry into a person's life, Jesus comes and demonstrates that He is still healing the broken-hearted.

Because of these three areas, the fourth area of **Demonic Oppression** exists. The enemy of our soul has access into our lives because of the "place"[1] given by the first three problem areas. The ancestral sins and curses provide Open Doors[2] in our lives through which the enemy comes to influence and bring "stealing, killing, and destroying."[3] We will have much more to say about the subject of demons and other evil forces in the next section of this book.

Ancestral Sins and Curses, Ungodly Beliefs, Soul/Spirit Hurts and Demonic Oppression: these four areas work together for our destruction. As we ourselves gain freedom, we can begin to bring to others understanding of how inter-related and interconnected these four problem areas are. As we minister to these areas, we will be used as the Lord's instrument[4] to bring deep and permanent healing and freedom.

---

[1] Please note Ephesians 4:27.

[2] This concept comes from Genesis 4:7, where God warns Cain that "sin is crouching at your door; it desires to have you, but you must master it." (NIV)

[3] This comes from Jesus' words recorded in John 10:10.

[4] Paul writes in Second Timothy 2:21 about how to be a useful instrument in the Lord's hand.

Appendix D

Selection Criteria for Case Studies

We believe the Transforming Your Business (TYB) ministry approach will work with any business/ organization and cause a significant improvement in its capacity to fulfill destiny and purpose. However, please refer back to the Beginning (page), for practical considerations when deciding whether to implement the Transforming Your Business process or not.

When we approach the issue of selecting the case studies for inclusion in the second edition of this book, it is important to be able to measure the effect of the TYB ministry on the business within a one to two year period. This automatically narrows down the possibilities. We want businesses that are not too big or too small in every dimension. The criteria listed below will be used to guide us as we make the final selections.

Before presenting the selection criteria, however, if you are considering offering to be a candidate case study, there are several important things to consider and agree to before moving ahead.

Relationship/Commitment
It is important that the business desire a ministry relationship with the author and that it is willing to commit to a 2-3 year relationship. The details of the relationship will be worked out with each business selected as a candidate case study business.

Baseline Data
In order to measure the effectiveness of the TYB ministry, it is important to determine the historical "base line" data parameters of the business. This will require extensive analysis of the company's financial records, employee records, customer and vender records, etc.

Ongoing Data
After the initial TYB ministry, and during the ongoing ministry, intercession and vigilance, it will be important to continue to measure/monitor the same business data in order to determine what and by how much the baseline parameters are changing. This data would also be used to identify areas of the business needing special attention and perhaps additional ministry.

Action Plan
From the ministry relationship and baseline data, plus interviews, prayer, revelation and intercession, the author will work with the business owners/managers/leaders to formulate an Action Plan that will help remove hindrances and obstacles to the business reaching its full potential and destiny. The author will lead the effort to develop the Action Plan and will begin the ministry to the organization. It is necessary that the ministry relationship continue with the business for at least two to three years to provide ongoing consultation and ministry as the Action Plan is carried out.

Selection Criteria

The things to look at for both the author and the candidate business as they consider entering into a ministry relationship/commitment include:

1. Are the owners/managers/leaders willing to allow us to research and publish selected detailed and summary business data concerning their business, knowing that the information will be published using a fictitious name and location for the business?

2. Are the owners/managers/leaders willing and do they desire to come into unity and humble themselves publicly such that they, from their heart, repent for themselves and any former owners/ managers/leaders?

3. Are the owner's willing to open their company records so that we can dig into the details of the business, including all financial records (by departments: sales, profit, expenses), employee information, customer and vender information, etc.?

4. Overall Business: Gross income (Sales by departments, by time, by products, by price), expenses (officer salaries, management salaries, employee salaries and wages, inventory valuation, inventory COGS, expense breakdowns by activity/budget including taxes by jurisdiction/type).

   a. Marketing: budgets, channels, percent of sales, percent of expenses, estimated effectiveness.

   b. Employees: number of employees, growth rate, turnover rate; satisfaction level; salaries and bonuses (as percent of total expenses), growth rate; gifts and personalities matched with jobs (using spiritual gifts and personality determination questionnaires).

   c. Customers: number of customers, growth rate, satisfaction level, spending levels and amounts, frequency of purchasing, personalities and attitudes survey, loyalty.

   d. Vendors: number of venders, growth rate, satisfaction level, cost levels and amounts, frequency of orders, personalities and attitudes survey, loyalty.

5. Is the business a reasonable size? Not too small and not too big. Gross revenue in the range of $1 => 20 million. A steady growth rate in the range of -5% to +5% would be an added benefit, as it would be easier to measure the effect of the TYB ministry.

6. Is the business a family owned business? With at most three generations of owners/ managers/leaders?

7. Does the business have at least 10 years of operation history against which we can measure the effect of the RTF ministry? On the other hand, a company that has been in business

for more than 30 years represents more complexity and thus may require a longer ministry time than we can spend for a case study.

8. Does the business have at least 4-5 employees besides the owners/managers/leaders, yet not more than 20-30 employees? A large number of employees would complicate the ministry and time required, just as mentioned in the previous item.

9. Is the business operating within one region? Multiple locations may be okay if they are in the same general region. A multi-state or multi-national business would involve more complexity than is suitable for the case study

Appendix E

Seminar Outlines for Transforming Your Business

The following outlines may be used to conduct a seminar to convey the concepts, principles, and practices expressed in *Transforming Your Business*. Obviously, they closely follow the outline of this book, however, also included is small group activity to involve the attendees and activate them to apply what they are learning in the seminar.

There are two outlines. Which one to use depends on whether the seminar is "open-to-the-public" or it is a private, "in-house" seminar, with focus on the sponsoring business or organization.

The outlines are based on a four-session format, with each session approximately three hours in duration. One possible schedule is to have a Friday evening session from 6:30 PM to 9:30 PM, plus three Saturday sessions from 9:00 AM to 12:00, from 1:30 PM to 4:30 PM, and the last session from 6:30 PM to 9:30 PM.

Pre-Seminar

1. Preparation of Leadership

Insure host Leadership understands and accepts their role and potential consequences of seminar and Transforming Your Business; good and bad.

2. Check List[1]

Go through Check List with host organizer/coordinator. Cover all arrangements.

---

[1] TYB Seminar Leaders trained by Proclaiming His Word Ministries have the Checklists.

325

Public TYB Seminar Outline[1]

I. Session 1

A. Beginning

1. Overview

2. Real Solutions to Real Problems

3. Apply TYB to Attendee's Business (start process)

B. Things We Need To Know (Part One)

1. Basic Definitions

2. Fundamental Concepts: Negative

3. Fundamental Concepts: Positive

C. Spiritual Dynamics of Organizations (Part Two)

1. Negative Spiritual Roots

2. Principles of Principalities

3. Spiritual Solutions

4. Birth and Ongoing

II. Session 2

A. Action Plan for Transforming Your Business (Part Three)

B. Common Principalities (Part Four)

C. Activation for Attendees' Business/Organization (or other Case Study)

Action Plan Information Gathering for One Problem/Issue

---

[1]   We recommend the seminar leader have RTF helpers to oversee the Activation small groups.

Compile Spiritual "Mapping" Information for a Business/Organization

- Select one Attendee desiring help with his/her business/organization
- Add 3-5 people to create a small group for spiritual mapping activation
- Assign one small group leader to assist group.

    a. Research Historical Material
    b. Seek Supernatural Revelation
    c. Each group report to entire group

III. Session 3

A. Intercession—Spiritual Warfare (Part Five)

B. Activation for Attendees' Business/Organization

Help Attendees continue the Information Gathering sub-phase for their Action Plan

IV. Session 4 (this session is optional)

A. Review of Seminar Contents and Case Histories

B. Activation for Attendees' Business/Organization (continued)

Continue to help Attendees develop their Action Plan

Private TYB Seminar Outline

I. Session 1

A. Beginning

1. Overview

2. Real Solutions to Real Problems

3. Apply TYB to Host Business/Organization (one Issue)

B. Things We Need To Know (Part One)

1. Basic Definitions

2. Fundamental Concepts: Negative

3. Fundamental Concepts: Positive

C. Spiritual Dynamics Of Organizations (Part Two)

1. Negative Spiritual Roots

2. Principles of Principalities

3. Spiritual Solutions

4. Birth and Ongoing

II. Session 2

A. Action Plan for Transforming Your Business (Part Three)

B. Common Principalities (Part Four)

C. Activation for Host Business/Organization (or other Case Study)

Action Plan Information Gathering for One Problem/Issue

1. Compile Spiritual "Mapping" Information for Host Organization

- Form a small group of 4-8 people for spiritual mapping activation.
- Assign one small group leader to assist group.

    a. Research Historical Material
    b. Seek Supernatural Revelation
    c. Each group report to entire group

2. (Optional) Seminar Leader(s) pray prophetically through compiled information on behalf of the business/organization.

III. Session 3

A. Intercession— Spiritual Warfare (Part Five)

B. Activation for Host Business/Organization

1. Interview Leaders

2. Complete Planning portion of Action Plan for the One Issue

IV. Session 4

A. Review of Seminar Contents and Case Histories

B. Present Action Plan for Host Business/Organization for One Issue

C. Implement Action Plan for Host Organization for One Issue

Ministry Action Plan to Host Organizational

Bibliography and References

Collins, Jim, "Good to Great: Why some Companies make the Leap... and Others Don't," Collins, October 2001.

Dawson, John, "Taking Our Cities for God: How to Break Spiritual Strongholds," Charisma House, September 1, 2001.

Doudera, Ralph, "Wealth Conundrum," Spectrum Financial, February, 2006. (You may visit his web site at www.WealthConundrum.com and order his book.)

Fleming, Jerry, "Profit at any Cost? Why Business Ethics makes Sense," Baker Books, 2003.

Frangipane, Francis, "The Three Battlegrounds," Arrow Publications, 1989.

Hamon, Bill, "Prophets and Personal Prophecy," Destiny Image Publishers, October, 1987.

Hamon, Bill, "Manual for Ministering Spiritual Gifts," Christian International Ministries, 1st edition, 1991.

Hamon, Bill, "The 10 M's: Maintaining and Maturing in Your Ministry," Christian International Ministries, 1st edition, 1990, tape set.

Hislop, Alexander, "The Two Babylons," 1917.

Jacobs, Cindy, "Possessing The Gates of the Enemy: A Training Manual for Militant Intercession," Grand Rapids: Baker House Books, 1991.

Jacobs, Cindy, "The Voice of God," Regal Books, July 1995.

Jacobs, Cindy, "Deliver Us from Evil," Regal Books, Nov 2001.

Kylstra, Chester and Betsy, "Restoring the Foundations," Proclaiming His Word Publishing, 1994, 2000.

Kylstra, Chester and Betsy, "Biblical Healing and Deliverance," Chosen Books, 2005. (In parts of the world other than USA, this book is released as, "Integrated Approach to Biblical Healing Ministry," Sovereign World Publishers, 2004.)

Kylstra, Chester and Betsy, "Shame-Fear-Control Stronghold," Proclaiming His Word Publishing, 1998, tape set and soon-to-be book.

Kylstra, Chester, "Knowing and Releasing Our Authority," Proclaiming His Word Publishing, 1999, tape set.

Marshall, Tom, "Understanding Leadership," Sovereign World, Ltd, Tonbridge, England, 1991

Moyer, Daniel and Eugene Alvarez, "Just the Facts, Ma'Am: The Authorized Biography of Jack Webb," Seven Locks Press, April, 2001.

Otis, George, Jr., "The Twilight Labyrinth: Why Does Spiritual Darkness Linger Where It Does?" Chosen Books, October 1997.

Otis, George, Jr., "Informed Intercession: Transforming Your Community Through Spiritual Mapping and Strategic Prayer," Renew Books, a Division of Gospel Light, Ventura, CA, 1999.

Otis, George, Jr., "God's Trademarks," Chosen Books, October 2000.

Parkinson , C. Northcote, "Parkinson's Law", Buccaneer Books, February 1993.

Peretti, Frank, "Piercing the Darkness," Crossway Books, September, 1989.

Peretti, Frank, "This Present Darkness," Crossway Books, August, 1996.

Petrie, Alistair, "Releasing Heaven on Earth," Chosen Books, Oct 2000.

Qaumaniq and Suuqiina, "Warfare by Honor," Healing the Land, PO Box 73, Scotland, PA, 17254, 2005.

Schaef, Anne Wilson and Diane Fassel, "The Addictive Organization: Why We Overwork, Cover Up, Pick Up the Pieces, Please the Boss, and Perpetuate Sick Organizations," Harper & Row, 1988.

Smart, Bradford, "Topgrading: How Leading Companies Win by Hiring, Coaching, and Keeping the Best People," Portfolio Hardcover; Revised edition, April 2005, 592 pages.

Tam, R. Stanley, "God Owns My Business," Horizon House, January, 1969 (out of print, available from US Plastic at www.usplactic.com. Click on Corporate Information at bottom of home page. Used versions are also sold at Amazon.com.)

Virkler, Mark and Patti, "Dialogue with God," Bridge-Logos, Gainesville, FL, 1986, 2005.

Virkler, Mark and Patti, "How to Hear God's Voice," Destiny Image Publishers, Shippensburg, PA, 2005.

Wagner, C. Peter, "Prayer shield: How to intercede for pastors, Christian leaders, and others on the spiritual frontlines," Regal Books, 1992.

Wagner, C. Peter, "Apostles of the City: How to Mobilize Territorial Apostles for City Transformation," Wagner Publications, 2001

Wagner, C. Peter, "Changing Church: How God Is Leading His Church into the Future," Regal Books," August 2004.

Wagner, C. Peter, (editor), "Freedom from the Religious Spirit: Understanding How Deceptive Religious Forces Try to Destroy God's Plan and Purpose for His Church," Regal Books, April 2005.

Index

Ministry Resources

We know there are many quality ministries "out there." God is insuring that we have all we need to be healed and equipped in this present time, where ever in the world we might be. However, we can only recommend the ministries we know. The following list contains ministries that we know that have reputations of integrity, quality, cutting edge, anointing, and calling. These ministries are available to help you gain knowledge, practice, and experience in the various areas of equipping we need to implement Transforming Your Business in your company.

Personal Ministry/Training

Healing House Network – 800-291-4706 – www.HealingHouse.org

> The network of qualified and seasoned Restoring the Foundations ministry teams. Network founded by Chester and Betsy Kylstra to bring healing and freedom to leaders and saints in the Body of Christ. Training cell/small group leaders, church teams, and those called to ministry through the Healing House Network.

Hearing God's Voice/Flowing in the Prophetic

Christian International Ministries – 800-388-5308 – www.christianinternational.org

> Bishop Bill Hamon has a passion to raise up saints that hear the voice of the Lord and prophets that bring God's word with integrity and honor. The CI apostolic and prophetic training modules have helped many saints advance in their ability to hear God's voice and express God's heart.

Communion with God Ministries – 716-652-6990 – www.cwgministries.org

> Mark and Patti Virkler's books and seminars have helped more people hear God's voice than any other ministry.

Gifts of the Holy Spirit

Christian International Ministries – 800-388-5308 – www.christianinternational.org

Bishop Bill Hamon has developed a course to equip saints to operate in the gifts of the Holy Spirit. Thousands have benefited from the Manual for Ministering Spiritual Gifts course as they have learned to hear His Voice and cooperate with the Holy Spirit.

Intercession/Prayer Networks/Spiritual Warfare

Generals International – 972-576-8887 – www.generals.org

Cindy Jacobs is an internationally recognized leader in Intercession. She travels extensively raising up Intercessors and mobilizing prayer networks for cities.

Maximum Significance International – 918-491-6400 – www.MaximumSignificance.com

Bruce and Karen Mow provide businesses with intercessors, daily or weekly inspirational emails (promoting Godly Organizational Culture in line with companies vision/values), training, consultation in establishing ministry departments, and other spiritual services.

Watchman Ministries International – 425-687-0994 – www.WatchmanMinistries.org

Tim Taylor is a retired naval officer, corporate trainer, and change management expert. Strategic leadership training is delivered through the Spiritual War College and has been adapted to both ministry and business. The same Biblical principles used to serve customers like Ford, GM and GE were also used to develop strategic prayer and outreach plans for cities.

Restoring the Foundations Resources

Please visit our Online Resources Sales at
www.phw.org
for all the resources or call 828-**693-9626 ext 522**.

Restoring the Foundations
An Integrated Approach to Healing Ministry

The foundations are damaged and twisted. God's solider has His plan for restoring them with anointing and grace. The heart of the Lord is to restore His people with deep and lasting healing. Are you willing to cooperate with the Holy Spirit to receive your healing? Work through the four problem/ministry areas and watch yourself shed old hurts, fears, shame, and other hindrances to the abundant life.

Twice Chosen

Twice Chosen gives a vivid portrayal of God's providential purpose being worked out in Betsy's life. She is adopted and raised in a godly home, yet tormented by deep rejection and demonic fears. Laugh, cry, and be profoundly encouraged as you learn how God restores her and brings her into her destiny.

345

Restoring the Foundations Resources

Please visit our Online Resources Sales at
www.phw.org
for all the resources or call 828-**693-9626 ext 522**.

Integrated Approach to Biblical Healing Ministry

This is a reduced version of *Restoring the Foundations*. Same core chapters but without the applications chapters. Great to share with others because of its smaller size and lower cost. Still facilitates receiving healing as they work with the Holy Spirit to clear out the four problem areas.

Shame-Fear-Control Stronghold

This "super" stronghold afflicts over half of the Body of Christ with a counterfeit identity. Is this stronghold lying to you about who you really are? You can learn how to identify, disassemble, and demolish it. As you listen to the second tape, participate in the one hour ministry and start on the road to freedom.

About the Author

When Chester and his wife Betsy heard God's call on their lives, the passage about "two becoming one" took on new meaning. Already well established in their careers of aerospace software engineering and mental health counseling, they left that behind for new "careers" as teachers and healing ministers in the Body of Christ.

Chester grew up in a ranching and farming community in Eastern Oregon. He attended Oregon State University in Engineering, including Air Force ROTF. Soon after graduation, the Air Force moved him to Cape Kennedy, Florida, where he was a member of the Titan Launch Control Team. After the  Air Force, he continued his education at the University of Florida for advanced degrees in Nuclear Engineering. He became a researcher and technical manager in the aerospace industry spending most of his time in California during the space boom years of the '60s. Between managing projects, developing software, writing proposals and reports, and traveling often to Washington, DC, life was full. He returned to the University of Florida in 1967, where he became a professor in the Nuclear Engineering Department. There he taught classes and conducted research in a number of different areas, including working closely with the Environmental Engineering Department.

In 1979, Chester and Betsy left Florida for North Carolina, wanting to move their family out of the intense drug culture of the university setting. Chester's entrepreneurial gifts begin to emerge as he managed and operated his own engineering consulting business and air-taxi business. He also worked as the software engineer for a Navy fighter ejection seat manufacturer. The central thread connecting the many different projects throughout the years was "problem solving," usually through the creation of engineering research software.

And then came the Call. In 1984 they left the mountains of North Carolina and begin their preparation time at Liberty Bible College.[1] God, wasting no time, begin doing a dual work in them. He brought them into a restoration and healing process, revealing the elements of "Christian Prophetic Prayer Counseling." They shared what they were learning with others, training other couples to bring the healing and freedom ministry to church members.

Since 1990, when they began to minister full-time, God continues to expand their vision. While still active in personal ministry, they have now established healing ministry programs within churches in many locations. They conduct Healing/Deliverance, Activation, and Training Seminars throughout the USA and internationally. They continue to train healing ministry teams and trainers of the teams.

1993 became a significant year when Chester and Betsy were called to Christian International (CI) in Florida by Dr. Bill Hamon to minister to the CI leadership. The leadership was so pleased with the results that CI asked them to organize and lead a "Prophetic Counseling" conference, held in March of 1994. This was a major indicator of things to come, as the first edition of the *"Restoring the Foundations"* book was completed and given to all conference attendees. Also, thirteen leadership couples remained after the conference and received ministry as part of the launch of the "Christian International/Proclaiming His Word Healing House." Chester and Betsy remain in association with CI and Dr. Bill Hamon, serving on the CI Board of Governors.

---

[1] Betsy has degrees in Counselor Education (MA, EdS). Chester has degrees in Mechanical (BS) and Nuclear Engineering (MS, PhD). They earned their Masters Degrees in Theology at Liberty Bible College, Pensacola, Florida.

"Proclaiming His Word, Inc." was founded in 1992 in response to God saying that others would be joining them and to prepare a covering organization to take care of them. This happened after the Prophetic Counseling conference. Teams begin to join them to minister in the Healing House. Many leaders came to receive healing in a safe place at the CI/PHW Healing House. By 2000, over sixteen trained ministers and trainers, as well as office staff, worked with Proclaiming His Word. Chester and Betsy were traveling extensively by this time, bringing the good news of how to receive God's Healing to many parts of the world.

Several major changes occurred in 2000. "Christian Prophetic Prayer Counseling" became "*Restoring the Foundations*" (RTF) ministry, the title of their first book. All references to "counselor" and "counseling" in their published materials were changed to "minister" and "ministering." Most significant, however, was that the Lord directed them to release all of the teams working with PHW into their own ministries and to launch the Healing House Network, Inc. (HHN) as the new covering organization. It started with 25 very capable, qualified RTF ministers working together as teams.

In 2004, the prophecies concerning an eventual training center came to fulfillment. Echo Mountain Inn in Hendersonville, NC, was purchased as the home of the "Restoring the Foundations International Training Center, Inc." and became the new ministry base, as the entire ministry moved from near Christian International in Florida to North Carolina. This training center has allowed a great acceleration in the preparation and release of RTF ministers into the Body of Christ.

By the start of 2006, the number of qualified HHN team members propagating the *Restoring the Foundations* ministry has grown to over 120 people. These teams are being used by the Lord to minister to leaders and others in the Body of Christ using the RTF ministry "Integrated Approach," usually in an intensive, one-week format. In addition, many church teams have been trained as Issue-Focused and/or Thorough Format ministers. They are serving their local churches, volunteering three to six hours a week, ministering to church members, doing their part to help prepare the "Bride without spot or wrinkle."

Then the RTF revelation expanded again. The Lord was bringing insight that the same types of problem areas afflicting individuals were also hindering and even blocking groups of individuals, or organizations (such as churches and businesses). It was keeping them from reaching their potential and destiny in life. It became more evident that before a city could be transformed, its organizations must be transformed. They begin to teach and spread the word about how to free organizations. It was from these revelations and teachings that this book was compiled. The detailed procedure for transforming an organization is now available to many so that the principles can be shared and put into practice.

They have developed a number of resources to help bring healing to individuals as well as train RTF ministers. ***Restoring the Foundations, An Integrated Approach to Healing Ministry***, is the flagship training and self-ministry manual. A smaller version, suitable for Christian book stores, was released through Sovereign World Publishers (UK) in September, 2004, as "An Integrated Approach to Biblical Healing Ministry." Subsequently, Chosen Books (USA) released a version titled "Biblical Healing and Deliverance." Please visit the PHW online store at **www.phw.org** (or see page 345) for many of their resources as well as other resources used to train RTF ministers. There are also many resources to help individuals receive the Lord's healing and freedom.

Betsy and Chester have four adult children; James, Lewis, Eric and Pam.

You may contact Betsy and Chester through:

> Proclaiming His Word Ministries
> 2849 Laurel Park Highway
> Hendersonville, NC 28739
>
> 877-214-8076
> office@phw.org
> www.phw.org

You may learn more about the several ministries they have founded at the following web sites.

Restoring the Foundations (central web site for all ministries)
> **www.RestoringTheFoundations.org**

Healing House Network
> **www.HealingHouse.org**

RTF International Training Center
> **www.RTFTrainingCenter.org**

Transforming Your Business
> **www.TransformingYourBusiness.org**

Issue-Focused Ministry
> **www.IssueFocused.org**
> **www.CellGroups.org**

The Restoring the Foundations International Training Center is located at Echo Mountain Inn in Hendersonville, NC. This facility is operated year-round as a B&B Inn. You may learn more about the Inn and its rooms at:

Echo Mountain Inn Bed & Breakfast
> **www.EchoInn.com**

Printed in the United States
57654LVS00001B/133-216